IDEAZ

A 2020 Vision Perspective
ON THE Rastafari Movement
Revisiting the Field
& Taking Steps Forward

VOL 15 • 2020
ISSN 0799-1401

GUEST EDITORS

Michael Barnett, Giulia Bonacci *and* Erin C. MacLeod

ARAWAK
publications
KINGSTON • JAMAICA

A 2020 Vision Perspective on the Rastafari Movement:
Revisiting the Field & Taking Steps Forward

GUEST EDITORS
Michael Barnett, Giulia Bonacci *and* Erin C. MacLeod

IDEAZ
Editor Ian O. Boxill

Vol. 15 • 2020

ISSN 0799-1401

ISBN 978-1-7252-9702-9

●

Ideaz-Institute for Intercultural and Comparative Research /
Ideaz-Institut für interkulturelle und vergleichende Forschung
Contact and Publisher: **www.ideaz-institute.com**

●

IDEAZ—Journal
Publisher: Arawak publications ● Kingston, Jamaica

●

Credits
-Cover artwork "Emperor Haile Selassie and Empress Menen"
 (November 2019) ° acrylic on canvas *by courtesy of*
   Seconde Chance, aka Dominique Mark
-Photos reproduced in text *by courtesy of*
   Clinton Hutton (p. vi)
   Derek Bishton (p. 180)

Contents

•

Acknowledgments

The Editors would like to express special thanks to the Office of the Principal and the Special New Initiative Grants Committee as well as the Research and Publications & Graduate Awards Committee of The University of the West Indies, Mona Campus for their contribution of funds towards the publication of this special issue of *IDEAZ*.

We would also like to thank Sister Seconde Chance, aka Dominique Mark from the Republic of Mauritius who offered the artwork for the cover of the volume. Thanks also must be extended to Derek Bishton for his photograph of Ivan Coore, and to Professor Clinton Hutton for his "Coronation Re-enactment" photo of November 2014, featuring Priest Dermot Fagan of the School of Vision House of Rastafari, Jamaica, among others. In addition, we would like to extend special thanks to all of the authors for their important contributions to this issue.

We would like to dedicate this volume to the people of Ethiopia, and of Shashemene in particular, where recent unrest has provoked much damage, loss and pain.

May justice and peace bless Ethiopia once more.

Re-enactment of the Coronation of Emperor Haile Selassie I,
featuring Priest Dermot Fagan of the School of Vision,
House of Rastafari, Jamaica
handing an imitation Orb to Ras Roy Ivory.

••

Photo taken on November 2, 2014 on the Occasion of the 84th
Anniversary of the Coronation of Emperor Haile Selassie I, at Scott's
Pass Nyahbinghi Centre, Clarendon, Jamaica.

Photo © 2014 by Clinton Hutton

INTRODUCTION

A 2020 Vision Perspective on the Rastafari Movement: Revisiting the Field and Taking Steps Forward

MICHAEL BARNETT, GIULIA BONACCI & ERIN C. MACLEOD

- Guest Editors -

This issue was completed in 2020—a year of much tumult.
From a pandemic reaching all corners of the globe,
to calls for racial justice and the fight against white supremacy
in light of the brutal murder of George Floyd,
to unrest in Ethiopia affecting so many.
The week of the issue's submission was the week of the tragic blast in Beirut.
It is difficult to tell what more 2020 has to offer.
As editors, we wish to acknowledge these events and recognize the need
to see and think differently—something Rastafari consistently offers.
There is a need for reasoning and more reasoning.
Let this issue be a small contribution to that need
to provide new, alternate perspectives.

Black Lives Matter

I n 1978, *Caribbean Quarterly* published a "Preliminary Rastafari Bibliography", authored by Joyce Gordon and Roger Hughes, neither of whom were scholars of the movement. The list of thirty-three books and periodical articles ran for only three pages. Of the works listed, many were simply focused on description of the movement, such as Jamaican professor of religion Leonard Barrett's then out-of-print classic *The Rastafarians* (1968) and British scholar Dick Hebdige's occasional paper "Reggae, Rastas and Rudies: Style and the Subversion of Form" (1974). The bulk of the items on the list were not wholly dedicated to Rastafari, but might have provided some information that would have been contextually relevant—such as publications on Marcus Garvey and what the authors described as "Rastafarianism within the wider social context" (p. 56).

Since this publication, the last four decades have introduced a period of extensive development so far as Rastafari studies and Rastafari publications are concerned—a point at which an online bibliography of works related to "reggae and Rastafari" consists of over one thousand entries.[1] 2020 offers us the ability not only to take stock of what has happened in the past, as far as the Rastafari movement is concerned, but also very importantly to address the current state of the movement as it stands today.

1

Just a decade ago, in 2010, the first Rastafari Studies Conference was held at the University of the West Indies, Mona campus. It was also the year of Professor Barry Chevannes's passing—his landmark work *Rastafari: Roots and Ideology* (1994) is a foundational text for many of the scholars who gathered in the summer of 2010 to discuss the movement, fifty years after the controversial 1960 report by M.G. Smith, Roy Augier and Rex Nettleford—*The Ras Tafari Movement in Kingston, Jamaica.* These events of gain and loss demonstrated a watershed for Rastafari studies. Scholars that had learned from the foundation of previous work began to produce new texts—all three of the editors of this issue were presenters at that conference and published books on Rastafari within the subsequent decade (Barnett 2012, 2018; Bonacci 2015; MacLeod 2014), not to mention the many other new works such as *Jah Kingdom* (2017) by historian Monique Bedasse on Rastafari, pan-Africanism and Tanzania and *Revolutionary Threads: Rastafari, Social Justice, and Cooperative Economics* (2018), a book that links Rastafari to a range of social issues, from activist Bobby Sullivan. Bedasse's work, in particular, is exemplary of the extent that the Rastafari movement has become a global phenomenon, as evidenced by the reality of the movement's international connections and livities. In addition, every year sees new MA dissertations and PhDs on various aspects of Rastafari being submitted and defended in the Caribbean, the United Kingdom, the United States, as well as the Netherlands, Mexico, Brazil, France and Australia.[2]

Beyond recognizing the worldwide existence of Rastafari and the ever-growing literature on the topic, this collection of essays represents a means of connecting past research with present work, gesturing to the fruitful future of Rastafari studies. Making use of the venue of *IDEAZ*, a journal whose involvement with Rastafari studies led to a landmark 2008 publication of a special issue *The Globalization of Rastafari*, is significant. The essays that were selected for that 2008 issue were derived from a Rastafari in Global Context Seminar of the Academy of American Religion. From 1998 to 2001, the seminar brought together scholars who presented work on the topic of the internationalization of Rastafari. This was a wide-ranging group of scholars from many backgrounds and disciplines, and the resulting text provided what the editor hoped would

> serve as groundwork for additional research on Rastafari's global context, including specifically additional ethnographic work on the forms Rastafari takes in various communities worldwide, an increased emphasis on the dynamics and change within Rastafari as it continues to grow, and an increased self-awareness by scholars of Rastafari of how Rastafari's global context might reshape methodology (Boxill 2008, 1).

The scholars involved, however, felt that one of the weaknesses of the work was the lack of Rastafari practitioners as scholars.[3]

As well as building on other collections such as *Chanting Down Babylon: The Rastafari Reader* (1998) and the more recent *Rastafari in the New Millennium: A Rastafari Reader* (2012), this volume appears to answer the call—and to add to what came before as best as possible. Here, we want to thank Darren J.N. Middleton, Religious Studies scholar, for being instrumental in mobilizing some of the scholars whose work is featured in this volume. In addition to the involvement of a range of scholars who identify as Rastafari, there is an attempt to take stock of Rastafari at the present moment from unique perspectives. All papers in this collection make use of what might be now called classical references—for example, Leonard Barrett (1968), Joseph Owens (1976), Horace Campbell (1985), Barry Chevannes (1994)—and then build on this past to create yet further foundations for future work. Presently there is a new generation of Rastafari scholars and scholars of Rastafari who are emerging in the field of Rastafari studies. They come from various linguistic and cultural backgrounds and from various disciplines: sociology of religion—unsurprisingly—but also history, linguistics, cultural studies, sound studies, political science and anthropology. As a matter of fact, this edited collection reflects multiple perspectives on the movement developed over the past decade, and it also charts a trajectory towards further learning.

Also, very importantly, it affirms that the global dispersion of followers of Rastafari does indeed constitute a fully fledged movement.[4] In fact, at least two of the articles in this volume emphasize the peculiar structure and nature of Rastafari, that it is simultaneously non-homogenous (presenting a large spectrum of interpretations and practices) and polycephalous (presenting numerous organizations and congregations). Furthermore, the various articles successfully highlight its multidimensional quality: Rastafari undoubtedly has a spiritual dimension, but it also contains other dimensions, notably cultural and political. Thus, not only can Rastafari be considered as a social movement in its own right, but also as a religious movement, with its own theological orientation, as well as a "livity"—a term coined by Rastafari to represent their way of life, akin to what Michel de Certeau (1990) would call the "social practices of everyday life". In this regard, the movement lends itself to multidisciplinary approaches and methodologies of study.

In terms of the ordering of the articles in this volume, to begin, Shamara Wyllie Alhassan speaks of the role of women in Rastafari, and provides an important perspective that engages with gender equality and the movement. A testimony follows, penned by Deena-Marie Beresford, who shares the unfolding of grassroots meetings held by Rastafari sisters in the United States. Ennis B. Edmonds provides an analysis of the differing mansions of Rastafari that is based in rich, practical experience alongside the development of essential historical trajectories that provide connections between past and present. For his part, Michael Barnett argues that the long-standing tradition of charismatic leadership, which has been a part of the movement since its inception, has been both a blessing and a curse. Jahlani Niaah's work on herb camps in Kingston grows out of that of Carole Yawney, Dennis Forsythe and Barry Chevannes, not only centring the importance of ganja to Rastafari, but also demonstrating how the use of ganja shapes community and culture. Dean MacNeil's work provides an analysis of Rastafari in the work of the legendary reggae singer, Bob Marley. Diving into the early works through to the end of Marley's life and career, MacNeil charts the development and expression of Marley's Rastafari beliefs. Charles Price, whose 2009 work *Becoming Rasta* provides an ethnographic and psychoanalytic perspective on the development of Rastafari identity, expands this perspective in his essay, demonstrating how Rastafari identity formation links with Black racial identity. Richard C. Salter thinks about the relationship between the Rastafari concept of *livity* and the law. His work not only provides insight into how Rastafari theology and ideology link with particular social contexts, but also raises questions about the development of Rastafari concepts and belief.

Even though Africa is so pervasive in the Rastafari movement, channelling both historical and symbolic significance, and it is also rich with vibrant Rastafari communities that continue to develop all over the continent, research on Rastafari in Africa is just beginning. Significantly, three papers in this issue contribute to firmly anchoring the continent in the conversation. Giulia Bonacci, whose groundbreaking work on the history of repatriation to Ethiopia is well known, takes a wide look at repatriation throughout the African continent and beyond, demonstrating the role of Rastafari and repatriation in shaping perspectives on Africa as well as in shaping the movement itself. Erin C. MacLeod returns to her 2014 work on the Ethiopian perception of Rastafari, and updates the approaches taken by Rastafari to find acceptance, legally and otherwise, as citizens in Ethiopia.

The eleventh piece in this special volume is from British journalist and photographer Derek Bishton, who was contacted by us as editors because of the essential oral history that he had collected from Ivan Coore. We had decided, upon hearing of Ivan's sad passing during the month of September 2019, that we wanted to pay tribute in some shape or form to his contribution to the Rastafari movement. Unfortunately, Ivan never got to complete his life memoirs that he had been working on earnestly, even through sickness. Derek's piece suitably provides room for the voice of Coore about his sojourn in Ethiopia. What is specifically included here are recollections of life in Shashemene at the time of the 1974 revolution in Ethiopia. The significance of his memories, his contribution to the historical and intellectual record, underlines the importance of Rastafari scholarship in collecting and transmitting such experiences. There is a need for these stories to be told—from many perspectives. Rastafari as a movement may be relatively young, but many of its adherents and practitioners are increasing in age.

The last issue of *IDEAZ* that focused on Rastafari was published as a means of encouraging further publication, further research. Let this issue do the same. There is a need to revisit previous research and renew, build and rebuild. We the editors of this collection have titled it *A 2020 Vision Perspective on the Rastafari Movement*, as that is exactly what we hope it turns out to be at this very important juncture in the trajectory of the movement—a perspective that not only accounts for and interrogates the past, but also by extension effectively provides a clear spotlight on the present dynamics of the movement, as it stands today. It is said that hindsight is 2020 vision, as it is imperative to always look back. We can use this clear view of what came before to guide what comes next—just as the Akan concept of Sankofa suggests that returning to the past is what enables any movement forward. This will not only put Rastafari studies in good stead for the future, but also very importantly the Rastafari movement itself, without which there would be no Rastafari studies.

Notes

1. Harold Hammarstrom, "Reggae and Rastafari Bibliography", https://cl.lingfil.uu.se/ ~ harald/alphaomega.htm. The number of items is 1,070 as of 2018.

2. Some recent graduate work at the Master's and PhD level includes Aarons 2017; Araujo 2018; Ayele 2018; Contreras 2018; De Kaiser 2016; Gomes 2011; Halimi 2018; Lamaison-Boltanski 2017; Montlouis 2013; Mulder 2015; Renaud-Grignon 2016; Stratford 2018; and Wakengut 2013.

3. According to the editor's note:

   > We were an eclectic and interdisciplinary group, coming from fields as far ranging as religious studies, anthropology, sociology, cultural studies, theology and literature. We were also an inclusive group, inviting onlookers and other interested parties to our meetings, and doing our best (but in the end failing) to also include Rastafari voices in our discussions (Boxill 2008, 1).

   The group did invite and find funding for Rastafari Elder Mortimo Planno; however, he was consistently denied a US visa, so could not attend.

4. If we wish to define movement, as many sociologists do, as "purposeful, organized groups striving to work toward a common social goal" (Little 2014, 652), Rastafari is certainly a movement. That being said, it is also possible to consider Rastafari as having provided its own definition of movement, as is described herein.

References

Aarons, David. 2017. "Chanting Up Zion: Reggae as Productive Mechanism for Repatriated Rastafari in Ethiopia". PhD diss., University of Washington.

Araujo, Felipe Neis. 2018. "'Every Man Do his Ting a Little Way Different': Poética, política e dissenso entre Rastas em Kingston, Jamaica". PhD diss., Universidade Federal de Santa Catarina, Brazil.

Ayele, Mahlet. 2018. "The Rastafari in Ethiopia: Challenges and Paradoxes of Belonging". MA diss., Leiden University, Netherlands.

Barnett, Michael. 2012. *Rastafari in the New Millennium: A Rastafari Reader*. Syracuse, NY: Syracuse University Press.

_____. 2018. *The Rastafari Movement: A North American and Caribbean Perspective*. London: Routledge.

Bedasse, Monique. 2017. *Jah Kingdom: Rastafarians, Tanzania, and Pan-Africanism in the Age of Decolonization*. Chapel Hill, NC: University of North Carolina Press.

Bonacci, Giulia. 2015. *Exodus! Heirs and Pioneers, Rastafari Return to Ethiopia*. Kingston, Jamaica: University of the West Indies Press.

Boxill, Ian, ed. 2008. *The Globalization of Rastafari*. Edited by Ian Boxill. *IDEAZ* (Special Issue) 7. Kingston, Jamaica: Arawak publications.

Campbell, Horace. 1985. *Rasta and Resistance: From Marcus Garvey to Walter Rodney*. Trenton, NJ: Africa World Press.

Chevannes, Barry. 1994. *Rastafari: Roots and Ideology*. Syracuse, NY: Syracuse University Press.

Contreras, Alberto Romero. 2018. "Etiopes en el extranjero: ¿Ciudadanos en casa? La repatriación de la diáspora Rastafari a Shashemene, Etiopía". PhD diss., Centro de Investigaciones y Estudios Superiores en Antropología Social, Mexico.

De Certeau, Michel. 1990. *L'invention du quotidien*. Vol. 1. *Arts de faire*. Paris: Gallimard.

De Keizer, Victoria. 2016. "Music, Voice, and Agency: Response Mechanisms of Politically Marginalized Groups and the Case of the Rastafari Minority in Ethiopia". Senior Capstone Project. New York University, Abu Dhabi Campus.

Forsythe, Dennis. 1983. *Rastafari: For the Healing of the Nations*. Kingston, JA: Ziaka Productions.

Gomes, Shelene. 2011. "The Social Reproduction of *Jamaica Safar* in Shashemene, Ethiopia". PhD diss., University of St Andrews, UK.

Gordon, Joyce, and Roger Hughes. 1978. "A Preliminary Rastafari Bibliography". *Caribbean Quarterly* 24 (3–4): 56–58.

Halimi, Lina. 2018. "Rastafari, (En)Quête de définition(s): Histoire(s), transnationalistation(s) et définition(s) du mouvement. Une historiographie du mouvement Rastafari, des années 1950 à aujourd'hui". MA diss., Université Paris 1 Panthéon-Sorbonne.

Lamaison-Boltanski, Jeanne. 2017. "Les communautés politique parallèles: Mouvement Rastafari et cultures Hip Hop au Burkina Faso". PhD diss., Université Paris Nanterre.

Little, William. 2013. *Introduction to Sociology: First Canadian Edition*. Houston, TX: Rice University.

MacLeod, Erin C. 2014. *Visions of Zion: Ethiopians and Rastafari in the Search for the Promised Land*. New York: NYU Press.

Montlouis, Nathalie. 2013. "Lords and Empresses In and Out of Babylon: The EABIC Community and the Dialectic of Female Subordination". PhD diss., School of Oriental and African Studies, University of London.

Mulder, Lianne. 2015. "Rastafari as a Counter-Hegemonic Practice: A Qualitative Comparative Analysis between Black and White Rastafari". MPhil diss., The University of the West Indies, Cave Hill, Barbados.

Owens, Joseph. 1976. *Dread*. Kingston, JA: Sangster.

Renaud-Grignon, Geoffroy. 2016. "Les Rastafaris dans les poumons de l'hégémonie: Matérialisme symbolique d'une négation idéologique". MSc diss., Université de Montréal.

Smith, M.G., Roy Augier, and Rex Nettleford. 1960. *The Ras Tafari Movement in Kingston, Jamaica*. Institute of Social and Economic Research, Department of the University College of the West Indies (Jamaica).

Stratford, Maria. 2018. "Rastas' Journey 'Home': Investigating the Lived Experience of the Rastafari in Ethiopia Through an Ethnographic Documentary". PhD diss., RMIT University, Australia.

Sullivan, Bobby. 2018. *Revolutionary Threads: Rastafari, Social Justice, and Cooperative Economics*. New York: Akashic.

Wakengut, Anastasia. 2013. "Rastafari in Germany: Jamaican Roots and Global-Local Influences". *Student Anthropologist* 3 (4): 60–83.

Yawney, Carole. 1985. "Strictly Ital: Rastafari Livity and Holistic Health". Paper presented at Annual Meeting of the Society for Caribbean Studies, Hertfordshire, UK, 2–4 July 1985. Working draft, sourced from Smithsonian Institution.

"THIS MOVEMENT IS NOT ABOUT THE MAN ALONE"[1]
Toward a Rastafari Woman's Studies

SHAMARA WYLLIE ALHASSAN

This piece is livicated to Blakk Madonna,
Empress Ama and Don Dread

Abstract Sistren[2] are partners in the development and maintenance of the Rastafari movement despite scholarly refusal to engage with balanced gender narratives. This refusal reinforces patriarchal notions that sistren have nothing significant to contribute to overstanding[3] Rastafari livity, philosophy or other world phenomena. Increased scholarly engagement with the intellectual contributions and livitical practices of sistren will allow balanced narratives of the movement to come to the fore, deepen our overstanding of Rastafari philosophy and livity and help rectify existing patriarchy within the livity.

Keywords • Woman • sistren • androcentrism • omega balance • gender balance • patriarchy

✦✦

"The omission of the Rastafari Woman's voice in literature about
Rastafari makes the assumption that either her voice is the echo
of the Rastafari man or it is so minimal that it does not
impact the movement in any serious way."
— Jahzani Kush (2011, 2)

Sistren are partners in the development and maintenance of the Rastafari movement despite scholarly refusal to engage with balanced gender narratives. In the epigraph to this essay, Rastafari woman scholar Jahzani Kush points out the implications of the lengthy omission of woman in Rastafari studies. Sistren[4] have had to struggle not only with patriarchy within the movement, but also against androcentric scholarship produced about the movement. I focus on the Rastafari movement, not because it is exceptional in terms of patriarchy and male-centred scholarship, but because literature in the field continues to elide the organizational capacity and philosophical contributions of sistren. Scholarly engagement with balanced gender narratives in the Garvey,[5] Negritude,[6] Communist,[7] Black Power[8] and other movements has transformed and enhanced our knowledge of the history of Black resistance and resilience. With only a handful of articles, a few dissertations, and even fewer published books about sistren, woman in

Rastafari are virtually rendered invisible in studies of Black women's activism, Rastafari studies and Pan-Africanist discourses.

A few questions to ponder while reading this piece are: 1) What role do researchers play in the perpetual silencing and erasure of sistren and whose purpose does this erasure serve? 2) How are research methods (research questions, selection of respondents, coding data, writing and analysis) influenced by a focus on masculine narratives? Some researchers have mentioned that sistren refused to be interviewed by them or that they found it more difficult to interview sistren (Christensen 2014, 142). If sistren refuse to participate in academic research, what is the impetus behind their refusal, and if they are hard to find, where are they? These methodological and epistemological issues should be grappled with because they present common reasons why woman are not included or remain marginal in prevailing scholarship. While this short contribution is not an exhaustive study of this issue, it provides a critique of the state of gender analysis in the field and presents ideas worth grappling with for future scholarship in Rastafari studies.

As a Rastafari woman scholar, I have worked with Rastafari sistren and brethren in Jamaica, Ghana and Ethiopia for the past twelve years. My access to sistren is primarily the result of relationships built over the years, referrals and my research agenda which focuses on the ways sistren use their livity to build Pan-African communities of social justice and combat anti-Black gendered racism. While it has not been my experience that sistren are harder to interview than brethren,[9] sistren are often more difficult to find. Most of my interviews occurred in the homes or places of employment of sistren. Over the course of my work, I found that sistren have helped shape livity and reasonings from the earliest formations of the movement. Analysing Rastafari from woman's perspectives changes the way constitutive elements of livity are conceptualized. Scholars and Rastafari people overstand Rastafari to be anti-imperialist, pro-Black and Africa-centred, but when considering woman's philosophical and livitical contributions to Rastafari, it is also pro-woman's health and wellness and pro-masculine and feminine energy-balance. A woman's perspective of the movement requires scholars to centre the practical quotidian work or materialization of Rastafari ideas as critical to the development of livity and philosophy. Sistren have been leaders and partners in building the grounds for reasoning and ritual activity by contributing financially to Rastafari events and organizations, leading Rastafari organizations, planning international conferences, cooking, clearing the land, gardening, caring for children and reasoning at Rastafari gatherings, among other forms of communal work.

ANDROCENTRIC NARRATIVES
IN RASTAFARI STUDIES

Driving down the winding streets of Kingston in the August heat, sweat dripping down my brow, I was gratified to reach the Ashanti Oasis Restaurant in the heart of the city in 2014. After eating the most delicious ital food[10] created by Sister Yvonne, owner of the restaurant, we sat down to reason about her life and gender dynamics within Rastafari. When I asked Sister Yvonne why she thinks woman have been omitted from much of the historical narrative of the movement, without hesitation she said,

> People, on a whole, are not interested *at all* in the views of Rastafari woman. I remember coming up in the '70s, '80s and people start—Bob Marley around—people start get excited about the whole Rastafari movement. None of these anthropologists, because you had anthropologists, you had some journalists, you had some researchers come down to interview and they just ignore the woman. They bypass you and they don't think that you have a voice. A lot of these researchers help to marginalize the woman and a lot of them were woman as well. They just feel that you were just breeders; just have to have children and sit in the corner. So they help the men to continue —rather than say let me hear what this sister have to say—to include her in this, because this movement is not about the man alone, it's about the man, woman and children, the family, the whole person. They just ignore you. So that is why there is not enough documenta- tion or documentary or research or any of those things being done on Rastafari woman and to hear what they have to say or how they think. You understand me. So they just encourage the men to continue so long and that is why we have to put a stoppage to it!![11]

I was surprised when Sister Yvonne said researchers helped perpetuate patriarchy within the movement through their refusal to interview woman. I suspected this given the lack of citations for woman participants in ethnographic research, but hearing Sister Yvonne vocalize the profound pain of being seen, but not taken seriously, was devastating. Her experiences led me to a central finding which is that while patriarchy exists in Rastafari, male dominance in the movement is aided by the way knowledge about the movement is produced. This is not to say all scholars of Rastafari studies have aided patriarchy by neglecting woman's narratives—I will discuss researchers who foreground the contributions of sistren in their work. However, it is important to question the ways knowledge is produced in Rastafari studies and how this knowledge directly impacts Rastafari people, particularly the most vulnerable members of the movement.

In Rastafari studies, androcentric scholarship can be defined as 1) insistence on Rastafari as solely linked to masculinity, 2) the omission of sistren and/or minimization of the contributions of sistren in narratives of the movement and 3) majority-use of male participants as authorities in constructing knowledge of Rastafari (Simpson 1955, 167-171; Barrett 1977, 2; Kitzinger 1969, 12; Sterling 2012, 147-148). Since 1955, male participants have been used as the sole or majority representatives from which generalizable knowledge is created in much of the literature on the movement (Simpson 1955, 167-171). The lack of inclusion of woman as research participants for studies about Rastafari and the minimization of their contributions when they are included are two of the ways androcentric thought informs scholarly analysis and writing. Contemporary scholars of Rastafari must tread carefully when relying on data produced with an androcentric lens because they may continue to reach the same conclusions with many of the same primarily male citations.[12] Upon reading against the grain of secondary literature, I discovered that there is evidence to support both the early participation and influence of woman if questions of inquiry centre gender.

There is a debate in Rastafari studies regarding the role, quantifiable presence and degree of influence sistren have had in the development of Rastafari philosophy (Kitzinger 1969, 12; Barrett 1977, 2; Campbell 1987, 199; Chevannes 1994, 257, 265; Lake 1998, 59, 93, 98–102; Rowe 1998, 78–81; Tafari-Ama 1998, 104–105; Erskine 2005, 58; Edmonds 2012, 95; Lewis 2012, 236–243; Christensen 2014, 3–4, 129–149; Niaah 2016, 1, 3, 9). Several scholars have used quantitative data to posit that sistren comprise a minority of the movement and therefore have had little influence on the formation of Rastafari (Edmonds 2012, 95; Niaah 2016, 1, 3, 9). Some scholars have argued that sistren were not numerically significant in Rastafari because of patriarchal norms and that they were involved in other more sistren-centred spiritual traditions like Pentecostalism (Austin-Broos 1987). Statistical representations of members within the movement are difficult to assess; therefore, I cannot say with certainty the exact number of sistren in the movement at any given time. However, I can say that small numerical presence does not equate with lack of influence. Considering some sistren do not attend organizational meetings or affiliate with major Rastafari mansions, it may be especially difficult to quantify their presence in Jamaica and in other countries. This point is important because many Rastafari scholars study the movement through mansions,[13] like The Order of Nyahbinghi, The Twelve Tribes of Israel and the Ethiopia Africa Black International Congress. However, some sistren do not attend mansional gatherings for a variety of reasons, like lack of access to childcare or transportation. Some sistren do not identify with a particular mansion and, therefore, will not be found at these gatherings. A researcher attending gatherings may not see many sistren, but the few sistren in attendance at these gatherings may not reflect actual membership of sistren within these mansions or their influence in terms of the ideas shared at gatherings.

Much of the literature in Rastafari studies supports the early presence and influence of Rastafari sistren, even though gender was not an important mode of analysis. In his recent book, Michael Barnett (2018, 73) confirms that sistren were a large part of the earliest membership that built the foundation of Leonard Howell's and Robert Hinds' pioneering organizations. Although the authors of the 1960 Report on the Rastafari Movement produced by the University of the West Indies (UWI) spoke with largely male respondents, they confirm the presence and organizational capacity of sistren by documenting that there was an organization that comprised only woman, writing: "Local 41 consists of women only" (Augier & Salter 2010, 12). Although the authors of the report do not highlight the significance of Local 41, they do document its presence, which suggests it was important enough to be recorded. A few years after that report was published, there was another reference to a woman-only camp in Sheila Kitzinger's work: "Women are peripheral to the Rasta movement, although at one time there was a camp consisting solely of women" (1969, 252). While it is unclear if Kitzinger is referencing the same camp as the authors of the 1960 UWI report, it is clear that a camp consisting of only woman existed in the 1950s and 1960s.

These sources confirm the numerical presence of Rastafari sistren, but do not provide a gendered analysis about how sistren contributed to the movement and the ways they influenced the early development of Rastafari livity or philosophy. Other examples from the prevailing scholarship actively discuss woman's contributions but do not fully engage the importance of those contributions. Some scholars contend that Rastafari woman's marginality is due to her lack of appearance in the typical visual iconography of Rastafari as well as male respondents not regarding her as central (Kitzinger 1969, 252). These findings suggest that the combination of patriarchal male respondents and preconceived notions of how a Rastafari woman should appear contributed to woman's marginality within the movement and in studies of Rastafari. Sister Ilaloo recalls,

> I remember like '71 and so... [t]here was no such thing as a Rasta-woman. There were cultural daughters and sisters primarily. Then all of a sudden about '72 or '73 all the little West Indian daughters in the high schools started wrapping up dem head and chant Rasta, an' mili-tantly a see Rasta fi demselves, and independently of any man (Niaah 2016, 10).

Ilaloo's testimony suggests that producing numerical data and qualitatively documenting woman's presence relies on the ability to see and recognize Rastafari sistren. Sister Ilaloo's comments distinguish between "cultural daughters or sisters" and a "Rastawoman". While it is unclear how "cultural daughters or sisters" are different from Rastafari woman, she does mention that wrapping their heads and chanting Rastafari independently of a man were important markers of delineation. Although she suggests that sistren only became Rastawoman in the 1970s, there is sufficient evidence of her own presence and the presence of other sistren to confirm that this perception is limited. Maureen Rowe points out that brethren deliberately kept younger sistren away from older sistren to stymie any feminist impulses they may have and restrict their access to only male interpretations of Rastafari philosophy (1998, 80-81).

The question of naming and recognition is important when examining much of the literature concerning Rastafari. There continues to be a clear masculinist interest in the ways data is interpreted and research participants chosen. The systemic focus on masculinity elides other gendered narrative representations about the movement and supports patriarchal dominance within the movement. This does not mean I negate the fact of Rastafari patriarchy, but it does mean that I reject the claim that Rastafari sistren were not co-constitutive parts of creating Rastafari philosophy. For example, Leonard Barrett whose research was conducted between 1963 and 1966, provides amazing examples of how woman contributed to the development of the livity but does not analyze the importance of these contributions. He writes:

> Women play a very minor role in Rastafarianism... In special meetings women act as mistresses of songs or. . . they may be used as recording secretaries. In all other respects, the male assumes the responsibilities of the movement, though at present, a large segment of Rastafarian women now sell Rastafarian products (Barrett 1977, 2).

While Barrett asserts several times that woman are peripheral in the movement, he documents their central roles as mistresses of songs at special meetings, as secretaries and as entrepreneurs.The rampant unemployment of poor Black communities in 1960s Jamaica and the pervasive discrimination against Rastafari during the time of Barrett's fieldwork indicates that woman's ability to lead ritual songs, generate economic revenue and document organizational activities was central to the spiritual, financial and historical sustenance of Rastafari organizations. Reading familiar texts in Rastafari studies with an eye toward sistren presence and influence provides evidence of the contributions they have made to Rastafari livity since its earliest formations. These findings allow for new questions of inquiry to emerge that centre sistren livitical and intellectual contributions.

Ethnographic data in the secondary literature provides evidence to support Rastafari woman's influential roles in the development of the movement by 1) maintaining Rastafari enclaves during periods of mass male incarceration, 2) remaining employed or mobilizing financial resources to support Rastafari communities, 3) working as secretaries and mistresses of songs in ritual and organizational gatherings and 4) organizing and comprising their own organizations. To this list, I would add reasoning, writing, cooking, child rearing and maintaining space for Rastafari gatherings. Androcentric analysis coupled with Rastafari patriarchy has made it quite difficult to recover Rastafari woman's history. Much of the early studies of the movement might mention sistren briefly or include one chapter on gender, but do not include analyses of how woman's contributions informed research questions and transformed research conclusions.[14] Charles Price's work on how ones and ones become Rastafari is an example of contemporary scholarship seeking to strike a balanced narrative that features both brethren and sistren (2009, 213–216). Rather than singling out a focus on either gender, he argues that his empirical research demonstrates that woman become Rastafari "primarily through their own experiences, interests, and pursuits. In this they deviated from the widespread view that women are to become Rastafari through the assistance of men" (ibid., 216). Price allows his ethnographic research to inform his analysis and transform his research conclusions. Rather than insisting on a single masculine narrative of Rastafari or debating qualitative influence and quantitative presence of woman, it would be useful to investigate the ways woman participated, developed and sustained the Rastafari movement since the early years.

SISTREN AS PARTNERS IN THE FOUNDATION AND MAINTENANCE OF THE MOVEMENT

Most scholars agree that there were no explicit gender roles prescribed in the early years of the movement (Edmonds 2012, 95; Rowe 1998, 75–81). Rastafari patriarchy congealed during the late 1960s and 1970s and coincided with Rastafari woman's mobilization around gender balance in their families and communities. The rigid masculinity in Jamaican society mirrored the institutionalization of male dominance in the movement and the rise of international feminist movements. Brethren began to "react negatively to feminist ideology. Many of the elders began to see women's liberation as the reason for every action that did not appear appropriate" (Rowe 1998, 81). Maureen Rowe documents the ways sistren were discouraged from taking initiative, were disciplined when they did not conform to social mores and were subjected to greater restrictions because brethren were concerned that sistren wanted equal treatment in the movement. It is important to note that Rastafari is not a monolith and different mansions have developed gender norms that suit their particular ideology. While some scholars have concluded that sistren have appropriated and internalized patriarchal practices of subjugation, citing dress codes and menstruation norms as the primary ways patriarchy is practised, this is inadequate because some sistren find solace and empowerment in modest dress and being relieved of certain responsibilities while menstruating. For example, when I interviewed Sister Lily, who has been trodding the path of Rastafari for forty-three years and lived at Bobo Hill for many years, but has since repatriated to Ethiopia, about whether she felt the twenty-one day principle[15] was oppressive, she said she found it to be liberating because she had time to develop herself and her entrepreneurship.

. . . I had a business from within my twenty-one days. Yea. I was working while I was within house. . . So I wasn't idle. For my first eight days, which is my time, I could read my Bible. After that I could fast, start my industry. I could do crochet. I could do embroidery. I could make mats and I can sew. So Rastafari woman, you know, we excel. We could run a country if you gave it to us.[16]

Sister Lily makes all her own elaborate clothing with intricate embroidery. The day I met her, she wore a red, gold and green accented khaki dress and a beautiful hair wrap and fall of the same colour. Some would argue she is internalizing patriarchy by covering herself and not showing skin, but she was proud of having designed her own clothing. While not all sistren will agree with Sister Lily's stance and scholars can critique her claims, dismissing her reflections on her experiences as internalized patriarchy reinforces androcentric forms of scholarly analysis by refusing to listen to her own interpretation of her experiences. Continuing to solely cite menstruation and dress codes as evidence of patriarchy elides other insidious forms of male dominance, such as dehumanizing treatment, gender-based violence and lack of access to resources or opportunities based upon gender.

Sister Lily continued her interview by discussing how she ran the Women's Freedom Liberation League (WFLL) of the Ethiopia Africa Black International Congress (EABIC) for a few years. The WFLL was established by King Emmanuel in 1980 and has become one of the primary centres of power in the Congress.

In her groundbreaking, yet unpublished, research, Nathalie Montlouis has shown the ways woman were able to use the WFLL "to create a reliable international network, in order to promote the EABIC livity from a female perspective" (Montlouis 2013, 149–150). In fact, Montlouis contends that sistren in the EABIC never were known as the Rastaman's woman but were always Rastafari woman sighting Rastafari and contributing to livity on their own terms. There was and, in some ways, there continues to be a debate within the field about whether woman were solely dependent on men for Rastafari philosophy or whether they could sight Rastafari for themselves. While some sistren do sight Rastafari through their Kingman, my research and that of Montlouis reveals that there are numerous single Rastafari woman who come to livity on their own accord. The scholarly absence of woman's intellectual and philosophical contributions to Rastafari formation, maintenance and livity continues to suggest that woman do not sight Rastafari on their own, that their voice is an echo of brethren, and that their unique perspectives have nothing of importance to contribute.

Jahzani Kush argues that there has been more misinformation spread about Rastafari than information because of a lacuna in scholarship produced by Rastafari scholars: "Until Rastafari scholars take the forefront in writing about INI[17] livity, INI will forever reside on the periphery of works that supposedly represent the Rastafari way of life" (2011, 6). Kush's argument that Rastafari scholars must take control of knowledge production concerning Rastafari is connected to broader questions of how the subject-position of the researcher shapes the research questions, methods, participant selection and analysis of the project. How does scholarly bias render vulnerable populations like Rastafari susceptible to misrepresentation and mischaracterization and how is this tied to broader notions of who controls the production of knowledge? These provocative questions are not posed to discourage ones and ones from researching with Rastafari, but are posed to inspire reflexivity and conscious choices while embarking on ethnographic research and writing.

Scholars have argued that the patriarchal norms pervading Rastafari exclude sistren from meaningfully contributing to the formation of the movement. Some scholars have argued that sistren face unique oppressions stemming from Christian, European and African gender constructions (Lake 1998, 98; Rowe 1998, 80–81; Christensen 2014, 3–4, 129–149). Although Obiagele Lake's empirical research indicates that most Rastafari woman she interviewed do not see themselves as subordinate to their male counterparts, she argues "their lack of personal mobility and their secondary social and cultural status relative to men belie this notion" (Lake 1998, 98). Lake's scholarship makes astute insights about the nature of patriarchy, but it forecloses analysis of Rastafari woman's mobilization because of male dominance. Most societies are dominated by patriarchy or systems that advantage man over woman and gender non-conforming individuals, but patriarchal dominance does not prevent woman from organizing against these systems of oppression.

Dr. Jahzani Kush writes that this mythic image of the Rastafari woman as subordinate, passive and oppressed is the dominant interpretation that people outside Rastafari have of woman within the movement (2011, 2). Kush's identification of a stereotypical "Rastafari woman trope" is critical to understanding why sistren are not represented in movement literature. By challenging this dominant representation, sistren break new epistemic ground, which allows for balanced and comprehensive depictions of the movement.

While sistren in the 1960s found it challenging to navigate the new rules and restrictions that solidified male dominance within the movement, this did not hinder their ability to influence Rastafari philosophy. Imani Tafari-Ama argues, "Rastafari sistren have been primarily responsible for the persistence of livity in the private sphere, which also influences the public maintenance of Rastafari as a viable social entity" (1998, 196). Tafari-Ama suggests public invisibility or restrictions on sistren did not necessarily correlate with their ability to influence the development of Rastafari philosophy through reasoning with their partners, raising the next generation of Rastafari and engaging in community organizing. Rastafari woman scholar Maureen Rowe writes, "A number of elderly females have identified themselves as early trodders within the movement, that is, they have been with it from the early years" (1998, 75). She argues that sistren participated in all activities in the early stages of the movement, including the chalice, ritual reasonings (conversations) and witness-bearing (ibid., 75–78).

Rastafari woman's oral testimonies from Pinnacle to the contemporary moment have affirmed their presence and their influence. When I interviewed Mama Irone in 2017, she recalled her time living in the first Rastafari community at Pinnacle. She confirmed women's presence and participation in both building and maintaining the community. Nana Farika Berhane, elder in the Nyahbinghi House, confirmed that elder sistren like Sister Ina, Sister Daphne and Sister Esmin held gatherings at their homes where people would visit them to seek knowledge of Rastafari during the late 1960s to 1980s. These elder sistren, including Ma Ashanti, raised chants and psalms in the Nyahbinghi tabernacle during the same period. This is significant because there is a long-standing notion in Rastafari studies that sistren did not reason. Nana Farika demonstrates that not only did sistren reason, but some were also leaders with their own followers. This is not to suggest that patriarchal restrictions were not present or that all sistren had similar experiences within the Nyahbinghi House. Nana Farika often points out that the history of Rastafari woman is not linear and must take into consideration class, status and age. In her award-winning historical account, Monique Bedasse documents Sister May as being one of the founding members of the Twelve Tribes of Israel during the late 1960s (2017, 30). We have already discussed the way woman felt empowered by the Women's Freedom Liberation League (WFLL) of the Ethiopia Africa Black International Congress (EABIC). This copious evidence offers fresh avenues for a renewal in Rastafari studies, which focuses on the balanced narratives of the ways brethren and sistren have organized as partners in revolutionary struggle.[18]

RASTAFARI WOMAN'S GENDER CRITIQUE

In Jamaica, the 1970s was the era of Michael Manley and experimentation with democratic socialism. Manley ran on a political platform that conveniently used selected Rastafari symbols to secure political office. The political establishment's use of Rastafari, alongside the popularity of reggae music at the time, created a space for more people, like women and the middle class to become Rastafari. During this era of new nation-building, new forms of governance, and continued struggles for economic and psychological sovereignty, the Rastafari movement became the premier site of radicalism in Jamaica and much of the Caribbean (Campbell 1987). With the rise of Rastafari in the UK, repatriation to Africa and the stardom of reggae musicians like Bob and Rita Marley, Peter Tosh, Judy Mowatt and Marcia Griffith (among others), Rastafari became the face of Black liberation in Jamaica and internationally. Some scholars have referred to Rastafari as the new iteration of Pan-Africanism in the Caribbean and Africa (Campbell 1988, 75–88). Black women with a desire to participate in the Black liberation struggle of the time were attracted to Rastafari, but once in the movement, they realized they would have to struggle against international neocolonial forces, white supremacy *and* sexism both internally and externally. Sistren had to use their radical imaginations to think beyond colonial, post-independence and internal gender constructions to create their own egalitarian visions of social justice. In fact, sistren were central to manifesting a Rastafari Black liberation agenda for the entire family.

Working to document Rastafari woman's political involvement in anticolonial resistance, Terisa Turner makes a distinction between two sequential stages of the movement—old Rastafari and new Rastafari (1994). While I contend that the stages she pinpoints act concurrently, her analysis is important to consider. She writes that the old Rastafari is characterized by male dominance and biblical rationalization for woman's oppression. On the other hand, an egalitarian woman-centred transnational network led by the visionary organizing of Mau Mau women in East Africa, who are seeking to dismantle all forms of oppression, characterize the new Rastafari (ibid., 47).

Advocating for control over land, equitable relationships, sisterly networks and freedom to sustain life are essential components of Rastafari woman's activism in continental Africa and the African Diaspora. Turner calls this activism Rasta feminism although many Rastafari woman have an aversion to the label "feminist" (Kush 2011, 2). Some scholars have tried to advance arguments situating Rastafari woman firmly within a feminist discourse (Turner 1994; Yawney 1994; Julien 2003). Rastafari woman have divergent opinions on the issue of feminism with some actively identifying themselves as feminists and others vehemently arguing against the label. Many Rastafari woman have issues with the term feminism because they associate it with white women's single-issue feminism. Black women have long critiqued white women for organizing in ways that only highlight their gender, but do not attend to other vectors of oppression experienced by Black women and other women of colour. In addition, Rastafari woman and many Black women are struggling with their male counterparts against white supremacy and other forms of oppression. White feminism is perceived as creating a woman-only silo, whereas Black women are fighting for the entire family.[19]

While I argue that there are similarities between Rastafari woman's thought and Black feminism, Africana feminism, Africana Womanism and Pan-African feminism, I use Imani Tafari-Ama's notion of a "rebel woman continuum", which she uses to describe the array of gender philosophies sistren ascribe to, some adhering to more patriarchal forms of womanhood and others identifying as feminist. Sistren exist on a continuum with many iterations in the middle and some occupying multiple positions on the continuum given the issues they are addressing. Based upon my ethnographic research, I use sistren's notion of balance to think through their fight for gender justice within Rastafari. As scholars, it is important to privilege the terms and categories of analysis that research participants use to describe themselves. Rastafari woman's notion of balance (sometimes referred to as Omega balance) denotes the equity and synchronicity between masculine and feminine energies. Both sistren and brethren have equal roles to play in the fight for Black liberation, and it is only through balance between them that this can be achieved.

Sistren challenged the "downpression"[20] of woman within the movement and colonial notions of gender more broadly (Christensen 2014, 142). Colonial notions of gender are challenged by their theorization of a balance between masculine and feminine energies within the body without regard to sex. "Rastafari feminists understand 'feminine' and 'masculine' as ways of conceptualizing energy that ought not to be conflated with male and female bodies" (ibid., 143). Christensen's formulations allude to Oyèrónkẹ́Oyěwùmí's argument that the obsession with links between anatomical sex and gender in Western episteme is a critical part of the colonial project and the imposition of the Western nation-state. The epistemic critique of the notions of gender nurtured by the tripartite domination schema of Christianity, colonialism and slavery are central to forming Rastafari woman's gender consciousness. In England, Rastafari woman created "a new politics, which integrated a Rasta analysis of a 'Babylon' system with [B]lack women's experiences of gendered oppression to create a new and unique oppositional vision" (Sudbury 1998, 89). The integrated critique of the imperial capitalist patriarchal white supremacist world order combined with the experience of being Africa-centred Black women, allows Rastafari woman to create Black "rebel woman" spaces for strategizing ways to achieve Black liberation. Patriarchy elevates men and dehumanizes other genders. In my ethnographic research, I have not found sistren who ascribe to their own dehumanization. Sistren I have spoken with overstand man and woman to have different roles or spheres of power but equity in their common humanity.

Theological notions of gender balance inform Rastafari woman's critiques of patriarchy. Rastafari woman scholar, Barbara Makeda Blake-Hannah, writes: "The Rastafari Wo(mb)man is the other half of Creation that is God-Jah. Jah is both male and female, Alpha and Omega, Yin and Yang, two halves united in one whole as Creation and Creator (2012, 61). The notion of sistren sharing divinity with brethren calls into question conceptions of divinity being based on masculinity.[21] It is important to mention that Hannah does not argue that Rastafari men and women are powerful or divine in the same ways. Hannah develops her analysis by writing that sistren control the domestic domain, while brethren control the public domain, but there is equity in their shared divinity and power (Blake-Hannah 2012). Her notions of gender balance are liberating in one sense and reinforce certain patriarchal understandings of gender norms in another. Liberating in that brethren and sistren share divinity, but patriarchal in that woman are still cast as domesticated, while brethren control public spheres. The shared feminine and masculine features of divinity in Rastafari theology were first introduced by Leonard Howell, who many consider to be the first Rastafari. In his 1935 foundational text, *The Promised Key*, Howell writes, "King Ras Tafari and Queen Omega are the foundation stones of the Resurrection of the Kingdom of Ethiopia" (Maragh 1935, 7). Howell's conceptions of Rastafari included brethren and sistren as foundational to the building of a new world. He did not make the distinction between the domestic and public domain here. While more research needs to be done on whether this theological notion materialized in livitical practices at Pinnacle, it is important to note that theological gender balance was integral to Rastafari from the beginning. Michael Barnett has documented the ways certain Rastafari now invoke Empress Menen Asfaw alongside Emperor Haile Selassie to concretize their overstanding of the 2 November 1930 coronation where Emperor Haile Selassie became the first Emperor coronated alongside his wife, Empress Menen Asfaw (Barnett 2018, 74). While more research needs to be done on exactly when Empress Menen began to appear on the altar beside His Majesty during Rastafari gatherings, it is important to note that sistren advocacy for gender balance materialized in Empress Menen Asfaw's presence on the altar. At Bingis or ritual gatherings within the Rastafari community, I have noted Empress Menen Asfaw's portrait alongside that of Emperor Haile Selassie I. Therefore, theological rationale for balanced conceptions of divinity are present, even if these notions are not always practised. In *Roaring Lionesses*, Jahzani Kush quotes Sister Janelle as saying,

> There is no Rastafari movement without Rastafari Women. . . . We are the co-Creators of this entire experience. . . . The success of nation requires that man and woman work together to create a harmonious life that begins with family, whose cup runneth over into the community, and then the nation, in that order (2011, 64).

Sister Janelle links the strength of the Rastafari family to the creation of a new world. It is only through the liberation of the entire family that Black people can achieve freedom. Rastafari woman's interventions in conceptualizing both divinity and the movement are critical correctives for future scholarship in Rastafari studies.

TOWARD A RASTAFARI WOMAN'S STUDIES

The last forty years have seen philosophical, livitical and organizational vision and leadership by Rastafari woman as they have continued to be household breadwinners, published authors of their experiences, international conference founders and organizers, leaders of Rastafari mansions, and spearheads for contemporary Pan-Africanism, reparations, environmentalism, decriminalization of marijuana and trade initiatives. For example,[22] prominent Rastafari woman scholar, writer and organizer Masani Montague was the lead organizer of the first Rastafari international conference in Canada in 1982 and organizes the Rastafari Rootz Festival in Canada. Nana Farika Berhane was the lead organizer of the second international Rastafari conference at the University of the West Indies, Mona, Jamaica in 1983, and she spearheaded the organizing of the first Rastafari Women's Conference in 2003 at Howard University. Among her many accomplishments, Barbara Makeda Blake-Hannah was appointed independent senator in the Jamaican parliament in 1984 and continues to be instrumental to Rastafari organizing internationally. Sister Mitzie Williams served as the head of the Rastafari Millennium Council,[23] which was the umbrella organization for the Rastafari movement in Jamaica. She also serves as the chair of the Nyahbinghi Mansion Administration Council in Jamaica. Sister Nanny serves as the secretary for the Coral Gardens Benevolent Society, which spearheads the move for reparations on behalf of the survivors of the Coral Gardens Incident of 1963. Mama Desta Meghoo serves as the liaison between the Diaspora African Forum and the African Union. Empress Marina Blake serves on the executive board of the World African Diaspora Union (WADU). Queen Mother Moses serves as the CEO of the Empress of Zion organization and as Rastafari chaplain in prisons around the world. Empress Imara organizes the Empress Menen celebrations every year in Ghana. Sister Safi serves as the Commissioner in the Rastafari Council of Ghana's Women's Commission. Blakk Madonna helped found the Rastafari Council of Ghana and the Black Starline Cooperative Credit Union in 2009. Sister Minnie Phillips helped establish the Emancipation Day celebration in Ghana, which has been held every year since 1998. Sister Akilah Jaramogi became a leader in the environmental movement in Trinidad and Tobago with her work establishing the Fondes Amandes Community Reforestation Project (FACRP). Among many other initiatives, Sister Ijahnya Christian and others planned the first All Africa Rastafari Gathering in Shashemene, Ethiopia, in November 2017, which led to the establishment of the Rastafari Continental Council in 2018. Giulia Bonacci cites sistren in the United Kingdom, like Sister Faith, Sis Liveth, Sis Wellete Medhin and others who organized the Rastafari Focus in 1986 and the Centenary Trod to Ethiopia in 1992.[24] There are numerous sistren across Europe, South America, Africa, the Caribbean, North America, Asia and Australia, who have done and are doing groundbreaking work.

I have provided only a few examples here to highlight the vast types of organizing sistren are engaging in and to inspire scholars to consider new arenas of analysis concerning gender dynamics within the Rastafari movement. I encourage increased analysis of Rastafari woman's organizations such as Roots Dawtas, King Alpha and Queen Omega Theocracy Daughters I, International Twelve, Dawtas United Working Towards Africa (DAWTAS) (Edmonds 2012; Kush 2011), the Empress of Zion organization and the Empress Menen Foundation. Increased book-length documentation of Rastafari woman's activism is crucial for debunking the persistent commitment to eliding Rastafari woman's roles in movement formation.[25]

As demonstrated by the work Rastafari woman are doing and the scholarship centring gender within Rastafari studies, women have been active participants in pushing the social justice agenda of the movement to include gender justice. Actively seeking sistren as respondents in ethnographic research, citing Rastafari woman's scholarship and scholarship about sistren, and using gender as an analytic are ways we can produce more balanced narratives of the movement. This politics of citation, combined with encouraging and providing venues for Rastafari woman to publish their own work, establishes equitable practices of knowledge production, which will lead to a renewal within Rastafari studies.

Black woman in Rastafari have produced an intellectual tradition that reaches as far back as the earliest years of the movement. The implications of recognizing this tradition for Rastafari studies, Caribbean studies and African studies in the twenty-first century debunks readings of Rastafari as solely about the redemption of the Black male. Placing Rastafari woman's organizing traditions in the context of Black women's Pan-Africanism and meditating on the intellectual contributions of sistren offer opportunities to think anew about Rastafari philosophy and livity.

Notes

1 From interview of author with Brother Trika, Shashemene, October 2002.

2 Rastafari scholars in Woman's studies use the term "woman" as singular and plural and repudiate the pluralized "women" because it indexes Babylonian gender designations and in certain contexts can be seen as an insult. For more on this issue please see the work of Jahzani Kush (2011) and Imani Tafari-Ama (1998). While there are scholars who use the terms women and men to describe Rastafari, this article uses the forms woman and sistren to write in solidarity with Rastafari philosophical linguistic norms.

3 "Overstanding" is a Rastafari word that transforms the English term "understanding" so that the sound of the word matches the meaning. Understanding, sounds like one is under the message being communicated and Rastafari believes that if one is under something, the message cannot be properly received, but if one overstands something, then they are able to receive the message and extend the meaning with their own thoughts or opinions.

4 Sistren is a word that refers to a group of Rastafari woman.

5 The historiography of the Garvey movement was written from a male-centred perspective before the interventions of scholars such as Keisha N. Blain (2019), Nzingha Assata and Amy Jacques Garvey (2008), Ula Yvette Taylor (2002) and others who worked to document the important roles women played in founding and maintaining the Garvey movement.

6 Please see Tracy Denean Sharpley-Whiting (2002).

7 Please see Carol Boyce Davies (2008) and Erik S. McDuffie (2011) for more on Black women's transformation of communist organizing.

8 Please see Robyn Spencer (2016) and Ashley Farmer (2019) for more on Black women's organizing in the Black Power struggle.

9 The term "brethren" refers to a group of Rastafari men.

10 Rastafari use the term "ital" to describe their dietary habits which contain no salt and are vegan with a primary focus on organic raw fruits and vegetables.

11 Sister Yvonne, in discussion with the author, Kingston, Jamaica, August 2014.

12 For example, on the first page of Smith, Augier & Nettleford (1960), the authors write that George Eaton Simpson's 1953 and 1955 studies helped expedite their study. Therefore, they were essentially updating Simpson's work.

13 Mansions are what organizations are called in Rastafari.

14 These studies mention women, but do not analyse how gender informs their approach to data or research conclusions: Smith, Augier and Nettleford (1960, 12); Kitzinger (1969, 252); Barrett (1970, 2); Campbell (1987, 199). For further analysis about the ways that scholarship has left out the narratives of sistren, please see Dwyer's ground-breaking work (2013).

15 In the EABIC, there is a biblical notion that woman are unclean seven days before, during and after their menstruation each month. During this time woman live in seclusion and are only permitted out of seclusion after the twenty-one day period concludes.

16 Sister Lily, in discussion with the author, Shashemene, Ethiopia, November 2017.

17 InI is a Rastafari word which refers to the connection between the self and divine.

18 Please see the work of Dwyer and her notion of a Black womanist framework for overstanding Rastafari (2013, 29–38).

19 Feminism is a broad area of study with many publications. A full discussion here of the complexities of Rastafari understandings of feminism cannot be undertaken given the limited format, but there are trends of thought such as bourgeoisie feminism, African feminism, Black Left feminism, Black internationalist feminism, Motherism, Womanism, Africana Womanism, Caribbean feminism, liberal feminism, left feminism, Black transnational feminism, which all have distinct histories that express different ideas around gender justice. For more on the debate between Black feminism and Africana womanism versus white feminism, please see Patricia Hill Collins (2000), Lisa-Anne Julien (2003), Audre Lorde (1984), Oyèrónké Oyěwùmí (1997), Barbara Bailey and Elsa Leo-Rhynie (2004), Clenora Hudson-Weems (2004).

20 The term "downpression" is a Rastafari term that reforms the English term "oppression", which has a positive sonic connotation because it is pronounced "uppression". Rastafari linguistics function on the belief that the meaning of the word should match the sound of the word so "oppression" becomes "downpression".

21 For more on the divine feminine, please see the work of Jahzani Kush who develops the notion of Blue Fyah energy that Empress Menen Asfaw has bestowed upon Rastafari woman to enact their revolutionary vision and step into their ivine feminine energy.

22 The activities pointed out in this section by a select few women are not indicative of the extent of their work or the work that sistren have done or continue to do. This list serves as a powerful reminder and example of sistren working as partners in shaping the philosophy and evolution of the movement over time. These examples suggest areas for further scholarship around the ways sistren transformed the movement.

23 For more on the significance of Sister Mitzie William's appointment, please see Barnett (2018, 45).

24 Giulia Bonacci, in phone conversation with the author, Fall 2019. Please see also Bonacci (2015, 244).

25 The following list includes some of the few scholars who have written extensively about Rastafari woman's contributions: Makeda Silvera, Imani Tafari-Ama, Maureen Rowe, Obiagele Lake, Barbara Makeda Blake-Hannah, Nana Farika Berhane, Carol Yawney, Terisa Turner, Mansani Montague, Lisa-Anne Julien, Loretta Collins Klobah, Jahzani Kush, Asheda Dwyer, Sonia Lye-Fook, Anjahli Parnell, Diana Fox and Jillian M. Smith. There are also a few documentary films directed by Barbara Makeda Blake-Hannah, Renee Romano and Elliott Leib, D. Elmina, Bianca Nyavingi Brynda, Diana Fox and the author that have explored Rastafari woman's thought. This is not an exhaustive list of scholars who focus on gender or have significant analyses of women in their work.

References

Assata, Nzingha, and Amy Jacques Garvey. 2008. Women in the Garvey Movement. Mitcham: N. Assata.

Augier, Roy, and Veronica Salter. 2010. *Rastafari: The Reports*. Kingston, Jamaica: *Caribbean Quarterly* Monograph series. https://uwi.edu/cq/monographs

_____, M.G. Smith and Rex Nettleford. 2010. "The Rastafari Movement in Kingston, Jamaica." *Caribbean Quarterly* 12.

Austin-Broos, Diane J. 1987. "Pentecostals and Rastafarians: Cultural, Political, and Gender Relations of two Religious Movements". *Social and Economic Studies* 36 (4): 1-39.

Bailey, Barbara and Elsa Leo-Rhynie. 2004. *Gender in the 21st Century: Caribbean Perspectives, Visions and Possibilities*. Kingston, JA: Ian Randle Publishers.

Barnett, Michael. 2012. *Rastafari in the New Millennium*. NY: Syracuse University Press.

_____. 2018. *The Rastafari Movement: A North American and Caribbean Perspective*. NY: Routledge.

Barrett, Leonard. 1977. *The Rastafarians*. Boston: Beacon Press.

Bedasse, Monique A. 2017. *Jah Kingdom: Rastafarians, Tanzania, and Pan-Africanism in the Age of Decolonization*. Chapel Hill: The University of North Carolina Press.

Berhane, Nana Farika. 2018. *Africa on the Move: Communiqués on the AU Global African Diaspora Summit and the OAU/AU 50th Anniversary Highlighted with Pan African Visionary Reasoning*. Washington, DC: Queen Omega Communications.

Blain, Keisha N. 2019. *Set the World on Fire: Black Nationalist Women and the Global Struggle for Freedom*. Philadelphia, PA: University of Pennsylvania Press.

Blake-Hannah, Barbara Makeda. 2012. *Rastafari: The New Creation*. Kingston, Jamaica: Jamaica Media Productions Limited.

Bonacci, Giulia. 2015. *Exodus! Heirs and Pioneers, Rastafari Return to Ethiopia*. Kingston: University of the West Indies Press.

Campbell, Horace. 1987. *Rasta as Resistance: From Marcus Garvey to Walter Rodney*. Trenton, New Jersey: Africa World Press.

_____. 1988. "Rastafari as Pan-Africanism in the Caribbean". *African Journal of Political Economy* 2 (1): 75–88.

Chevannes, Barry. 1994. *Rastafari: Roots and Ideology*. Syracuse: Syracuse University Press.

Christensen, Jeanne. 2014. *Rastafari Reasoning and the Rasta Woman: Gender Constructions in the Shaping of Rastafari Livity*. Lanham, MD: Lexington Books.

Collins, Patricia Hill. 2000. *Black Feminist Thought: Knowledge, Consciousness, and the Politics of Empowerment*. Second Edition. Abingdon, UK: Routledge.

Davies, Carol Boyce. 2008. *Left of Karl Marx: The Political Life of Black Communist Claudia Jones*. Durham, NC.: Duke University Press.

Dunkley, Daive A. 2016. "Leonard P. Howell's Leadership of the Rastafari Movement and his 'Missing Years'". *Caribbean Quarterly* 58 (4):1-24.

Dwyer, Asheda. 2013. "Left Waiting in Vain for Y/our Love: Situating the (In)Visibility of Black Women of Rastafari as Lovers, Partners and Revolutionaries in *Brooklyn Babylon* and *One Love*". *Caribbean Quarterly* 59 (2): 25–38.

Edmonds, Ennis. 2012. *Rastafari: A Very Short Introduction*. Oxford, UK: Oxford University Press.

Erskine, Noel Leo. 2005. *From Garvey to Marley: Rastafari Theology*. Gainesville, FL: University Press of Florida.

Farmer, Ashley. 2019. *Remaking Black Power: How Black Women Transformed an Era*. Chapel Hill, NC: University of North Carolina Press.

Hudson-Weems, Clenora. 2004. *Africana Womanist Literary Theory*. Trenton, NJ: Africa World Press.

Julien, Lisa-Anne. 2003. "Great Black Warrior Queens: An Examination of the Gender Currents within Rastafari Thought and the Adoption of a Feminist Agenda in the Rasta Women's Movement". *Agenda: Empowering Women for Gender Equity* 57: 76-83.

Kitzinger, Sheila. 1969. "Protest and Mysticism: The Rastafari Cult of Jamaica". *Journal for the Scientific Study of Religion* 8 (2): 240-262.

Klobah, Loretta Collins. 2008. "Journeying Towards Mount Zion: Changing Representations of Womanhood in Popular Music, Performance Poetry, and Novels by Rastafarian Women". *IDEAZ* 7: 158–196.

Kush, Jahzani. 2011. *Roaring Lionesses: Rastafari Woman, Journeys of Self Liberation*. Self-published.

Lake, Obiagele. 1998. *Rastafari Women: Subordination in the Midst of Liberation Theology*. Durham, NC: Carolina Academic Press.

Lee, Hélène, and Stephen Davis. 2003. *The First Rasta: Leonard Howell and the Rise of Rastafarianism*. Chicago, IL: Chicago Review Press.

Lorde, Audre. 1984. *Sister Outsider: Essays and Speeches by Audre Lorde*. Trumansburg, NY: Crossing Press Feminist Series.

Maragh, G.G. 2017. The Promised Key. N.p. EWorld Incorporated.

Marley, Rita, and Hettie Jones. 2004. No Woman, No Cry: My Life with Bob Marley. New York: Hyperion.

McDuffie, Erik S. 2011. Sojourning for Freedom: Black Women, American Communism, and the Making of Black Left Feminism. Durham, NC: Duke University Press.

Montague, Mansani. 1994. Dread Culture: A Rastawoman's Story. Toronto: Sister Vision Press.

Montlouis, Nathalie. 2013. "Lords and Empresses In and Out of Babylon: The EABIC Community and the Dialectic of Female Subordination." PhD diss. SOAS, University of London.

Murrell, Nathaniel Samuel. 1998. Chanting Down Babylon: The Rastafari Reader. Philadelphia: Temple University Press.

Niaah, Jahlani A.H. 2016. "'I'd Rather See a Sermon than Hear One...': Africa/Heaven and Women of the Diaspora in Creating Global Futures and Transformation". Africa Development / Afrique Et Développement 41 (3): 1–24.

Oyĕwùmí, Oyèrónkẹ́. 1997. The Invention of Women: Making an African Sense of Western Gender Discourses. Minneapolis: University of Minnesota Press.

Price, Charles. 2009. Becoming Rasta: Origins of Rastafari Identity in Jamaica. New York University, NY: New York University Press.

Rowe, Maureen. 1998. "Gender and Family Relations in Rastafari: A Personal Perspective". In Chanting Down Babylon: The Rastafari Reader, edited by N. S. Murrell, W. D. Spencer, and A. A. McFarlane, 78–81. Philadelphia: Temple University Press, 1998.

Sharpley-Whiting, Tracy Denean. 2002. Negritude Women. Minneapolis, MN: University of Minnesota Press.

Simpson, George Eaton. 1955. "The Ras Tafari Movement in Jamaica: A Study of Race and Class Conflict". Social Forces 34 (2): 167–171.

Smith, M.G., Roy Augier, and Rex M. Nettleford. 1978. The Ras Tafari Movement in Kingston, Jamaica. Reprint. Mona, Jamaica: University of the West Indies, Dept. of Extra-Mural Studies.

Spencer, Robyn. 2016. The Revolution Has Come: Black Power, Gender, and the Black Panther Party in Oakland. Durham, NC: Duke University Press.

Sterling, Marvin D. 2012. Babylon East: Performing Dancehall, Roots Reggae, and Rastafari in Japan. Durham, NC: Duke University Press.

Sudbury, Julia. 1998. Other Kinds of Dreams: Black Women's Organisations and the Politics of Transformation. London and New York: Routledge.

Tafari-Ama, Imani. 1998. "Rastawoman as Rebel: Case Studies in Jamaica". In Chanting Down Babylon: The Rastafari Reader, edited by N. S. Murrell, W. D. Spencer, and A. A. McFarlane, 89–106. Philadelphia: Temple University Press.

Taylor, Ula Yvette. 2002. The Veiled Garvey: The Life and Times of Amy Jacques Garvey. Chapel Hill, NC: University of North Carolina Press.

Turner, Terisa E. 1994. "Rastafari and the New Society: Caribbean and East African Feminist Roots of a Popular Movement to Reclaim the Earthly Commons". In Arise Ye Mighty People!: Gender, Class and Race in Popular Struggles, edited by T. E. Turner and B. J. Ferguson, 9–55. Trenton, NJ: Africa World Press.

Yawney, Carole D. 1994. "Moving with the Dawtas of Rastafari: From Myth to Reality". In Arise Ye Mighty People!: Gender, Class and Race in Popular Struggles, edited by T. E. Turner and B. J. Ferguson, 65–74. Trenton, NJ: Africa World Press.

Testimony

CHARTING THE MATRIARCHAL SHIFT IN THE RASTAFARI MOVEMENT

DEENA-MARIE BERESFORD

The existence of a "Matriarchal Shift" within the Rastafari
Movement is not surreptitious. Paradoxically, its presence is evident
both regionally and universally and consequently is poised to trans-
form the fundamental tenets of this Revolutionary Movement
(Beresford 2019).

RASTAFARI WOMAN REBORN

Rastafari women are on the rise and their evolution cannot be stayed. Today, the emergence of the "Blue Fyah" energy by Rasess Jahzani Kush, PhD has reawakened their latent Divine Feminine and given them a path to self-actualization within the Rastafari Livity. Through a trinity of gatherings, known as the Empress Menen Asfaw Blue Fyah Leadership Retreat, Rastafari women gathered, shared skills, developed projects, and reinforced the Teachings of The Ivine (Divine) Majesties, Haile Selassie I and Empress Menen Asfaw.

The three-day long inaugural event began with Sister Trea presenting the morning MEDI (Menen Enlightenment Dawning Iwa). This offered opportunities for meditation, affirmation and Ises (Praises). Thereafter, Dr. Asantewaa Oppong-Wadie delved into the Ivine (Divine) nature of Empress Menen Asfaw, showing a clear path to her Divinity. I later presented workshops on crochet, offered lavender foot wash, and led the Chant Writing workshop. It was truly heartwarming to witness the presentation of chants livicated (dedicated) to Empress Menen Asfaw. Dawtas were chanting choruses such as "Let her rise, rising high, teach I n I (us) your virtue, raise her up on high" and "Empress Menen, Empress Menen, Blue Fyah, Blue Fyah...." Some additional highlights included Mama Thea's ASLI Pure Body Salts workshop. Therein, Dawtas explored the infusion of Himalayan pink salt with lemongrass, lavender, mandarin, peppermint and a plethora of other essential oils and dried flowers. Sister Montez' Waist Beads workshop shared some great historical information on the significance of the beads as sistren (sisters) created beads in a variety of colours and according to their Irits (mindset). Sister Diane shared some great insight on womb care. And lastly, Empress Ruth blessed

27

the event with her melodious songs entitled "Inner/Deeper" and "Lioness".

Earlier signs of a matriarchal shift were observed at the Brooklyn, NY-based Church of Haile Selassie I (CHSI). According to Halpern (1998), the Daughters of Zion women's group met on Saturdays to discuss women's issues and family concerns and to plan events for the entire congregation. This is an active and growing church that aspires to lead the larger Rastafari movement, which it views as hopelessly mired in factionalism and an outworn traditionalism. In an August 1994 official Church newsletter addressed to the broader Rastafari movement, Sister Sonya, a Jamaican immigrant and mother of five, wrote:

> Rasta woman, the time is now to stop calling yourself a Rasta woman. That name represents a colonial name given to the woman of a Rasta man. The Daughters of Zion realize this name represents a domiciled conception which only undermines the socio-religious development of the daughters and subjects them to medieval practice. Today we the Daughters of Zion need to take an active part in the development of the Rastafarian community. We should follow the footsteps of our women like the Queen of Sheba, and Empress Menen Asfaw, and Sarah. Our children need an example to follow. Let us be that example for them and the future generation of daughters to come (CHSI Daughters of Zion Document 1994).

OUTSIDER PERSPECTIVES

Although Rastafari women themselves remain vigilant in their quest for liberation, her positioning continues to be the focus of outsider perspectives. Becky Michelle Mulvaney states that "Rastafari's capitulation to mainstream patriarchal attitudes, and its spiritually imbued glorification of subservient women's roles work in direct conflict to Rasta's own stated purpose" (Mulvaney 1990, 2). This quote illustrates the disparate problem with the Rastafari struggle for equality globally. This power and equality as a people will never be reached if current Rastafari views on women persist.

She further suggests that gender discrimination against Rasta women can be dated back to the early days of slavery. Evidence shows that early Kenyan tribes in Africa, such as the Mau Mau recorded unequal treatment of women and the resulting rebellions of the colonized women and men who refused to continue being treated so poorly by their British colonial masters. Likewise, the same dynamic existed in Jamaica, but after slavery was abolished there, these primitive forms of gender discrimination remained in Jamaican society, because the formerly enslaved had inadvertently adopted the White man's Christian views on gender (Greville 1998). In terms of race and human rights, Jamaicans have, for the most part, risen above their previous position. However, they have done this without their women, and Rastafarianism has emerged as a male philosophy. The women associated with Rastafarianism immediately took on a subordinate role in the Rasta culture and society. Rastafarianism's traditional and oppressive gender roles have limited Jamaican women from achieving an equal identity in Jamaican society.

In order to fully understand the roles of Rastafari women, it is helpful to examine the evolution of Rastafari women from the early days of slavery up to the current situation in Jamaica and around the world. The standards and philosophy that the "old Rastafari" held for women continue to limit Rasta women today. However, with the help of certain influential female leaders and music artists, the old Rastafari society has evolved into the Black feminist movement-shaped "new Rastafari" society. Feminist Rastas' written, spoken and musical expression has universalized their goal of being a direct concern in Jamaican society towards the Rastafari progression. In Teresa Turner's words, "New Rasta has come from the recognition that central to the struggle for women's rights is the resistance of black women, north and south, against the gendered, racial and racially-gendered hierarchies of slavery, colonialism and today's super-exploitation" (Turner 1994, 19). Therefore, from the days of slavery up to today, the old, gender-oppressive philosophies remain and continue to limit Black women. For this history of oppression to finally come to its end, people must open their minds to the understanding of the origins of gender discrimination against women as well as accept the inevitable positive future of the new Rastafari (Greville 1998).

According to filmmaker and Rastafari Kassa Hynes, "Rasta women are at the forefront now, more than ever. Old school Rastas took away women's voices because of the Bible" (quoted in O'Gilvie 2019). Hynes asserts that his generation focused more on the teachings of Haile Selassie I and Garvey. Hynes noticed the shift in the 1990s when women and little girls were included in playing drums and voiced opinions in reasoning sessions.

In recent years much has been written on the subject. According to Lake (1998), men who have advocated for the liberation of African people in the African Diaspora are not exempt from sexist attitudes and behaviours toward African women. Rastafari stand out as an example *par excellence* of this contradiction since they are viewed by many as being in the vanguard of revolutionary movements. Rastafari men have dominated leadership positions within the organization and consider women to be secondary in all matters pertaining to Rastafari. This position, although anathema to the idea of freedom, is not surprising given the existence of global patriarchy and the entrenchment of sexism in Jamaica. These uneven relations are significant as they indicate the male propensity to exclusively struggle for male power—a focus that has historically pervaded all Diaspora African movements.

The views held by many early Rastafari men closely mirror Biblical passages which sacralize the subordination of women. The most direct passage was given by Paul in 1 Corinthians 14:34–35: "Let your women keep silent in the churches, for they are not permitted to speak: but they are to be submissive as the law also says, and if they want to learn something, let them ask their own husbands at home, for it is shameful for women to speak in church."

INSIDER PERSPECTIVES

One insider perspective proclaims, "When Norman [Manley] and Bustamante and the citizens of Jamaica used to bust Rasta men's heads and throw them in the gully, it was the Rasta woman who had to hold down the family and the community. There is no Rastafari without woman" (Hynes, idem).

Interviews I conducted recorded varied perspectives on the roles of Rastafari women. A sistren who owned and operated a small business, and who is raising her children on her own, asserted, "A woman must know when to speak in the congregation, but that don't say she don't know truth and right. But for me, this [not being able to speak until allowed by men] won't work. For other Dawtas [daughters] like me, we are more independent. We are economically independent."

Another stated, "You have the Order of the Nyahbinghi[1] where at one stage women were not really permitted to be vocal in the sense of making statements and contributing to reasoning (conversations) in the house. This has now changed where women are now seen and heard."

As someone who has trod within the Theocracy Reign Ivine Order of the Nyahbinghi for several decades, I too have witnessed this welcome "Matriarchal Shift". I received confirmation during a Groundation Nyahbinghi Ises on 23 July 2017, when a Rastafari sistren led the chanting into the morning. Attendees chanted and harps rolled as she recalled chant after chant lasting close to two hours. In the early days of the movement, and still today, generally this would have been unheard of. It is these isolated moments that validate that a "Matriarchal Shift" has indeed occurred, and give hope to those who feel a sense of hopelessness.

Rastafari, like most cultures, is mutable, and changes are coming slowly, just as they are in Jamaica as a whole. The slow pace of change in large part is due to male domination which has been internalized by Rasta women. The following interview excerpts (from interviews that I conducted) speak volumes:

So, man is the head of women. The Bible clearly says that the man must respect the woman. But you must have that head in the family. I know some feminists have a problem with that, but I don't see a problem with it. I don't remember exactly where, but somewhere in Corinthians it says that man is the head of woman and God is the head of man.

Another Rasta woman offered a different perspective. While she stated that she "honor[s] and respect[s] a man", she added:

I think the statement that a man should be the head of the household is a wrong statement. The reason is that the majority, in the whole earth set up, it is the woman who passes on education, philosophy and all information to the youths. So, I see the woman as one of the main builders of the nation. So, I think in Black and White issues, we got some things wrong, and I think we got some things wrong in gender issues also. But it's a thing that people don't want to investigate.

Yet another asserted that Dawtas who come through their Kingman: "They shave their heads when their Kingman leaves them. Some of them fade out of the Rasta movement. But those who come through Jah [God] themselves, they are strong. We are equals with men."

Clearly, there are different views and experiences among Rasta women relative to male supremacy, although the majority with whom I spoke agreed that the man is the spiritual leader among Rastafari and within the household. Women who were part of common living arrangements (two or more families living in the same household or small communities) tended to adhere to this way of thinking more than others, although women cannot be strictly categorized in this way. Even though part of Rastafari ideology posits that women cannot enter Rastafari except through a man, Rastafari women can, and do, join all the groups at will. A Rastafari woman in Kingston who owns a public relations business put it this way:

> I came into Rasta through self-exploration. If it didn't come out of that, I'd be accepting dogma. And those elders who are true Rasta elders would have less respect for somebody who is going to put themselves a certain way to gain acceptance than for somebody who is naturally following where their heart is leading (Lake 1994, 233-256).

The role of women in Rastafari has been a complex, yet orderly, system of knowing one's place. Although the Kingman is seen as the head of the home, and of his community, women in Rastafari are greatly respected as Queens, and their duty is to raise their children and provide a stable community for the men. By teaching health, nutrition and various elements of life, women contribute greatly to Rasta culture. Though the rules for women seem strict, a Rasta woman must be able to tell herself apart from the larger society of women in Babylon whose ways, style of dress and approach to life is altogether different.

Rasta women realize their potential as Queens and honour that title with respect: no short dresses, no pants, no adding chemicals to the hair, and no make-up or artificial cosmetic use. Rasta women maintain a sense of identity with nature, their community and their children. The faith requires women to know their place when they are among men, while being as wise as any man. In Rasta culture women are not geared into vanity and are frowned upon when it comes to exploiting their bodies. This exploitation destroys the great potential that women have in becoming leaders and becoming closer to God. You can't travel two roads and expect to get to Jah. You must travel the narrow road, and for women in Rastafari this is often not easy. For the temptations of western society that says a woman can dress any way, show her flesh, that she can talk any kind of way, and use obscene words to express herself, or that she can denounce her community and her children for vanity are misleading concepts that can tear the nation apart. The Rasta woman is the holder of the nation, and her awareness of this allows her to live a simple lifestyle while upholding her duties as a woman; she is always revered for that.

It is safe to say that women who recognize Rastafari as their faith do not have to be told what to do but have learned what works for them. It's unimaginable that every woman will adhere to every single law of the culture, but it is imaginable that Rastafari women have found a faith that brings them closer to Jah and binds them to uplifting themselves toward positive I-spirations.

ACCORDING TO DR. JAHZANI KUSH, "THERE IS NO JAH WITHOUT A JAHESS"

Today Rastafari women hold firm to this principle and have established a framework that interprets Their Ivine Majesties (Haile Selassie I and Menen Asfaw) in a balance. The Omega presence is now intricately posited within the Livity and she is called on for strength and guidance.

Empress Menen Asfaw is a modern woman of her time from her hairstyles to her outlook on the power of educating young girls and women. The Empress built the nation's first childcare centres and trade schools for working mothers. During this process, she single-handedly started the nation's conversation of equipping women with the necessary tools to lead through education and understanding the complexities of not only motherhood, but womanhood and its power.

Although written half a century ago, the information contained in the article "Rastafari: Way of Life" (Dubb 1970) remains relevant today. Rastafari women are referencing Empress Menen Asfaw as the standard by which they should live their lives. She is viewed as a perfect example and one that should be emulated without apology. Change is always difficult, as cited in some religions, but the idea that Rastafari is any different is just not accurate. Continuing to be vocal on equality to provide and create a path that offers Rasta living to everyone will allow it to remain consistent with their message of peace, freedom and love.

THE STRUGGLE CONTINUES...

A few organizations have been formed over the last two decades that are centred on elevating Rastafari women. The Empress of Zion (EOZ) was an early representation and had the goal of establishing an African-centred curriculum.

The Rastafari Council of Ghana Women's Commission is another such organization. Many have lost their footing in that the work is not as visible, but on occasion they surface and reinforce the familiar quote, "the race is not for the swift but for those who endure to the end".

The early Rastafari movement was not void of stalwart voices who advocated for Rastafari women. Dawtas such as Nana Farika Berhane, Mama Bubbles, Ma Shanti, Sister Mitzie, Sister Pearl, Sister Minnie and Mama Baby I never ceased to remain visible and relevant voices in the movement. Some Rastafari men also held strong opinions about how women should be treated. In his latter days, Bongo Rocky encouraged Rastafari women to rise and let their voices be heard. I had the privilege of interviewing both him and Mama Baby I during a visit to Shashemene, Ethiopia, in 2009. During the interview, he stated the following: "Father says, in the last days, I will pour out my Spirit on all flesh, and my sons and daughters shall prophesize. Later he added, as he recalled his mother: "When Mama tek up her breast and pray for you, it done." I interpreted this to mean, women play a very significant role in the lives of men and it is important to hold them in high esteem.

Bongo Rocky also said there were no Rasta women or very few. People would come from near and far to see Mama Baby I. The reason is that women who sight Rastafari would risk losing everything. They were disowned by their families and were put out of their homes. They were further ostracized by society and considered outcasts.

This poem by Faybiene Miranda expresses her strength and pride as a "new-Rastafari woman" (quoted in Faristzaddi 1987, 9):

> I am not your Venus de Milo
> Perfectly sculptured from marble to be carefully pedestal placed.
> My name is not Eve. I offer you no temptation
> I am not your concubine by night
> Transformed to memory by day
> I am not the milk you thirst for
> Now dry in your mother's breast
> Nor could you call me queen
> For I have no dominion over beast, earth, or man
> I am not a receptacle for the seed
> You indiscriminately cast in the wind
> I ask no sacrifice of Lamb's blood for the stain would be mine
> Do not toss gold trinkets at my feet
> They do not shine for me
> I am no slave to a promise written in ink
> Where there is no master there are no chains to be broken
> Bondage is no glory
> I am woman
> Bone of your bones, flesh of your flesh
> When I lay sleeping in your rib
> You called me no name
> I AM THAT I AM

Note

1 In addition to referring to a group of elders, "Nyahbinghi" is also used to refer to important Rastafari meetings which are presided over by a "leading brother" (Barrett 1977, 120). The term Nyahbinghi is East African and referred to a religious-political group who resisted colonial domination in the first part of the twentieth century. "In Jamaica the term means 'death to the Black and White oppressors'" (Barrett 1977, 121).

References

Barrett, L. 1977. *The Rastafarians*. Boston: Beacon Press.

Dubb, Adjua. 1970 (January 1). "Rastafari-Way of Life". www.jahworks.org (accessed November 10, 2019).

Faristzaddi, Millard. 1987. *Itations of Jamaica and I Rastafari*. London, UK: Judah Anbesa International.

Greville, Georgie. 1998. "The Evolution of a New Rastafari". Essays from the University of Vermont Class. *Rhetoric of Reggae Music*. University of Vermont: Dread Library. https://debate.uvm.edu/dreadlibrary/dreadlibrary.html

Hepner, Tricia M., and Randal L. Hepner. 1998. "Gender, Community and Change among the Rastafari of New York City". In *New York Glory: Religions in the City*, edited by Tony Carnes and Anna Karpathakis, 333-356. New York & London: NYU Press.

Lake, Obiagele. 1994. "The Many Voices of Rastafarian Women: Sexual Subordination in the Midst of Liberation". *NWIG: New West Indian Guide / Nieuwe West-Indische Gids,* 68 (3/4):235-257, Brill. www.griotsrepublic.com (accessed November 10, 2019).

_____. 1998. *Rastafari Women: Subordination in the Midst of Liberation Theology*. Durham, NC: Carolina Academic Press.

Mulvaney, Rebekah Michele. 1990. *Mental Slavery: A Feminist Response to Rastafari*. Miami, FL: Women's Studies Center, Florida International University.

O'Gilvie, Diana. 2019. "Tug of War: Traditional Rastafarian Women in Modern Jamaican Society". www.griotsrepublic.com (accessed November 10, 2019).

Turner, Terisa E., with Bryan J. Ferguson. 1994. *Arise Ye Mighty People!: Gender, Class, and Race in Popular Struggles*. Trenton, NJ: Africa World Press Inc.

SHIFTING MODELS OF GROUP FORMATION
Communes, Houses and Mansions of Rastafari

ENNIS B. EDMONDS

Abstract   The acknowledged houses and mansions of Rastafari do not exhaust the many named Rastafari groups in Jamaica and around the world. They do illustrate, however, that Rastafari is not a homogenous movement with a hierarchical structure and a binding creed. As I have argued elsewhere and others have affirmed, the Rastafari concept of I and I (that is the innate divinity of each person) has engendered a radical kind of individualism in the movement. This entrenched individualism has proven resistant to rigid organizational structures and has given rise to a kind of social fissiparity. Some have even pursued the Rastafari lifestyle without recourse to or identification with any house or mansion of Rastafari. Velma Pollard has aptly designated these as "own-built" Rastafari, indicating that these are solo travellers on the path of Rastafari.

Over the years, the desire for a more cohesive and organized structuring of Rastafari has been repeatedly voiced and attempted. This desire often emerges from the realization that for Rastafari to gain respect and exercise social influence, it needs to present a united front to the world. For example, the Rastafari Movement Association, formed in the 1970s, attempted to unify Rastafari into a political force that could vie for parliamentary representation in Jamaica. In all cases, the emphasis has been on the need to develop a coordinated voice and a collective strategy to further the interests of Rastafari vis-à-vis the wider society, and not so much on the need to develop organizational structures to administer the internal affairs of Rastafari. While most Rastafari are united around certain philosophical and social ideas, a collective identity represented by certain symbols and a commitment to certain practices, to date, the movement as a whole remains heterogeneous without the institutional structures to undertake effective collective actions.

Keywords • Nyahbinghi • Twelve Tribes of Israel • Bobo Shanti • Youth Black Faith • School of Vision • Church of Haile Selassie • identity • group formation

At a Rastafari gathering in the early 1990s, I listened as a Rasta related an anecdote concerning a conversation between two other Rastas who were meeting for the first time. The first ended the introduction of himself by stating "I n I belong to the Twelve Tribes of Israel". Then he queried, "Which tribe the I [you] belong to?" With sharp wit, the second Rasta responded, "I n I belongs to the first". With much puzzlement in his voice, the first Rasta inquired, "What the I mean by that?" The second Rasta explained, "You passed I right here at first and gone to twelve". Admiring the cleverness of the other's reasoning, the first Rasta slapped hands with the second acknowledging his wit and wisdom.

This exchange illustrates the banter that often takes place among Rastas and between Rastas and others. It highlights how carefully one has to be with words, and how a Rasta may choose to understand words in ways unintended by the speaker and then uses that to make his own point, often to gain the upper hand in a discussion. This exchange also brings to the fore that beyond the broad identity of Rastafari, various sub-identities exist in Rastafari. These sub-identities often occasion jockeying for recognition as a "true Rasta" and reveal a characteristic of the interaction between "bredrin" from different groupings. As is widely acknowledged by scholars, Rastafari has never been homogeneous. In its nascent days, several groups coalesced around charismatic personalities. As Rastafari became entrenched in Jamaica and spread around the world, Nyahbinghi, Twelve Tribes of Israel and Bobo Shanti (EABIC) have surfaced as the three distinct groups to which most Rastas subscribe. However, many Rastas pursue the Rastafari lifestyle without allegiance to these groups, and many other groupings of Rastas exist alongside or in addition to these groups. Foremost among these are the Church of Haile Selassie, School of Vision and Fulfilled Rastafari.

IN THE BEGINNING: CHARISMA AND DIVERSITY

Max Weber, one of the founding fathers of the discipline of sociology, avers that a charismatic personality is often the moving force for the emergence of new religious/social movements (Weber 1963, 46–47). The case of Rastafari adds an interesting twist to Weber's theory of charisma. Instead of a single charismatic leader forging a new movement, a number of itinerant preachers appeared on the streets of Jamaica in the early 1930s proclaiming the newly crowned emperor of Ethiopia, Haile Selassie I, as a divine Messiah vested with effecting the liberation of oppressed Black people around the world. Foremost among these itinerants were Leonard Percival Howell, Joseph Nathaniel Hibbert, Robert Hinds, and Henry Archibald Dunkley. Howell, Hibbert and Dunkley seemed to have arrived at the conviction of Selassie's divinity independently. Initially, Hinds was associated with Howell, but like the others, he eventually attracted his own following and pursued an independent "ministry".

For some reason, Leonard Percival Howell (1898–1981) looms larger in the literature on Rastafari and has gained the designation, "The First Rasta" (Lee 2003). This ascendency is probably due to his frequent encounters with Jamaica's law enforcement from 1934 to the late 1950s. These encounters are amply documented in police records, courts records and local newspapers, especially the *Daily Gleaner*, Jamaica's premier publication. Furthermore, interviews with Howell, members of his family and followers have contributed greatly to the relative abundance of information about him (Hill 1983; Lee 2003).

Howell was in his mid-thirties when he came to prominence as a leader in the new cultural and religious movement known as Rastafari. Gaining exposure to Black nationalist ideas from his sojourn in Panama during his teens and early twenties, his travels with the United States Army Transport Service, and his residency in New York during the 1920s, Howell returned to Jamaica in December 1932. The following year, he started proclaiming that Ras Tafari (Haile Selassie) was the Messiah (Jesus Christ) in his second coming with the mission of liberating the Black race (Hutton 2015, 10). At first, Howell attracted followers by preaching on street corners in Kingston and in the Parish of St Thomas, east of Kingston. For his verbal attack on the British colonial government and his insistence that Jamaica's Blacks should give allegiance only to Haile Selassie, he was arrested and imprisoned in 1934 on a charge of sedition. After his release from prison he formed the Ethiopian Salvation Society and retreated to Pinnacle, where he and his followers established a Rastafari commune in 1940 (Edmonds 2003, 37; Hill 1981, 360). Pinnacle initiated one of the primary modes of communality that has remained characteristic of Rastafari. After the destruction of Pinnacle by law enforcement agents in 1954, the communal tradition persisted in the Wareika Hills settlements of the 1950s and 1960s, and continues today in the Bobo Shanti communal spaces in several countries and in Dermot Fagan's School of Vision in the Blue Mountains.

At Pinnacle, Howell provided guidance and governance to a community estimated between five hundred and two thousand. Howell's charisma was the principal force that precipitated the establishment of Pinnacle and the adhesive that enabled its existence for about twenty years. Through the power of persuasion, he convinced hundreds of people to abandon their previous residences and ways of life to join his experiment in a new way of life unencumbered by the oppressive forces of the then colonial Jamaican society. Though Howell appointed lieutenants to assist him in administering the commune, he exercised unrivaled power over the affairs of Pinnacle. He was not only its inspirational leader, but also its chief lawgiver, counselor and judge. His assumption of the title Gong Guru Maragh (eminent teacher of wisdom) indicated that he viewed himself as the conduit of the teachings and principles by which his followers should live.

Though Pinnacle was established as an autonomous village to escape the reach of the police agents of the wider Jamaican colonial society, which Howell considered illegitimate and undeserving of the loyalty of African-Jamaicans, law enforcement conducted frequent raids of the commune and eventually demolished most of the existing structures in 1954. The residents were displaced; some moving to the slums of West Kingston, some eventually resorted to Wareika Hills, where they replicated forms of communal living. Howell was arrested, deemed mentally unstable by the courts and committed to Bellevue, a psychiatric hospital. After his release, Howell spent the next twenty years of his life in relative obscurity, living with some of his followers in Tredegar Park near Spanish Town.

Like Howell, Joseph Hibbert (1894–1986) migrated from Jamaica to Central America (Costa Rica and Panama) in his late teens. While in Central America, he imbibed ideas about the centrality of Ethiopia to Black history and Black identity. This is evident in his membership in the Ancient Mystic Order of Ethiopia. Convinced that Ras Tafari was divine and that his enthronement as Emperor Haile Selassie in 1930 was a harbinger of Black liberation from White oppression, he returned to Jamaica in 1931 to proclaim his new message on the street corners of rural St Andrew and eventually the urban streets of Kingston (Barrett 1997, 82). Hibbert's proclamation of the divinity of Haile Selassie and his folk healing practices, which drew on his knowledge of the healing property of herbs and his ability to manipulate spiritual forces, attracted a significant following (Bishton 1983; Chevannes 1994, 124–125). Hibbert joined with others to form a short-lived chapter of the Ethiopian World Federation in 1938, but withdrew his support almost immediately, apparently because he was not accorded a high position of authority in the organization (Chevannes 1994, 126). Hibbert developed a strong conviction that the Ethiopian Orthodox Tewahedo Church was the appropriate Christian organization for Jamaicans of African descent and became a strong campaigner for its establishment in Jamaica. The Ethiopian Orthodox Tewahedo Church was eventually established in Jamaica in 1970, and in 1971, Hibbert was designated as a "Spiritual Advisor" of the Church in Jamaica by Archbishop Laike Mandefro (Chevannes 1999, 345). By this time, Hibbert was far removed from the forefront of the Rastafari movement and he seemed to have spent his later years reclusively in Bull Bay, Portland (Bishton 1983).

Henry Archibald Dunkley gained knowledge of the international struggle of Black liberation during his travels as a sailor for the United Fruit Company. Disembarking in Jamaica in Port Antonio in December 1930, he immersed himself in a study of the Bible to determine if the recently crowned Haile Selassie was the long-promised Messiah. He finally latched on to the designation of Christ as "Lion of the Tribe of Judah" and "King of Kings and Lord of Lords" in Revelation 2:5 and 19:16. Since Haile Selassie's titles read "King of Kings, Lord of Lords, Conquering Lion of the Tribe of Judah", he became convinced that this proved Haile Selassie's divinity. With this conviction, he started disseminating the message in Kingston around the same time as Howell and Hibbert. Dunkley formed the King of Kings Missionary Movement, which had neither headquarters nor officials other than Dunkley himself (Pullen 2011, 634). Like the other early proponents of Rastafari, Dunkley attracted and exerted influence over his followers by his personal magnetism and by his reputation as having spiritual powers. He was also subjected to repression by Jamaica's law enforcement as were other leading Rastas, and like them, he exited centre stage of the movement by the 1950s, though he lived until the early 1990s.

Of the four leading proponents of Rastafari in the 1930s, Robert Hinds was the only one who did not receive his initial Black consciousness and Black nationalist education abroad. Instead, his exposure came from a fiery, charismatic preacher named Alexander Bedward who admonished his followers in the 1920s to rise up against the White oppressors in Jamaica. Hinds was also exposed to the Black independence and Black self-reliance teachings of Marcus Garvey. Convinced of Haile Selassie's divinity and liberating mission for African peoples, he joined forces with Howell, becoming his lieutenant. After his imprisonment on charges of sedition in 1934 (along with Howell), he ceased his association with Howell and founded the King of Kings Mission. According to Barry Chevannes, Hinds' King of Kings Mission had as many as eight hundred members in the early 1940s. The ethos of the organization was patterned after Revivalism, a Jamaican folk religion. Final authority was vested solely in Hinds, who was considered a prophet, but he was supported by a number of functionaries whom he appointed. Water baptism and healing rituals were practised (Chevannes 1994, 127–128). To this Revival ethos, Hinds added the belief in the divinity of Haile Selassie and in the exilic status of Blacks in Jamaica. Internal disagreements over the degree of Rastafari involvement in politics and the status of Garvey eventually destroyed the King of Kings Mission (Chevannes 1994, 140–141). With the dissolution of the King of Kings Mission, Hinds quickly lost his stature in the movement, and when he died in 1950 none of his former followers showed up for his burial (Chevannes 1994, 142).

CONTINUED HETEROGENEITY:
HOUSES AND MANSIONS OF RASTAFARI

The initial diverse formations of Rastafari continued as the movement matured and gained traction in Jamaica and elsewhere. To highlight the lack of homogeneity in Rastafari, adepts often quote the words of Jesus from John 14:2: "In my Father's house are many mansions" (KJV). This speaks to the fact that the Rastafari is not organizationally cohesive. Instead, it is an aggregation of individuals and groups who identify themselves with the ethos of Rastafari and in some measure pursue a lifestyle deemed commensurate with its principles. While eschewing formal hierarchies, the movement has nevertheless coalesced into more or less distinct groups referred to as "houses and mansions". Sometimes "houses" refer to smaller groups of Rastas who interact regularly in particular locations or who belong to particular groups associated with individual inspirational leaders, while "mansions" suggest greater numbers of adherents who share similar orientations to Rastafari regardless of face-to-face interactions. Increasingly, both terms are used interchangeably, and so I will use them in that manner. Over the years, three houses have emerged as the broadest aggregations with which most Rastas identified: Nyahbinghi House (The Nyahbinghi Order or Haile Selassie I Theocratical Order of the Nyahbinghi Reign), Bobo Shanti (Ethiopia Africa Black International Congress) and the Twelve Tribes of Israel.

The Nyahbinghi Order

Even without numerical data, it is generally accepted that most Rastas, certainly in Jamaica, identify with the Nyahbinghi House, which holds to the most traditional or conventional ethos of Rastafari. Its roots can be traced to the ferment that occurred in Rastafari from the late 1940s to the early 1960s. The instigators of this ferment were a new generation of young Rastas who rejected elements of the approaches of the founding Rastas discussed above and who brought a much more radical edge and distinctive ethos to the praxis of Rastafari. At the forefront of this new "brigade" were a loose aggregation of young Rastas called the House of Youth Black Faith (YBF). As Barry Chevannes indicates, YBF members were dissatisfied with the old guards for not making a sufficient break with Jamaica's most widespread folk religion popularly known as Revivalism (Revival Zion). Instead, the founding Rastas tended to adopt some ritual forms from Revivalism and engaged in magical arts associated with witchcraft. The new generation of Rastas considered these practices an abomination and an indication of the alienation of Jamaicans of African descent from direct communion with Jah (God). As Chevannes continues, YBF viewed the founding fathers as not sufficiently repudiating the norms and mores of Jamaica's colonial society, and they embarked on a cultural project to demonstrate by their words and lifestyle their rejection of Jamaica's status quo (Chevannes 1998, 77). As anthropologist John P. Homiak contends, the break of the young brigade with the old guards also signaled a repudiation of the charismatic authoritarianism the founding fathers had exercised over their respective followings. The new cohorts of Rastas ushered in a new spirit of radical equality and collective pursuit of insights that have become characteristic of Rastafari as a whole (Homiak 1998, 132). While YBF seemed to be the vanguard of radical reform in Rastafari during the 1950s, Homiak has produced ethnographic evidence that at least two other groups, the I-gelic House and the I-tes of Rastafari were also agents of change during this period. Both were considered even more radical in their rejection of Jamaica's codes of propriety and civility than the YBF. Both groups embraced a radical asceticism which included living in the wild, a strict vegetarianism, and even sexual abstinence in some cases. I-tes of Rastafari, also called Higes Knots, wore only loincloths fashioned from crocus bags and walked barefooted because leather shoes came with the violence associated with killing animals (Homiak 1998, 139–140, 151).

The reforms initiated by YBF and other radical young Rastas of the 1950s and 1960s established the foundation of the Nyahbinghi ethos. Based on data collected from his informants, Chevannes has argued that the first generation of Rastas concentrated on espousing the divinity and messiahship of Haile Selassie. By insisting God was embodied in the Black king from Ethiopia, these early Rastas sought to counter the doctrine of White superiority and Black inferiority central to the cultural and religious ethos of Jamaica since the institution of British colonialism (Chevannes 1994, 145–146). While they challenged the status quo with their vituperative utterances at street meetings, marches and symbolic capture of public spaces, and withdrawal to communal spaces (Pinnacle), they did not effect a radical break with social customs and practices of society. The second generation of Rastas from the late 1940s onwards committed themselves to delegitimize the values and mores that held sway in Jamaica. As Homiak argues eloquently, "resistance shifted significantly to a process of signifying upon the authorized social codes that upheld the everyday commonsense legitimacy of the system" (Homiak 1998, 136). In other words, these Rastas inscribed rejection of the accepted standards of propriety in their "physical appearance, dress, speech, [and] gender relations" (Homiak 1998, 136) and embarked on forging new modes of being and behaviour that reflected their understanding of the world and their place in it. Underlying the new traditions forged by these reformers was the ideology of "naturality" or "naturalness", which in Rasta speech/ discourse became "Ital" or "Ital livity" (Homiak 1998, 138–145).

Ital is a commitment to a lifestyle that is in harmony with nature as opposed to the manufactured and artificial culture of the West and the socially constructed conventions of the modern world. For the most radical, this meant withdrawal to undeveloped areas such as Wareika Hills (northeast of Kingston) to live in the wild. This was not just to escape the Babylonian (corrupt and repressive) ethos of the city and the relentless pressures from local law enforcement, but also to pursue "a mystic alignment with nature" believed to be the conduit of the cosmic energy of the Most High (Homiak 1998, 154). Beginning in the late 1940s, YBF and other radicals ushered in the strict vegetarian or vegan diet that has become deeply engrained in the Nyahbinghi tradition. This dietary commitment disapproves of the consumption of animal flesh and manufactured foodstuff, especially that which is canned. While some Rastas consume small fishes with scales and fins according to Leviticus 11, most subsist on eating tubers, fruits, grains, nuts and leafy vegetables. Ital extends to the use of herbs for culinary and therapeutic purposes, particularly the use of the "holy herb" (marijuana/ganja) for medicinal and religious purposes. While ganja has been smoked recreationally in Jamaica for decades, YBF and other radical Rastas sanctified this practice making it part of their commitment to the use of natural products for healing and sacramental purposes. Undergirded by the Ital philosophy, ganja smoking became a tool in the resistance against the establish-ment's embrace of the artificial—for example, manufactured cigarettes and alcohol.

The philosophy of naturalness also gave impetus to the emergence of dreadlocks. First-generation Rastas had already encouraged the copious growth of hair on both the head and the face. However, while they discouraged cutting the hair and shaving in particular, they practised careful grooming with the assistance of a comb. Hence, they gained the appellation "combsome", as distinguished from "dreads" or "locksmen" which have become a moniker for those favouring uncombed matted tresses. While Leonard E. Barrett, who wrote the first book-length monograph on Rastafari, attributes the first appearance of dreadlocks among Rastas to Howell's commune at Pinnacle, the informants for both Chevannes and Homiak credit YBF and other second-generation Rastas of the 1950s for introducing and valorizing dreadlocks as essential to Rastafari "livity" or lifestyle (Chevannes 1998, 101; Homiak 1998, 133).

While not all Rastas insist on the necessity of locks, and while others who accept the ideal of locks have forgone "locksing" to escape discrimination in the workplace, the house of Nyahbinghi has promulgated dreadlocks, along with the divinity of Haile Selassie I, as an indispensable element of its ethos. Over the years, Nyahbinghi Rastas and others have put forth various rationales for and justifications of dreadlocks. Drawing on the philosophy of "naturality" or Ital, they aver that dreadlocks are the inevitable outcome of uncut and uncombed African hair. Washing one's hair and letting it grow naturally without the aid of grooming instruments is thus a protest against artifice. Dreadlocks are also traced to and justified by biblical passages concerning the Nazarites who were forbidden from trimming and shaving their hair during a limited period or during a lifetime (Numbers 6; Judges 13:5–7; Judges 16:17). Furthermore, dreadlocks by simulating the lion's mane symbolize the leonine attributes of confidence and courage. Haile Selassie's title "Lion of Judah", his use of the lion's images as his emblems and tales of his interactions with pet lions also undergird Nyahbinghi's association of dreadlocks with leonine qualities and closeness to Jah (God). In fact, dreadlocks are often considered a form of spiritual antenna for tapping into the cosmic powers of Jah immanent in nature.

The Nyahbinghi traditions initiated by the second generation of Rasta include the ritual complex of reasoning, chanting and drumming. Instead of the preaching of a single inspired leader, "reasoning" (a dialogic conversation) emerged as a collective exploration of inner consciousness, based on the conviction that all individuals have the same access to spiritual insights. In the ferment of the 1950s, some adherents added chanting to their reasoning sessions. Chanting denotes the slow rhythmic singing of religious folk melodies to which they added lyrics reflecting the consciousness of Rastafari. Within the same changing ethos, Count Ossie and others adopted drumming styles and rhythms from extant secular and religious drumming traditions to create what they dubbed Nyahbinghi drumming. This drumming style evolved as an accompaniment to the chanting at the Rastafari gathering called Nyahbinghi Issembly (Assembly). Both the drumming and the chanting were considered an effective means of countering oppressive forces. In fact, the term Nyahbinghi is of East African origin and was associated with groups resisting European colonial domination. In its usage by Rastas, it came to mean death to oppressors.

Another tenet of Nyahbinghi emanating from the radical reformists is the inferiority and subordination of women. The young Rastas of the 1950s and 1960s drew on the teachings of Paul concerning women's roles (1 Timothy 2:11–15; 1 Corinthians 14:34–35) and Levitical laws concerning menstrual impurity to formulate a discourse that imputes both physical inferiority and spiritual deficiency to women (Edmonds 2012, 97– 98). Some of these young Rastas considered women so inimical to their spiritual well-being that they embraced celibacy and refused any domestic contacts with women (Homiak 1998, 140–142). Though celibacy did not take hold as a required practice in Nyahbinghi, the discourse on women's impurity and inferiority resulted in their marginalization. For a long time, strict Rastas of the Nyahbinghi persuasion insisted that women could not independently arrive at the awareness of their inner divinity without being nurtured by their Rastafari partners (Kingman). This idea was inscribed in the pithy saying, "There was no such person as a Rastawoman, but a Rastaman woman" (Chevannes 1994, 260). Restrictions on women's participation in ritual ganja smoking, playing drums and dancing in the circle of Rastas at gatherings institutionalized their underclass status. In addition, they had to follow a dress code that prescribed the covering of their heads and the wearing of clothes that did not expose parts of their body, including arms and legs, considered sexually attractive. From the 1970s onwards, some women in Nyahbinghi have challenged their male counterparts concerning their gender discourse and practices. Some women have asserted their rights of equal participation in Rastafari and some brethren have supported or tolerated their position. However, gender equality is still a contested issue in the Nyahbinghi order of Rastafari.

While Nyahbinghi is a distinctive group within Rastafari, it is not an effectively structured organization. However, it has evolved a system of eldership to provide inspirational and disciplinary leadership to the house. Eldership is not gained by ordination or election, but by some combination of at least three factors: an exemplary life demonstrating and defending Rastafari, a reputation as a skilful and persuasive exponent of the principles of Rastafari, and some demonstrated ability to bring people together for collective inspiration or collective action for the Rastafari community. As Barry Chevannes writes, elders are "the most knowledgeable or the most forceful participants, whether this knowledge or forcefulness derived from venerable age and experience in the movement... or from native intelligence" (Chevannes 1994, 231). A central role of elders is to provide inspiration for those in their circles to live "upfull" (upright) lives and to inspire confidence and perseverance in the face of opposition. Elders also serve as protectors and promoters of the well-being and interests of Rastafari in relation with the wider society. The major administrative function of elders is to convene monthly meetings "to discuss internal affairs and plan events such as celebrations" or Nyahbinghi assemblies (Chevannes 1994, 231). When issues requiring a Rastafari response arise in the wider community, the most revered elders usually convene to formulate responses or plan events to address these issues.

House of Bobo Shanti

Though the house of Bobo Shanti, aka Ethiopia Africa Black International Congress (EABIC) was founded by a second-generation Rasta, it has preserved much of the charismatic ethos of early Rastafari. From the late 1950s until his transition (death), Prince Emmanuel (Emmanuel Charles Edwards, 1915–1994) exercised unrivalled charismatic leadership of the group in the manner of Howell, Hibbert and Hinds. The core group of this house now lives communally in a settlement established by Prince Emmanuel on the hillside of Bull Bay several miles east of Kingston. The religious ceremonies in this commune reveal close parallels to that of Revivalism much like some of the earliest Rastafari ceremonies did.

Bobo Shanti first came to public knowledge in 1958 when its founder, Prince Emmanuel, convened an assembly of Rastas to deal with the issue of repatriation. This assembly attracted a large number of Rastas from around the island. Many apparently came to Kingston with the expectation that their repatriation was imminent. Following a week-long "convention", the followers of Prince Emmanuel staged a symbolic capture of Queen Victoria Park in downtown Kingston by planting Rastafari flags of red, green and gold in much of its empty spaces. The police descended and forcefully cleared the park scattering the would-be occupiers (Chevannes 2012, 2; Edmonds 2003, 82–88). At that time, the commune was located in the West Kingston inner city enclave of Ackee Walk. After the Jamaican government razed the squatters' settlement of Ackee Walk in 1968, Emmanuel's commune reconstituted itself at various locations around the city. Eventually, Prince Emmanuel and his followers settled on "captured" government-owned land on a hillside in Bull Bay to the east of Kingston (Chevannes 1994, 173–174). While "Bobo Hill" or "Temon", as this commune is called by those who domicile there, remains the centre of the Bobo Shanti house, many who identify themselves as Bobo Dreads (followers of Prince Emmanuel) have their permanent residences elsewhere, but make frequent visits to the commune and support it with monetary and other material possessions. Since the 1990s, an increasing number of famous reggae artists have identified themselves with this house, though they do not live in the commune at Bull Bay (Bonacci 2015, 245). In addition, circles of followers of this house have also formed in Trinidad and Tobago, the United States, England, Ethiopia and West Africa. For Bobo Dreads who live outside of the commune in Jamaica and abroad, the Bull Bay commune has become something of a pilgrimage site. Many make pilgrimage there for special commemorations or just to see the site from which their inspiration flowed.

The most obvious difference between Bobo Dreads and other Rasta is their clothing. While other Rastas may wear a variety of clothing styles, Bobo Dreads usually garb themselves in robes of various colours. They also characteristically don head wraps that seclude their locks from public gaze. Almost as distinctive as their clothing is their association with the making and peddling of a variety of brooms throughout the city of Kingston. From all appearances, the selling of brooms is a vital source of income that supplements the subsistence farming that sustains the community.

Like other houses, Bobo Shanti has made repatriation to Ethiopia an essential tenet and a sustained focus of its activism. Since he called the "convention" in 1958, the issue of repatriation remained a constant preoccupation for Prince Emmanuel. The EABIC formed at the time of the "convention" was intended to be an organization that would advocate for and facilitate the return of Rastas and other Blacks in the Americas to Africa/Ethiopia, considered their ancestral homeland. Reportedly, Prince Emmanuel occupied himself with composing hundreds of letters to heads of government (Ethiopia, Jamaica and United Kingdom) and multinational organizations (United Nations and Organization of African Unity/African Union), urging them to effect the return of people of African descent exiled in Jamaica and the Americas as a whole (Bonacci 2015, 245). Ironically, only a few adherents of the house of Bobo Shanti have actually migrated to Shashemene, Ethiopia, where Haile Selassie granted land to people of African descent in the West who supported Ethiopia's military resistance against the Italian invasion and occupation from 1935 to 1941 and who wished to repatriate to Africa (Bonacci 2015, 246).

Another distinguishing feature of Bobo Shanti is its assertion that the Holy Trinity consists of Haile Selassie, Marcus Garvey and Prince Emmanuel. Selassie is King; Garvey is Prophet; and Emmanuel is Priest. Prince Emmanuel is therefore a divine personality who is considered a reincarnation of Christ. Prince Emmanuel's teaching on the Trinity may sound rather quixotic. However, it gels well with the Rastafari assertion that "Man is God and God is man" (Chevannes 1994, 181). Like the Nation of Gods and Earth or Five Percenters (a breakaway group from the Nation of Islam), Rastas insist that God is not a "spook"—some ethereal being—but the inner divine self of humans. Selassie's, Garvey's and Emmanuel's status as part of the Trinity arises from the fact that they actualized their divine-human consciousness to a higher degree than other humans.

While Black supremacy and White inferiority no longer figure prominently in Rastafari as a whole, Bobo Shanti adheres to the theory that Blacks were the original people from which all others sprung. To support this assertion, Bobo Dreads argue that the offspring of a Black person and a person of any other race is invariably Black (Chevannes 1994, 180). From this, they conclude that the Black race is inherently superior to other races, especially Whites.

Yet another distinguishing feature of Bobo Shanti is its strict and extensive ritual observances. In fact, religious rituals modulate the whole rhythm of life in the Bull Bay commune. Members punctuate every day with three prayers—in the morning, at midday and at the going down of the sun. Evenings bring the members together for services in an outdoor ritual space. These services are comprised of drumming, singing/chanting, "ovations and tributes" to the Trinity, and Bible readings and sermons by Prince Emmanuel while he was still alive, and presumably now by his successor. In addition to two weekly fasts, the community observes a fast on the first Saturday of every month. This is a complete fast in which neither food nor drink is consumed all day. On fast days, Bobo Dreads dress in their ceremonial white and participate in a service in the temple or tabernacle. This service lasts from noon to six and consists of Bible reading and singing accompanied by drumming. The fast ends with ablutions, ceremonial eating of bread, closing prayers, and reverential greetings of the leader and one another (Chevannes 1994, 180–183).

Unlike the house of Nyahbinghi, the Bobo Shanti community is rigidly structured. While Prince Emmanuel was alive, he was the supreme leader to whom reverence and obeisance were routinely given. His teachings became the tenets of Bobo Shanti, and the social structure and practices of the community were all dictated by him. Male members are assigned statuses and roles as priests and prophets. According to Chevannes, "The function of the prophets is to reason, the function of the priests is to 'move around the altar', that is to conduct the services". In other words, the prophets engage in discussing and refining their understanding to the principles of Rastafari, while the priests are responsible for conducting the ceremonies of the commune. Some male members of the community are also assigned to carry out other duties (cooks, guards, storekeepers, maintenance persons, etc.) that are necessary for the welfare of the community (Chevannes 1994, 174). Since the passing of Prince Emmanuel, dissension has sprung up within ranks of Bobo Shanti concerning who should assume the mantle of leadership left by its founder and unchallenged priest for a half a century. While Priest Trevor

Stewart assumed leadership of the community at the passing of Prince Emmanuel, rivals have emerged declaring that they are the true successors. At least two factions have left the original settlement to establish their own further up the mountain.

Women occupy a decidedly marginalized space in the Bobo Shanti commune. A stronger sense of patriarchy and more restrictive policing of women prevail here than anywhere else in Rastafari. The discourse of women's physical and moral impurity in the house of Nyahbinghi becomes in Bobo Shanti a pathologizing of women because of their monthly menses and their perceived danger to men's pursuit of spiritual matters. This pathologizing of women is clearly evident in their confinement to the "sick house" or infirmary for a considerable time each month—the week before, the week during and the week after their monthly periods. The women of the community never cook for or serve men, are segregated from men during religious services, and are required to wear clothing that covers their entire torso and limbs. Their main duties in the commune are cleaning, caring for children and providing sex to their male partners (Chevannes 1994, 176–179).

The Twelve Tribes of Israel

The aggregation of Rastas known as the Twelve Tribes of Israel came to prominence in the early 1970s, when it moved its headquarters from the inner city of Kingston to Hope Road in close proximity to Bob Marley's house/studio and to the official residences of the prime minister and the governor general of Jamaica. However, its founding goes back to 1968 when Vernon Carrington, who was the head of Chapter 15 of Ethiopia World Federation (EWF) in Jamaica, effectively transformed the group into the Twelve Tribes of Israel. When questions arose concerning the authenticity of Chapter 15, Carrington dropped the EWF association and became the charismatic and inspirational leader of a new Rastafari group with a broad appeal to middle class youths who were engaged in the politics of cultural decolonization in the 1960s and 1970s (Barnett 2005, 67).

Vernon Carrington arrived at the designation the Twelve Tribes of Israel from his reading of the Bible, particularly the passage about Jacob's twelve sons who became the progenitors of the twelve Hebrew tribes that constituted the original nation of Israel. The significance of the number twelve seemed to have etched itself on his consciousness from his exposure to the teachings of the Unity School of Christianity and Rosicrucianism concerning the "twelve seats of power in the human body" (Bonacci 2015, 205). The fact that Jesus had twelve disciples in his inner circle and that there are twelve signs of the zodiac further cemented in his mind that twelve is a number with spiritual or mystical significance.

The identification of Rastas with the Children of Israel arises from the Rastafari belief that they (and other Blacks) either descended from or are the reincarnations of the ancient Hebrews. Proceeding from this conviction, Carrington assigned all his followers to one of the Twelve Tribes of Israel according to their birth date and associated them with particular colours and personality traits:

> April corresponds to the name Reuben and is associated with the color silver. May is Simeon and is associated with the color gold; June is Levi, whose color is purple; July is Judah, whose color is brown; August is Issachar, whose color is yellow; September is Zebulun, whose color is pink; October is Dan, whose color is blue; November is Gad, whose color is red; December is Asher, whose color is gray; January is Naphtali, whose color is green; February is Joseph, whose color is white; and March is Benjamin, whose color is black (Barnett 2005, 68).

In this schema, Carrington belongs to the tribe of Gad, and was often simply referred to as Gad or Prophet Gad, which, in the vocalization of most Jamaicans, sounded the same as God. This created an air of divinity around Carrington. In concert with the numerical significance of twelve, Twelve Tribes avers that the righteous elect will ultimately be 144,000 (12x12,000), a claim similar to that of the Jehovah's Witnesses and the Unification Church (Barnett 2005, 68).

Because of the location of its headquarters in a somewhat affluent area of Kingston and because many of its members had middle and upper-class pedigrees, Twelve Tribes members are popularly labelled "uptown Rastas". Auspiciously, the Twelve Tribes came along as many college and university students from Jamaica's upper and middle classes were becoming disenchanted with the corruption and the ineffectiveness of Jamaica's political system to address the poverty and inequality that plagued the society. Concurrently, these students were exposed to the radical politics and Black nationalism that characterized the Black Power Movement that was resonating throughout the African Diaspora. Many of these students along with many visual and performing artists embraced Rastafari and aligned themselves with the Twelve Tribes of Israel, signaling their embrace of an African identity and their repudiation of the bourgeois ideals foisted upon them by their parents and their elite education.

Twelve Tribes shares many of the central emphases of Rastafari in general: rediscovery of African identity, the oppressive nature of Western societies, the necessity of repatriation and the inner divinity of the individual. However, on several fronts, Twelve Tribes differs from other houses in its philosophy and practice. For this reason, it is considered a more moderate house of Rastafari than either Nyahbinghi or Bobo Shanti.

While the other groups espoused a militant Black identity politics and were hesitant to incorporate people of other races, especially Whites, Twelve Tribes applied its "I n I" philosophy (inherent divinity of the individual) to embrace people of all races. Hence Whites who profess "I n I" consciousness are much more likely to associate with Twelve Tribes than the two other main mansions.

Unlike Nyahbinghi that unequivocally embraces Haile Selassie as a divine persona, either as the second coming or appearing of Jesus Christ or Jah (God) himself, the identity and role of Selassie are not so clearly defined in Twelve Tribes. University of the West Indies sociologist Michael Barnett has noted that because of a lack of clear articulation on this point by Carrington, notions regarding the status of Selassie range from Christ reincarnated, to the Holy Spirit, to having the same spirit as Christ, to being divine but not Christ, to the latest occupier of the Throne of David (Barnett 2005, 76). Selassie as the latest occupier of the Davidic throne seems to have much currency in Twelves Tribes that sees it as the fulfilment of the prophecy enunciated in Genesis 49:10: "The scepter shall not depart from Judah"—David's and Selassie's ancestral lineage. Some even argue that "Christ" should be understood as an office, not a person. In the New Testament era, the office was occupied by Jesus and in more recent times by Haile Selassie. Whatever nuance may be attached to Twelve Tribes' understanding of the identity and status of Haile Selassie, Jesus occupies a place of prominence in the Twelve Tribes that he does not in other Rastafari houses, especially Nyahbinghi. For Nyahbinghi Rastas, and probably Bobo Dreads as well, the name "Jesus" is likely to evoke images of the pirate John Hawkin's slave ship, *Jesus of Lubeck*. In the 1990s, the term "bun Jesus" (burn Jesus) became the vociferous reaction of Nyahbinghi and other Rastas to the conversion of former Rastas (most famously Judy Mowatt and Tommy Cowan, former stalwarts in Twelve Tribes) to Christianity. Conversely, Twelve Tribes Rastas fully embrace the Jesus of the New Testament. Referring to him as *Yahshuah*, they declare that he is their Lord and Saviour. For this reason, Twelve Tribes are popularly dubbed "Christian Rastas".

Some Rastas have a complicated relationship with English translations of the Bible (especially the King James Version), employing some passages to support their beliefs and practices and rejecting others as interpolations by White translators to give divine sanction to oppressive institutions and practices. Twelve Tribes, however, fully accepts the authenticity and authority of the King James Version of the Bible and places a major emphasis on its reading. The mostly clearly enunciated requirement that Carrington has placed on his followers is to "read a chapter a day" from Genesis to Revelation.

Another aspect of Twelve Tribes that marks it as more moderate than Nyahbinghi and Bobo Shanti is that women are considered equal to their male counterparts and hence are equally involved in the activities of the house. This was evident in the initial organization of the group. To administer the affairs of the group, Carrington appointed an executive of twelve male elders and twelve female elders. Twenty-four alternates were equally divided along gender lines. For some unexplained reason, Carrington decreed in the early 1980s that the group would go on "rest status". Since then, the leadership of the organization became static (Barnett 2012, 7–8).

In the 1970s and early 1980s, the main public activity of Twelve Tribes was a monthly reggae dance at its Hope Road compound. This was a departure from the chanting and drumming that are front and centre of the ceremonies of other Rastafari groups. This was also an unmitigated embrace and utilization of reggae, the popular musical phenomenon, which some Rastas saw as a corruption of vintage Rasta music and hence not an acceptable medium of praising Jah. This embrace of reggae was clearly related to the fact that a number of celebrated reggae artists, including Bob Marley, belonged to the Twelve Tribe mansion. During the 1990s, the monthly reggae dance became irregular in Jamaica, while the dance programme has become a regular feature of the international branches of the house. With the passing of Carrington in 2005, Twelve Tribes has become less centrally organized and hence less cohesive. Nevertheless, it is still recognized as one of the major houses/mansions of Rastafari with followers throughout the Caribbean, North America, Europe, Africa, Australia and New Zealand.

OTHER SHEEP HAVE I WHICH ARE NOT OF THIS FOLD: BEYOND HOUSES AND MANSIONS

Beyond the houses of Nyahbinghi, Bobo Shanti and Twelve Tribes, various other groups with more limited following have dotted the "landscape" of Rastafari over the years. In the late 1950s and early 1960s, the Reverend Claudius Henry and his African Reform Church/International Peacemakers Association emerged rather suddenly on Jamaica's social stage. Though Henry's credentials as a *bona fide* Rasta have often been questioned, he certainly posed as an African nationalist with association to Haile Selassie. In 1959, Henry convened a gathering of Rastas that he pitched as preparation for repatriation. The "tickets" he sold as admission to this gathering displayed a picture of Haile Selassie and indicated that they will be the only "passports" needed for repatriation to Ethiopia. Jamaica's leading newspaper, the *Daily Gleaner*, reported that hundreds of Rastas, some having sold all their possessions, descended on Henry's headquarters in Kingston expecting to embark on ships heading to Ethiopia. When no ships appeared in the Kingston harbors to ferry the faithful to Zion, the whole affair ended in disappointment with Henry arrested, fined and placed on probation for a year (Barrett 1997, 95–98). The following year, Claudius Henry and his son Ronald Henry were implicated in a plot to overthrow the Jamaican government. In a raid on his Rosalie Avenue premises, the authorities discovered a cache of arms. Shortly thereafter, Ronald Henry and a group of armed men, including some Rastas, precipitated a national state of emergency in Jamaica when they killed two British soldiers who were part of a group sent to investigate their activities. Ronald and four of his confederates were apprehended, convicted and executed. Reverend Claudius Henry was convicted of treason and incarcerated until 1966. As quickly as Henry rose to prominence, he faded from centre stage on account of his conviction and incarceration. However, after his release from prison, he retreated to Sandy Bay, Clarendon, where he embarked on the establishment of a largely self-sufficient community. In addition to building a church, the International Peacemakers Association operated the Peacemakers Bakery, a concrete block factory, a fish shop and a farm. During its halcyon days in the late 1960s, membership of this community was estimated at four thousand, and its Sabbath services were reportedly crowded. Though the community has survived the passing of the Reverend Claudius Henry, it now exists on the margins of Rastafari and its membership seems to be mostly the elderly surviving followers of Henry (Paul 2012).

A rather controversial group associated with Rastafari is the Ethiopian Zion Coptic Church. Founded in the 1940s by Louva Williams, more affectionately known as Brother Love, the group had little connection to Rastafari until it adopted elements of Rastafari in the 1970s. While the group acknowledged Haile Selassie as an inspirational figure, it did not consider him a divine persona. Ethiopian Zion Coptic Church accepted the Rastafari idea concerning the divine nature of humans and the sacrality of ganja (marijuana). In the 1970s, this group distinguished itself by the influx and growing influence of White adherents. These were mostly former hippies from the United States, who embraced the ganja ethos of the group and turned it into an entrepreneurial venture. With their financial resources, they purchased large tracts of land in Jamaica on which they grew ganja and other crops. Soon the church became financially well off, reportedly from the international ganja trade it facilitated through the use of private airstrips on its properties. Before long, the White Rastas with their headquarters in Miami Beach became the dominant force in the church. In 1980, *60 Minutes* aired a sensationalist report about the Miami Beach group's association with criminality and particularly drug trafficking. A series of indictments and convictions of its members on drug charges by Florida's law enforcement eventually dismantled the Miami Beach group and dispersed its members elsewhere in the United States. While the Ethiopian Zion Coptic Church does not command the public attention it did in the 1970s and 1980s, it persists today with congregations in Jamaica, Iowa and California.

The Church of Haile Selassie I, founded in 1987 by Abuna Foxe, is a Rastafari group that seeks to bring routine structures to the otherwise diffused ethos of Rastafari. To that end, Abuna Foxe created a hierarchy of church leaders, established regular church services including Sunday school, and drew up articles of belief and codes of behaviour (The Church of Haile Selassie I 2018). Foxe's objective was to elevate the veneration of Haile Selassie to the same status as that of Jesus Christ and to secure the kind of official recognition for Rastafari that most nation states accord to churches. In New York for example, Foxe secured authorization to provide chaplain services to Rastas incarcerated in the state correctional institutions. In October 2013, the Jamaican parliament enacted a bill granting official status to the Church of Haile Selassie I, thus granting it the right to hold property and to perform services recognized by the government, such as marriages and funerals (*Jamaica Observer*, 30 October 2013). The Church of Haile Selassie I and its companion organization, the Imperial Ethiopian World Federation, also founded by Abuna Foxe, has congregations in several Caribbean countries, the United States and the United Kingdom.

In recent years, a new group of Rastas has emerged with the name Fulfilled Rastas. Information of this group is sparse and can be gleaned mostly from the internet. From online postings, it seems that Fulfilled Rastas are a multicultural group. While they embrace Rastafari identity, they differ in significant ways from widely acknowledged Rastafari principles. To begin with, like Christians, they declare themselves followers of *Yahshuah* (Jesus) who is the saviour of humankind. Haile Selassie is not lauded as divine, but as the defender of the Ethiopian Orthodox Tewahedo Church and an inspired leader who has given instructions on how to live as God's children in modern time. To that end, Fulfilled Rastas are committed to advancing the teachings and philosophy of Haile Selassie (gleaned mostly from his speeches) about the pursuit of justice in the world, the embrace of tolerance for all people, and a commitment to peaceful resolution of personal and political conflicts. For Fulfilled Rastas, some of the practices that are considered essential markers of Rastafari identity, such as the cultivation of dreadlocks, ganja smoking and Ital living, are not obligatory, but are left up to individual choice.

Founded in 1997 by Dermot Fagan, His Imperial Majesty (HIM) School of Vision falls within the ambit of the Nyahbinghi mansion. However, it is a particular camp or commune with its own distinctive approach to Rastafari. Located above Irish Town in the Blue Mountains that overlook Kingston, HIM School of Vision is a throwback to a time when the characteristic formation of Rastas was in camps located in depressed inner cities or on the periphery of urban areas. HIM School of Vision stands out from other Rastas because of the particular brand of apocalypticism that Fagan has elaborated. Fagan founded the school (which is technically not a school) out of the conviction that we are living in the apocalyptic era prophesied in the book of Revelation in the Christian Bible. Babylon (the institutions and forces of oppression in the world), he argues, is in the process of branding people with the "mark of the beast" (666) via a microchip planted in their hands or brains. The School of Vision seeks to educate people against submitting to this implantation and to provide a haven for the righteous in prepara-tion for their repatriation to Ethiopia (Zion). At the founding of the group, Fagan predicted that by 2007, Haile Selassie would show up with chariots in the shape of flying saucers to evacuate the righteous before unleashing fiery judgement on the forces and institutions of Babylon (Chevannes 2012, 26–27; Templehof 2017). Despite the non-appearance of Haile Selassie with his chariots, Fagan continues to preach an imminent apocalypse, preside over religious services in the camp, and conduct outreach in Kingston to get others to join in preparation for a miraculous repatriation.

CONCLUSION

The preceding discussion of the multi-formation of Rastafari does not exhaust the many named Rastafari groups in Jamaica and around the world. It does illustrate, however, that Rastafari is not a homogenous movement with a hierarchical structure and a binding creed. As I have argued elsewhere and others have affirmed, the Rastafari concept of I and I has engendered a radical kind of individualism in the movement. This entrenched individualism has proven resistant to rigid organizational structures and has given rise to a kind of social fissiparity (Barnett 2002, 54–61; Edmonds 2003, 71). Some have even pursued the Rastafari lifestyle without recourse to or identification with any house or mansion of Rastafari. Velma Pollard has aptly designated these as "own-built" Rastas, indicating that these are solo travellers on the path of Rastafari (Pollard 1982, 17).

Over the years, the desire for a more cohesive and organized structuring of Rastafari has been repeatedly voiced and attempted. This desire often emerges from the realization that for Rastafari to gain respect and exercise social influence, it needs to present a united front to the world. For example, the Rastafari Movement Association, formed in the 1970s, attempted to unify Rastafari into a political force that could vie for parliamentary representation in Jamaica. The famed Rastafari drummer, Count Ossie, formed the Mystic Revelation of Rastafari in the early 1970s to unite Rastas to develop a practical programme for repatriation as well as to provide cultural education of the young people. The formation of the Rastafari International Theocracy Assembly in 1983 and Rastafari Centralization Organization in 1995 represent similar efforts to bring some measure of centralization to Rastafari. In all cases, the emphasis has been on the need to develop a coordinated voice and a collective strategy to further the interests of Rastafari vis à vis the wider society, and not so much on the need to develop organizational structures to administer the internal affairs of Rastafari. Some Rastas, including the University of the West Indies sociologist Michael Barnett, advocate that these structures are needed to prevent the unending proliferation of Rastafari groups (Barnett 2002, 60). While most Rastas are united around certain philosophical and social ideas, a collective identity represented by certain symbols (dreadlocks, Haile Selassie) and a commitment to certain practices (ganja smoking, Ital or vegan diet), to date, the movement as a whole remains heterogeneous without the institutional structures to undertake effective collective actions.

Notes

1 See *Daily Gleaner,* 17 March 1934.

2 See the following sites: http://christianreggae.ning.com/profiles/blogs/why-are-fulfilled-rastafari, http://fulfilledrasta.blogspot.com/, and http://snwmf.com/phorum/read.php?1,209884 (accessed 13 February 2018).

References

Barnett, Michael. 2002. "Rastafari Dialecticism: The Epistemological Individualism and Connectivism of Rastafari". *Caribbean Quarterly* 48 (4): 54–61.

_____. 2005. "The Many Faces of Rasta: Doctrinal Diversity within the Rastafari Movement". *Caribbean Quarterly* 51 (2): 67-78.

_____. 2012. "Rastafari in the New Millennium: Rastafari the Dawn of the Fifth Epoch". In *Rastafari in the New Millennium: A Rastafari Reader*, edited by Michael Barnett, 1–12. Syracuse, NY: Syracuse University Press.

Barrett, Leonard E. 1997. *The Rastafarians.* Twentieth Anniversary Edition. Boston: Beacon Press.

Bishton, Derek. 1983. "Meeting Joseph Nathaniel Hibbert, July 23, 1983". https://derek-bishton.wordpress.com/2013/03/11/meeting-joseph-nathaniel-hibbert-july-23-1983/

Bonacci, Giulia. 2015. *Exodus! Heirs and Pioneers, Rastafari Return to Ethiopia.* Kingston: University of the West Indies Press.

Chevannes, Barry. 1994. *Rastafari: Roots and Ideology.* Syracuse, NY: Syracuse University Press.

_____. 1998. "Origin of Dreadlocks". In *Rastafari and Other African-Caribbean Worldviews*, edited by Barry Chevannes, 77–96. New Brunswick, NJ: Rutgers University Press.

_____. 1998. "The Phallus and the Outcast: The Symbolism of Dreadlocks in Jamaica". In *Rastafari and Other African-Caribbean Worldviews*, edited by Barry Chevannes, 96–126. New Brunswick, NJ: Rutgers University Press.

_____. 1999. "Between the Living and the Dead: The Apotheosis of Rastafari Heroes". In *Religion, Diaspora and Cultural Identity: A Reader in the Anglophone Caribbean*, edited by John W. Pulis, 337–356. Amsterdam: Gordon and Breach Publishers.

_____. 2012. "Rastafari and the Coming of Age". In *Rastafari in the New Millennium*, edited by Michael Barnett, 13–34. Syracuse, NY: Syracuse University Press.

Edmonds, Ennis. 2003. *Rastafari: From Outcasts to Culture Bearers.* New York: Oxford University Press.

_____. 2012. *Rastafari: A Very Short Introduction.* Oxford, UK: Oxford University Press.

Hill, Robert A. 1981. "Dread History: Leonard P. Howell and Millenarian Visions in Early Rastafari Religion in Jamaica". *Epoche, Journal of the History of Religions at UCLA* 9: 31–70.

_____. 1983. "Leonard P. Howell and Millenarian Visions in Early Rastafari". *Jamaica Journal* 16 (1)/February: 24–39.

Homiak, John Paul. 1998. "Dub History: Soundings on Rastafari Livity and Language". In *Rastafari and Other African-Caribbean Worldviews*, edited by Barry Chevannes, 127–181. New Brunswick, NJ: Rutgers University Press.

Hutton, Clinton. 2015. "Leonard Howell Announcing God". In *Leonard Percival Howell and the Genesis of Rastafari*, edited by Clinton A. Hutton, Michael A. Barnett, D.A. Dunkley, and Jahlani A.H. Niaah, 9–52. Mona, Jamaica: The University of the West Indies Press.

Lee, Hélène. 2003. *The First Rasta: Leonard Howell and the Rise of Rastafarianism*. Translated by Lily Davis. Chicago: Lawrence Hill Books.

Paul, Annie. 2012. "A Visit to Rev Claudius Henry's Church, Sandy Bay, Jamaica". https://anniepaul.net/2012/08/19/a-visit-to-rev-claudius-henrys-church-sandy-bay-jamaica/.

Perkins, Ann Kasafi. 2012. "The Wages of (Sin) Is Babylon: Rastafari Versus Christian Religious Perspectives on Sin". In *Rastafari in the New Millennium: A Rastafari Reader*, edited by Michael Barnett, 239–254. NY: Syracuse University Press.

Pollard, Velma. 1982. "The Social History of Dread Talk". *Caribbean Quarterly* 28 (2): 17–40.

Pullen, Elizabeth. 2011. "Rastafarianism". In *Encyclopedia of African American Religions*, edited by Larry G. Murphy, J. Gordon Melton, and Gary L. Ward, 632–637. New York: Routledge.

Templehof, Joshua. 2017. "Sci-Fi Rastas: UFO Cult/Bed and Breakfast". Accessed 11 August 2017. www.thetowner.com/sci-fi-rastas.

The Church of Haile Selassi I, and IEWF Inc. 2020. "CHSI Sabbath Worship Scriptures". http://www.himchurch.org (accessed 29 June 2020).

Weber, Max. 1963. *The Sociology of Religion*. Translated by Ephraim Fischoff with Introduction by Talcott Parsons. Boston: Beacon Press.

THE LEGACY OF CHARISMATIC LEADERSHIP IN THE RASTAFARI MOVEMENT

Michael Barnett

Abstract   This article intends to take a discerning look at the nature of Rastafari leadership throughout the movement's trajectory, arguing that it is by and large of a charismatic nature. Broadly speaking the Rastafari movement is largely considered by many Rastafari scholars to be decentralized and polycephalous; a movement wherein ritual/social/political authority resides in branches or mansions that act independently of each other. Having no centralized authority structure presents both advantages and disadvantages to the movement, and this article will help to highlight this. The article will utilize Max Weber's stance on the various types of authority to analyse the leadership dynamics of the first generation of Rastafari, as well as that of the second and third generation of Rastafari leaders, who brought with them new perspectives and outlooks in terms of the philosophy and orientation of the Rastafari movement.

Keywords • Charismatic leadership • Rastafari • types of authority

THE FIRST-GENERATION LEADERS OF THE RASTAFARI MOVEMENT

From its beginning in Jamaica, Rastafari was a decentralized and polycephalous movement as opposed to being homogenous as is often assumed by many present-day adherents and casual observers of Rastafari. As early as the middle of 1933, the movement was composed of two distinct congregations, one in Trinityville, St Thomas, which consisted of followers loyal to Leonard Howell and Robert Hinds, and the other consisting of followers based in the Benoah district of St Andrew, who were loyal to Joseph Hibbert. When Archibald Dunkley entered the fray and founded his King of Kings Mission in Kingston in late 1933, we had three distinct congregations or houses of Rastafari. Thus importantly, from its very inception, the Rastafari movement was a polycephalous one, with the early Rastafari congregations originating and developing independently under different leaders (Smith, Augier & Nettleford 1988, 6–7).

By titling her book on Leonard Howell *The First Rasta* (2003), the author Hélène Lee took a distinct position in the debate regarding the beginning of the Rastafari movement, namely that the movement originated with Leonard Howell and that all the other early leaders essentially became his lieutenants. This author has contended elsewhere (Barnett 2015, 56) that

Joseph Hibbert could well have been the first one to pronounce the divinity of Haile Selassie, and that he and Dunkley formed their own Rastafari organizations independently of Howell. However, having said that, it should be emphasized that it was Leonard Howell who was the most influential and successful of all the first-generation leaders of Rastafari. Notably, each of the prominent first-generation leaders, Robert Hinds, Leonard Howell, Joseph Hibbert and Archibald Dunkley, eventually had independent followings in Jamaica that existed relatively autonomously. There was no significant collaboration among the leaders, except for the case of Howell and Hinds who worked together as partners and were a tight-knit team right up until the time they were sentenced and jailed for sedition in a landmark court case in March 1934 (Barnett 2015; *The Gleaner*, 17 March 1934).

The Impact of Marcus Garvey on the First-Generation Leaders of Rastafari

The impact of Marcus Garvey overall on the Rastafari movement is immeasurable. He undoubtedly trail-blazed a path for the early Rastafari leaders in terms of leading an anticolonial movement of his own and exuding a charismatic leadership that has arguably been unmatched by any Black leader to date. Garvey provided not just rhetoric, but a tangible vision and template for the upliftment of Black/African people worldwide.

In his book chapter entitled "Marcus Garvey and the Early Rastafarians: Continuity and Discontinuity" (1998), acclaimed Garvey scholar Rupert Lewis details notable differences between Rastafari and Garveyism, but significantly he also details many areas of convergence between the two movements. For one thing, Lewis (1998) asserts that both movements were Afrocentric and unapologetically defended the beauty and dignity of Africa and people of African ancestry. Another was that both Rastafari and Garveyism showed great respect for the Bible and attempted to distance themselves from biased Eurocentric interpretations of scripture that contributed to the oppression of Black people.

Lewis (1998) also notes that two of the prominent first-generation Rastafari leaders, Leonard Howell and Robert Hinds, were followers of Marcus Garvey (Garveyites) prior to espousing Haile Selassie I as the divine King of African people in the early 1930s. Leonard Howell became a member of Garvey's UNIA in New York in the 1920s, where he sojourned for a few years before suffering the indignity of being deported to Jamaica towards the end of 1932. While Robert Hinds (as in the case of many other Bedwardites) became attracted to the pro-Black teachings of Garvey just as he was to those of Alexander Bedward.

In this author's opinion, Howell's and Hinds' exposure to Garveyism prior to taking on the mantle of leadership in the Rastafari movement served them in good stead in becoming effective, highly influential and charismatic leaders. Their relatively large followings when they were together and when they both went their separate ways stand as testament to that (Barnett 2015; Chevannes 1994).

An Overview of Leonard Howell

According to Robert Hill (2001), Leonard Howell was born on 16 June 1898 at May Crawle in the Bull Head mountain district of upper Clarendon. He was the oldest of ten children. His father, Charles Theophilus Howell, was an independent peasant cultivator and a tailor while his mother, Clementina Bennett, was an agricultural laborer. Howell was a former seaman who had been part of a Jamaican contingent to Colon, Panama, during World War I. He travelled back and forth between New York and Panama a few times before travelling to New York to settle in 1918. He remained there for several years, becoming a member of Garvey's UNIA and noting Garvey's organizational techniques. He was subsequently deported to Jamaica in 1932, whereupon he started preaching the divinity of the Emperor of Ethiopia, His Imperial Majesty Haile Selassie I.

Significantly, soon after Howell started to preach that Haile Selassie I was the manifestation of God in the flesh upon his return to Jamaica, he joined forces with the notable Bedwardite and Garveyite, Robert Hinds. Not only did Hinds have the distinction of being a staunch lieutenant for Howell during the early years of the Rastafari movement in the early 1930s, when the parish of St Thomas became the crucible for the movement, he also represented an important link between the rich Revivalist tradition in Jamaica and the emerging Rastafari movement (Erskine 2005; Hill 2001). Prior to his espousal of the divinity of Haile Selassie I, Hinds had been a devout disciple of Alexander Bedward, a notable revivalist leader from August Town who effectively led his Native Baptist Church movement from 1895 till 1921, at which time he was incarcerated in the Bellevue asylum. Notably Hinds was present during Bedward's final march from August Town in the spring of 1921, when the police halted the marchers and arrested them. When the marchers were tried at Half Way Tree court, Hinds by his own admission (*The Gleaner*, 17 March 1934) was fortunate, in that although he was actually committed to Bellevue along with Bedward, the doctors there determined that he was not mad and he was subsequently discharged (Barnett 2015). In stark contrast, Bedward remained in Bellevue until he died on 8 November 1930, no longer a force or an influence on the peasant/underclass in Jamaica. Oral history has it however that Bedward died a happy man after receiving news of the 1930 coronation of HIM Haile Selassie I in Ethiopia, believing this to be a sign that the redemption of African people was at hand, and that his work in the physical realm was now well and truly over. Aside from Hinds, many of Howell's early followers were Bedwardites. The possibility of religious convergence (i.e., Revivalism converging with Rastafarianism) clearly existed in the parish of St Thomas, and Howell and Hinds were able to find ready converts there. In fact, St Thomas had proven to be a good recruiting ground for Rastafari adherents as many revivalists were based in this parish as well as numerous Kumina practitioners, many of whom were descendants of nineteenth century Central African immigrants who came to Jamaica as indentured workers (Hill 2001, 46).

After his release from prison in 1936, Leonard Howell formed the Ethiopian Salvation Society and in 1940 established the first ever Rastafari commune called Pinnacle, in the vicinity of Sligoville in the parish of St Catherine. Pinnacle made a mark in Rastafari history having been a self-sufficient community with its residents able to grow everything they needed so far as food was concerned and making effective use of ganja as a cash crop to generate revenue for the group as a whole. Furthermore, the community at Pinnacle was a sizable one, comparable to that of a small town, with its numbers in the thousands. Many estimates have the population of Pinnacle at over two thousand (Barnett 2015).

Undoubtedly it was Howell's charismatic leadership that provided the glue to hold the Pinnacle community together as a cohesive community (Chevannes 1994, 123). Emblematic of his leadership status was the fact that Howell named himself Gangunguru Maragh which later became "Gong" Guru Maragh (which translated meant eminent teacher of wisdom), indicating that he saw himself as a supreme leader in his own right. Notably, this was the name under which he authored *The Promised Key* which he published in 1936 and which served as a spiritual guidebook for his congregation. Howell was often referred to as the "Gong" by his followers and ruled with the authority which the name suggests (Dunkley 2015). Though Howell appointed several deacons to help with the administering of the Pinnacle commune, it was he who ultimately exercised unrivalled power over the affairs of Pinnacle (Chevannes 1994, 123).

Unfortunately for Leonard Howell and his followers, Pinnacle was not to exist for more than some sixteen years. Many occupants left when it was first raided in 1954 by law enforcement agents under the pretext of ganja being an illegal and illicit drug at the time. Notably, however, many dwellings were burned down in addition to the ganja crop being burned out. And then in 1956 there was another raid in which nearly all the remaining Howellites (followers of Leonard Howell) were summarily evicted/ejected. According to Monty Howell (the first son of Leonard Howell), there was one final raid on Pinnacle in 1958, in which every single Howellite was evicted and all remaining houses on the vast expanse of land were destroyed (phone interview with author, 14 June 2020).

Some of the Howellites fled to nearby Tredegar Park, while others moved to the slums of West Kingston and some even found themselves in Wareika Hills where they attempted to replicate the communal lifestyle that they enjoyed at Pinnacle. Leonard Howell himself was arrested after the final raid of Pinnacle, deemed mentally unsound by the authorities and committed to Bellevue Hospital. After his release, Leonard Howell became a recluse, living the remaining years of his life in Tredegar Park with some of his followers, his spirit crushed by the devastation and desecration of his Rastafari community. Sadly for Howell, the remaining years of his life were spent in a relative state of obscurity, with him no longer a force or factor in the Rastafari movement as a whole.

Robert Hinds as an Independent Rastafari Leader

Barry Chevannes notes that Hinds went his own way from Howell when he was released from prison in 1935 by setting up his King of Kings Mission, first at 82 North Street, and then at 6 Laws Street, in Kingston (Chevannes 1994, 127). The King of Kings Mission was organized along the lines of a revival group, with the leader or the Shepherd being Hinds himself. Beneath him were the secretaries, two chaplains, an armour bearer, twelve male officers and twelve water-mothers. The secretaries were the recording officers. They were literate, which was not a given back then among the peasant/underclass. In addition to being responsible for general written correspondence, both for matters internal and external to the organization, they were responsible for reading lessons at the meetings. The chaplains, water-mothers and officers were indispensable at the baptism rituals, which took place twice a year to mark the reception of candidates into full membership. Baptisms were usually held at the Ferry River, on the border of St Andrew and St Catherine. According to Noel Erskine, it was in Hinds' King of Kings organization that the revivalist spirit was the strongest (Erskine 2005, 66). Additionally, it was because Hinds was able to skillfully merge Revivalism with Rastafari that his organization had a wide-scale appeal. The carry-overs of Revivalism were very much evident in Hinds' King of Kings mission (in which you had feasts, fasts and of course baptism). In addition, he introduced new practices and beliefs, such as the celebration of the Passover to remind his congregation that they were exiles in Babylon who sought to return to Ethiopia, and the introduction of Haile Selassie as the messianic figure who would redeem Black people all over the world from the shackles of colonialism and poverty.

A notable similarity between Hinds' and Howell's individual organizations was the relatively high number of women they had in their congregations. This arguably was an outcome of the high revivalist influence that was part and parcel of both Rastafari followings. A key feature of Revivalism is the preponderance of women in the congregations, and this characteristic was clearly transferred into the Rastafari organizations of Howell and Hinds (Erskine 2005, 66). Not only were women very much visible in Howell's Pinnacle community and Hinds' King of Kings Mission, but they were also key players, sharing in key responsibilities for these Rastafari organizations along with the men.

According to Chevannes (1994, 140), Hinds' King of Kings Mission began to decline as a result of internal conflicts. One of Chevannes' informants told him in relation to Hinds, "Brother Hinds start to carry on with some things, because you have to say him fall. Him take away all the brother-them wife and live with them, and the Lord vex with him" (Chevannes 1994, 140). Chevannes notes that there must have been some truth to this assertion as a son and a daughter were born to him within the space of a month in 1938, inferring multiple-partner sex. However, Hinds' organization never showed any visible signs of breaking down until the mid-1940s, indicating a gradual decline of his King of Kings Mission rather than a sudden abrupt one.

The major cause of the break-up of Hinds' organization, however, appears to have been due to conflict among the lieutenants of the organization that Hinds had appointed. Even though Hinds had devolved some of his authority to his trusted lieutenants, this apparently was not enough to suit them (Chevannes 1994, 142). Some of these lieutenants ended up forming their own organizations, and notably it was a brother Morris who ended up taking away most of Hinds' membership. Sadly, when Hinds took sick in 1950, he did not have one faithful member left to look after him. He died at the Kingston Public Hospital on 12 May 1950 and was given a pauper's funeral with none of the members of his former King of Kings Mission showing up and only one mourner in attendance, his sister (Chevannes 1994, 142). And so, sadly, after being one of the most prominent leaders of the Rastafari movement during its early years, Hinds died in a relative state of obscurity.

Joseph Nathaniel Hibbert

Joseph Nathaniel Hibbert was another of the early preachers of the divinity of Haile Selassie I. He was born in Jamaica in 1894, but traveled to Costa Rica with his stepfather in 1911 (Hill 2001). In 1924, Hibbert joined the ancient Mystic Order of Ethiopia, a Masonic Society based in Panama, which was not formally incorporated until 1928. Hibbert became a master mason of this order before he returned to Jamaica in 1931, when he then started to teach the divinity of Haile Selassie I, before Leonard Howell returned to Jamaica in 1932 (see preface of Ras Sekou Sankara Tafari, Hill 2001, 5). Leonard Barrett also alludes to the distinct likelihood that Joseph Hibbert started to preach that Haile Selassie I is divine at Benoah in the district of St Andrew, months before Howell returned to the island (Barrett 1997, 82). As such, it can be argued that Hibbert was the first Rasta preacher, and not Howell.

According to Chevannes, Hibbert was something of a mystic, to be more specific, a leader who built his organization along the lines of "occultism" (Chevannes 1994, 124). He professed that there were hidden secrets in the Book of Maccabees as well as in the publications of DeLaurence. Many of Hibbert's congregants were awed by his reputed powers and desirous themselves of learning his magical secrets. What led to the decline of Hibbert's organization (according to Chevannes) was a combination of two things. First, he was unwilling to impart his innermost secrets to his initiates; second, Hibbert did not tolerate anyone or anything that challenged his leadership (Chevannes 1994, 125). A prime example is that of the EWF, which came to Jamaica in 1939 through the initiative of Brother Paul Earlington. In an effort to establish a charter, which needed a minimum of twenty-five dues-paying members, Earlington first appealed to Hinds, then to Dunkley and then finally to Hibbert. As fate would have it, Hibbert agreed to lend his support to the initiative, having assumed that he would inherit a strong leadership role for the charter. However, after learning that the position being offered to him was as far down as third vice president, he ordered all his members out of this local branch of the EWF (Chevannes 1994, 125–126).

Notably in 1953, Joseph Hibbert's Rastafari congregation was one of the Rastafari groupings that was observed by George Eaton Simpson, who has the distinction of carrying out the first ever Rastafari ethnography in Jamaica in 1953 (Simpson 1955, 167–171). He noted that spirit possession, a popular occurrence in revivalist gatherings, never occurred at the Rastafari meetings that he observed. He also noted that the drums of the revivalists were replaced by rhumba boxes in the Rastafari congregations that he observed.

According to Chevannes, despite his significantly reduced influence on the Rastafari movement as a whole during the decade of the 1960s, Hibbert remained relatively active by becoming a strong and passionate campaigner for the establishment of the Ethiopian Orthodox Tewahedo Church in Jamaica. He was of the firm conviction that this was the most appropriate Christian-based church for Jamaicans of African descent (Chevannes 1999, 345). As a result of this, Hibbert was appointed as the "Spiritual Advisor" for the church in 1971 by Abuna Yesehaq, after the church was established in Jamaica in 1970. However, despite this appointment, Hibbert became somewhat reclusive during the 1970s and into the early 1980s, right up to his death in 1986. Notably, it was Derek Bishton (1983) who managed to secure an audience with Hibbert in the summer of 1983, when he interviewed and photographed him at his place of residence at that time, Bull Bay, St Andrew, shortly before he died.

Archibald Dunkley

Archibald Dunkley was another early proponent and preacher of Rastafari. He was formerly a Jamaican seaman on the Atlantic Fruit Company's boats until he quit the sea on 8 December 1930 when he landed at Port Antonio off the SS St Mary. Upon his arrival to Kingston from Port Antonio, Dunkley studied the Bible for two and a half years on his own to determine whether Haile Selassie I was the returned Messiah. Ezekiel 30, Revelation 17 and 19, and Isaiah 43 finally convinced him. In

1933, Dunkley opened his mission, preaching Rastafari as the King of Kings, the Root of David and the returned Messiah. A key point of consideration is that Dunkley arguably made stronger efforts to incorporate the entire Bible in his teachings of Rastafari than did the other three leaders. Thus in my opinion, Dunkley can be conceived of as a Rastafari leader who pre-empted the Twelve Tribes of Israel mansion in terms of this approach to the Bible (a mansion as it happens that was founded some thirty-five years later). I make this assertion on the basis that very few Rastafari mansions or houses encourage the entire reading of the King James 1 Bible, wherein the New Testament is given just as much credence as the Old Testament. Dunkley encouraged a complete reading of the Bible among his followers (a distinct trait of the Twelve Tribes of Israel mansion.)

According to Chevannes (1994), Dunkley, like Hibbert, was considered somewhat mystical in nature, and it was this alluring quality of his that ultimately allowed him to attract a congregation/following. (Notably, a similar claim was made about Leonard Howell.) Additionally, like Hibbert, Dunkley had an aversion to the revival practice of spirit possession and did not allow this at any of his meetings (Chevannes 1994, 126).

According to Erskine (2005, 65), it is instructive that Dunkley was clear that Rastafari was to be differentiated from the practices of revivalists. Spirit possession was a central revivalist practice, but this was certainly not the case with Dunkley (or Hibbert). While Rastafari has undoubtedly borrowed the traditions of chanting, drumming and dancing from Revivalism, the same cannot be said about the central practice of spirit possession. However, all said and done, both Hinds' King of Kings Mission and Leonard Howell's grouping at Pinnacle notably exhibited more elements of Revivalism than did Hibbert's and Dunkley's groupings.

Archibald Dunkley formed the King of Kings Missionary Movement, but his Rastafari organization was not in truth, by any means, an institutionalized one, as his organization had no formal headquarters nor organizational officials other than himself. It was a genuine one man led affair. However, it was his charisma and his (alleged) mystical powers that allowed him to attract and exert influence on his followers, just as was the case with the other three prominent first-generation leaders/proponents of Rastafari.

According to Chevannes (1994, 142), all four leaders—Howell, Hinds, Hibbert and Dunkley—ruled over their organizations with charismatic authority. Hinds was the only one to share authority with his lieutenants, and rather than subvert Hinds' King of Kings Mission, they chose to break away to form independent bodies.

One key aspect of charismatic leadership, asserts Chevannes (1994, 142), is in the belief of supernatural powers of the prophet or leader, and this was undoubtedly the case for Hibbert, Howell and Dunkley (if not Hinds).

THE SECOND-GENERATION LEADERS
OF THE RASTAFARI MOVEMENT

As we progress past the mid-twentieth century, we find that the influence of all the first-generation leaders of the Rastafari movement had decidedly started to wane. Robert Hinds notably died in 1950, while Leonard Howell drifted into obscurity when his Rastafari encampment Pinnacle was raided and destroyed in 1958. Joseph Hibbert continued to hold Rastafari meetings with a congregation during the 1950s but was no longer a force in the movement with the onset of the 1960s. And so far as Dunkley was concerned, he exited from centre stage of the movement during the course of the 1950s, although he did not die until as late as 1991, outliving all the other first-generation leaders.[1]

It should also be noted that none of the first-generation Rastafari leaders received medals from Haile Selassie I on the most memorable occasion of his visit to Jamaica in April 1966. This certainly was an indication of their departure from the spotlight, so to speak. It was instead the second-generation leaders of the Rastafari movement who received medals from HIM Haile Selassie I at King's House, at a notable occasion during the Emperor's Jamaica visit itinerary, with much joy and exuberance for the recipients and the Rastafari movement as a whole.

Of note, the Rastafari leaders and Rastafari brethren who had the actual honour of receiving medals from Haile Selassie I were: Ras Shedrach, Ras Daniel Heartman, Ras Trevor Campbell, Ras Graham, Ras Sam Brown, Ras Dizzy, Bongo Hill, Prince Emmanuel, Mortimo Planno, Filmore Alvaranga, Sam Clayton, Douglas Mack and Father Gooden (who ran the Rainbow Healing Temple on Spanish Town Road during the 1960s). There is also the case of Brother Kapo, who very likely received a medal as well, and finally we should not forget the EWF members Cecil Gordon and M.B. Douglas who travelled on the first fact finding mission to Africa in 1961, along with Mortimo Planno, Filmore Alvaranga and Douglas Mack, but who never proclaimed to be Rastafari. According to Rastafari scholar Jake Homiak (via an email conversation on July 28, 2020), it was very likely that they also received medals from Haile Selassie I, because of their allegiance to him by virtue of being members of the EWF. These thirteen (possibly fourteen, if we count Brother Kapo) Rastafari brethren along with the two EWF members had the lifetime honour of being bestowed medals by His Imperial Majesty Haile Selassie. Importantly, this gives us an indication of who were considered the movers and shakers of the Rastafari movement at that time.

In terms of Rastafari historiography I consider the second epoch of Rastafari history to be 1948–1968 (Barnett 2018), a period characterized by the emergence of the second-generation leaders of the Rastafari movement, as well as the major mansions of Rastafari—the Nyahbinghi Order, the Ethiopia Africa Black International Congress (EABIC) aka the Bobo Shanti Mansion, and the Twelve Tribes of Israel. It is noteworthy that it was Bongo Wato (also known as Ras Boanerges), the leader of the Youth Black Faith movement (a Rastafari group that emerged in the late 1940s), who eventually became the leading patriarch of the Nyahbinghi Order. This is significant because even though the Nyahbinghi Order is governed by a council of Rastafari elders, as opposed to a single leader, we should note that it was ultimately Bongo Wato who possessed the greatest degree of influence and garnered the most respect among his peers so far as this mansion was concerned.

The Nyahbinghi Mansion and Bongo Wato

The Nyahbinghi Order/Mansion came into its own once the influence of the Youth Black Faith movement grew significantly during the 1950s, attracting significant numbers of Rastafari members. This new amalgamation of Rastafari then morphed into the Nyahbinghi Order in the early 1960s.

The precursor to the Nyahbinghi Mansion, the Youth Black Faith movement was founded in 1949 by young Rastafari adherents who were notably more rebellious than the older guard represented by the first generation of Rastafari leadership. According to Chevannes (1994, 154), Bongo Wato described the leadership of the Youth Black Faith movement as being born out of their contempt for the waywardness of the first-generation leaders:

> I and Brother Anton used to go among Hibbert and them brethren and hear how them administrate. We walk among them many days and see them movements. And it always impress my spirit so much that I say of a truth, those men who carry the doctrine of Rastafari really preach and teach. But there was something in the midst. For I know one named Hibbert who have some other scientific ways to deal with, such as the burning of candles and we condemn those things. Man like Hibbert them have other powers that them use and the prophecy preach against those things. For those man used to burn candles (quoted in Chevannes 1994, 154).

This, as Chevannes correctly interprets, was a clear show of resentment against the elements of Revivalism that still lingered in the rituals of the first-generation leaders. Wato went further with his criticism of the first-generation Rastafari leaders when he spoke of Brother Downer, who was one of the former lieutenants of Robert Hinds who broke away from his congregation to form his own. Wato explained:

> Brother Downer now used to lick out against man who carry beard, for him don't carry beard—him shave clean. So in fi him house him never like to see much of the beard man come in. Him call we Ramgoat. So it is always fiery to I how you teaching about His Majesty Haile Selassie, and [him] is a man who carry beard (idem).

Thus there were two things that the Youth Black Faith stood for: (1) the denunciation of traditional practices of superstition, identified with earlier revival beliefs and the first-generation leaders of the Rastafari movement; and (2) the upholding of the right for Rastafari to wear beards. In fact the Youth Black Faith movement took things even further than this by introducing and institutionalizing the wearing of dreadlocks in addition to the wearing of beards (Chevannes 1994, 157).

From the 1930s wearing beards among Rastafari (inspired by Haile Selassie himself) became an established practice among many, but dreadlocks did not become visible in the movement until the 1950s. According to Chevannes (1994, 158), all Rastafari adherents combed their hair prior to the advent of the Youth Black Faith movement, whether they grew their beards or not, and became known as "combsomes". The young rebellious youthful members of the Youth Black Faith movement elected not to comb their hair, however, symbolizing a complete rejection of the social mores of what they considered a colonized society. They distinguished themselves from the combsomes by growing their hair into locks and becoming the Dreadlocks, the Dreadfuls, the Warriors or the Bonogees[2] as the members of the Youth Black Faith movement came to be known.

It is the contention of Chevannes (1994, 158) that with the arrival of the Youth Black Faith movement and the institutionalization of dreadlocks, and the subsequent popularization of matted hair, a schism developed within the Rastafari movement during the 1950s. A combsome Rastafari respondent told Chevannes (1994, 158) that: "The Warriors or Dreadfuls were so vociferous and quarrelsome that a split developed in which those who could not take the new order, 'Shif up', departed their separate ways."

Thus in the 1950s there were effectively two major groupings of Rastafari with different orientations, the "Combsomes" and the "Dreadlocks". Of interest is that in 1961 a fact-finding mission that was sent to Africa as a result of the *Ras Tafari* Report that was published by the University College of the West Indies in 1960 was composed of three Rastafari brethren, the leader of which was a Dreadlocks Rastaman, Mortimo Planno, while the other two, Douglas Mack and Filmore Alvaranga, were Combsomes. A decade later, in the early 1970s, it was dreadlocked Rastafari who dominated the movement in terms of numbers and the Combsomes who became a distinct minority (Chevannes 1994, 158).

For Chevannes (1994, 158), there was a distinctive difference in the type of leadership exuded/extoled by the dreadlocked council elders of the Nyahbinghi Mansion. They operated within a more open and democratic structure and they defended the principles of the organization and expounded the doctrine of the faith more forcefully and passionately than the leaders of the past. They also exhibited a different kind of charisma than that of the first generation of Rastafari leaders, one based not on mysticism, but rather on moral authority.

Prince Emmanuel Charles Edwards and the Ethiopia Africa Black International Congress

In 1958, Prince Emmanuel Charles Edwards officially founded another major Rastafari mansion, the Ethiopia Africa Black International Congress (EABIC). The emergence of this major Rastafari mansion, informally known as the Bobo Shanti Mansion, corresponded to a significant moment in Rastafari history, namely the first Nyahbinghi ritual, or "Groundation", during which many Rastafari gathered in a public space in West Kingston (Back-O-Wall). This landmark event was convened and chaired by Prince Emmanuel, and attended by members of the Youth Black Faith, including leading figures like Bongo Wato, Arthur and Pan-Handle.[3] This Groundation was officially named the Rastafari Universal Convention and was deliberately convened on 1 March 1958 to mark the sixty-second anniversary of the battle of Adwa, when Emperor Menelik II of Ethiopia defeated the Italians. The Groundation was originally intended to last throughout the month until April, but ended up going only until the third week of March because of constant police intimidation (Smith, Augier & Nettleford 1988).

Prince Emmanuel not only has the distinction of being the founder of the EABIC, but he is also revered as the returned Black Christ by the members of this mansion of Rastafari. Specifically, he is part of a triune of divinity, in other words one part of a trinity of divine personalities that is glorified by the Bobo Shanti (EABIC) Mansion. For the Bobo Shanti, the Holy Trinity consists of Haile Selassie, Prince Emmanuel and Marcus Garvey. While Haile Selassie is regarded as the Almighty himself, Prince Emmanuel is considered the Black Christ and Marcus Garvey is the modern-day equivalent of John the Baptist. The divine trinity of the Bobo Shanti is also referred to as a trinity of Prophet, Priest and King. Wherein Marcus Garvey is the prophet, Prince Emmanuel is the High Priest and Haile Selassie is the King. Prince Emmanuel was also referred to as the shepherd, because just as a shepherd leads its flock, it is argued that he came to lead the lost and scattered Black people in the West out of the wilderness and into the light (Barnett 2005). Symbolically, Prince Emmanuel always kept his locks wrapped in a turban and carried a shepherd's crook wherever he went, a distinct carry-over from Revivalism and a reminder of the historical linkage between Revivalism and Rastafari (Hutton 2015). In fact, I would go as far to say that the influence of Revivalism on the Rastafari movement is particularly evident in the Bobo Shanti Mansion with the notable jubilance that ensues at the ceremonial services conducted by Bobo Shanti priests. The adherents of this mansion are particularly distinctive in that all members wrap their locks in turbans when outside their dwellings, both man and woman, further reinforcing the revivalist underpinnings of this mansion.

The Twelve Tribes of Israel Mansion and
Dr. Vernon Carrington (aka Prophet Gad)

The establishment of the third major Rastafari mansion, the Twelve Tribes of Israel, took place on 25 February 1968. It was Vernon Carrington, known to his membership as Prophet Gad or Gad-man, who founded the Twelve Tribes of Israel, first located at Davis Lane in Trench Town.

A contributing factor to the popularization of the Rastafari movement during the 1960s in fact was the emergence of the Twelve Tribes of Israel in 1968. Dr. Vernon Carrington proved to be a significant second-generation Rastafari leader, as he founded a mansion that would distinguish itself as having the largest global membership of all the current Rastafari mansions and houses. This particular mansion was notably able to attract not only grassroots Jamaicans, but also middle-class Jamaicans and even Jamaicans from upper-class backgrounds. There has been much speculation as to why this was the case, with a diverse array of opinions. So far as I am concerned, however, it is arguably its more relaxed membership requirements that was a significant factor here. For instance, in this mansion of Rastafari, a strict vegetarian diet is not adhered to. Twelve Tribe members eat chicken, curry goat/mutton, oxtail and a variety of other meats. The only thing that is taboo is pork. Additionally, you are not required to have dreadlocks to be a member of the Twelve Tribes. Notably, Vernon Carrington, the leader and founder of the Twelve Tribes of Israel mansion, did not wear dreadlocks, and several prominent members of the Jamaica branch of the mansion up to today do not wear dreadlocks.

On this note we should recall the famous song by the reggae group Morgan Heritage, "You Don't Haffi Dread to be Rasta" (1999)—the key argument of the song fundamentally being that you don't need to wear dreadlocks to be Rastafari. The band members certainly could make this claim because their father, Denroy Morgan, is a long-standing member of the Twelve Tribes of Israel, and following in their father's footsteps, they themselves are of the same philosophical orientation so far as Rastafari is concerned. The Twelve Tribes of Israel membership, it should be noted, do not adhere to the Nazarite vow[4] as do the Bobo Shanti Mansion and the Nyahbinghi Mansion of Rastafari.

Reverend Claudius Henry

Of significance is that Claudius Henry, a noteworthy second-generation Rastafari leader, was invited to the first Groundation/Nyahbinghi event, held in March 1958, by Prince Emmanuel. His attendance at this landmark event proved to be effective in introducing him to the wider Jamaican Rastafari community. It would also be effective in inspiring him to start his own Rastafari organization. In fact it was early in the following year, 1959, that Henry set about establishing his own Rastafari grouping, the Africa Reform Church, in West Kingston (Barrett 1997). Henry, who had given himself the title "the Repairer of the Breach", was a Jamaican who had lived in New York City for a while. He became known for his charismatic leadership and was soon able to garner a large following of Rastafari—some of whom used to belong to other mansions. However, he created an atmosphere of controversy when he started to sell thousands of postcards which read:

> Pioneering Israel's scattered children of African origin, back home to Africa. This year 1959, deadline date—October 5th, this new Government is God's Righteous Kingdom of Everlasting Peace on Earth. 'Creation's Second Birth'. Holder of this certificate is requested to visit the Headquarters at 18 Rosalie Avenue... August 1, 1959, for our emancipation Jubilee commencing 9am sharp. Please reserve this certificate for removal. No passport will be necessary for those returning to Africa. We sincerely, 'the Seventh Emmanuel Brethren' gathering Israel's scattered and anointed prophet, Rev. C.V. Henry, R.B. Given this 2nd day of March 1959, in the year of the reign of His Imperial Majesty, 1st Emperor of Ethiopia, God's Elect, Haile Selassie, King of Kings, Lord of Lords, Israel's returned Messiah (Barrett 1997, 95–96).

Sold at a shilling each, thousands of these cards were acquired by hopeful masses. On 5 October 1959, people from all over Jamaica flocked to Rosalie Avenue, ready to depart to Africa. The Reverend Claudius Henry now, of course, found himself in a difficult situation. With thousands of people ready to depart, the atmosphere was highly charged with expectation. As the deadline transpired, Henry went to great pains to explain that the 5 October deadline had never been intended as a day of departure for Africa, but rather the day on which he expected the Jamaican government to explain how it would meet the demands of Jamaica's African peoples. Needless to say, the Jamaican press had a field day with this.

The controversy surrounding Henry was not to end here, as several months later, in April 1960, police raided Henry's headquarters and allegedly found twenty-five hundred electrical detonators, thirteen hundred detonators, a shotgun, a .32-caliber revolver, a large quantity of machetes sharpened on both sides and several sticks of dynamite. After Claudius Henry was convicted of treason and given a six-year sentence, his son, Ronald Henry, came to Jamaica from the United States with some self-trained military personnel, supposedly to break his father out of prison. An armed attack that transpired between Ronald Henry's group and Jamaica's armed forces was given much publicity by the Jamaican media, especially after the killing of two British soldiers, with the wider Rastafari movement being wrongfully implicated in this crime. Eventually, Ronald Henry was captured and summarily executed (Barrett 1997, 98–99).

In 1966 Claudius Henry was released from prison and went on to establish a new organization which he named the International Peacemakers Association and which was located at Green Bottom, Sandy Bay, in the parish of Clarendon. This Rastafari organization was highly distinctive in that it was not only religious, but also highly entrepreneurial—with its own block-making factory, a bakery, a farm, a fish shop, making the community largely self-sufficient. The organization also built several homes for families, a community centre, and a school—the Ethiopian Peacemakers School—established to provide the children of the community with an African education. During the peak years of its existence (1968–1970), Henry's International Peacemakers Association boasted a membership some 4,000 strong.

Claudius Henry died in 1986, and although the organization still exists today, it is notable that its dwindled membership consists primarily of now elderly original members who had joined the Peacemakers Association way back in the late 1960s (Paul 2012).

Ras Sam Brown

Ras Sam Brown was a Rastafari leader who distinguished himself as a political activist, running as an independent candidate in Jamaica's 1962 national election for a political party he created known as the Blackman's Party (Waters 1985). He lost by a wide margin to Edward Seaga in contesting for a constituency in West Kingston, but he made history as the first Rastaman to ever be involved in mainstream politics in Jamaica and for having the sheer audacity and independence of thought to enter the political arena (Barrett 1997).

Generally speaking, there are two notable dimensions that exist in the Rastafari movement, the "religious" and the "political", and Sam Brown notably represented the political dimension in a very profound way by actually attempting to enter the fray of mainstream politics in Jamaica. Ras Sam Brown ran his campaign on a political platform that he termed the 21 Points Platform, which clearly outlined his vision and mission to "rasticize" Jamaica (meaning that he wished to decolonize and Africanize the mentalities of the wider Jamaican populace). The document not only gave insight into his philosophy, but also a general Rastafari worldview.

He also headed up a Rastafari organization known as the Rastafari Movement African Recruitment Centre, which had its headquarters at 1000 Marcus Garvey Drive in Kingston (Barrett 1997). This organization served as a voice for Rastafari who were agitating for improved material and social conditions in Jamaica until repatriation was realized.

Ras Mortimo Planno

Ras Mortimo Planno is another notable second-generation Rastafari leader who had a considerable degree of influence on the movement although not formally heading up a Rastafari mansion or house of his own, but rather a more informal gathering of Rastafari that is commonly known among Rastafari as a "Yard". According to Edmonds (2003, 68), a Yard is comprised of a small independent group of Rastafari who gather frequently to smoke ganja and to reason about their faith as well as current or historical events that affect their understanding of their place in the world.

A Rastafari Yard may emerge when several Rastafari (usually males) attach themselves to a leading brethren. They may gather at the leading brethren's house or "yard" in informal settings to smoke ganja and to reason, or even in some cases more formally to observe and celebrate special Rastafari days of significance (such as the Birthday of Haile Selassie or the anniversary of Haile Selassie's coronation). The leading brethren or "Elder" is not conferred Eldership through election, but rather by inspiration (i.e., the members feel inspired to bestow the mantle of leadership upon a particular brethren).

According to Edmonds (2003, 69), Eldership is informally conferred when two criteria are met: 1) A record of uncompromising commitment to and defense of the principles of Rastafari and 2) the ability to expound the philosophy and worldview of Rastafari such as to inspire the members of the Yard to a greater understanding and appreciation of the Rastafari worldview and lifestyle.

In 1961, Mortimo Planno became one of the first Rastafari, along with Douglas Mack and Filmore Alvaranga, to have an audience with Haile Selassie in Ethiopia on 21 April while they participated in a fact-finding mission in Africa on the basis of a recommendation from a formal university report that was generated by the University College of the West Indies in 1960 (Smith et al. 1988).

Exactly five years later, on 21 April 1966, when Emperor Haile Selassie arrived in Kingston for an official state visit and his plane was sandwiched in the middle of a massive crowd of Rastafari and Jamaicans on the tarmac of the Palisadoes airport in Kingston, Mortimo was the Rastaman who was called from a public address system to meet His Majesty Haile Selassie at the steps of his plane and to facilitate his escort and exit from the plane. Mortimo motioned the crowd to make way for His Majesty to disembark and the gathering parted, just as though it was Moses parting the Red Sea, leaving a clear pathway between them. Then Haile Selassie and his royal entourage and Mortimo Planno were able to make their way through the crowd towards the airport terminal. During an interview with Mortimo Planno at the University of the West Indies (18 July 2003) in the course of an international conference known as the Global Reasoning conference (16–23 July 2003), he revealed to me that this was the most memorable and treasured memory of his life.

Planno also had the distinction of mentoring the young reggae group "The Wailers" (Bob Marley, Peter Tosh and Bunny Wailer) in the late 1960s at his Yard gathering (as well as many other local youth in the West Kingston area) and bringing them firmly and soundly onto the path of Rastafari. During the 1970s he helped to globalize the Rastafari movement when he made several trips to Africa.

Abuna Ascento Foxe –
Second- and Third-Generation Rastafari Leader

Ascento Foxe has the distinction of being both a second-generation and a third-generation Rastafari leader, in that he was an up and coming member of the Rastafari community in Jamaica from the mid 1950s, became a founding member of the British Rastafari Movement in England when he migrated there in the late 1950s, and then rose to prominence in the United States when he migrated there during the late 1980s (Adams 2002). Notably, Ascento Foxe and Norman Adams became prominent members of Local 37 of the Ethiopian World Federation in Jamaica, along with Roy Prince, Brother Tull, Ras Sam Brown as the President and Mortimo Planno as the General Secretary, before they migrated to England in the late 1950s (Adams 2002, 34).

The group of Rastafari brethren in England that Norman Adams (Jah Blue) and Ascento Foxe affiliated with were Roy Prince, Brother Tull, Clifford Gully, Keith (Shaggy) Berry, Earl Duke, Desmond Christie, Nicholas McKoy and Keith Miller. This group would meet regularly at 40 Powis Garden at Powis Square in the Notting Hill area, London, from 1958 onwards into the 1960s (Adams 2002). In 1960, after meeting for two years, the brethren were authorized by the Local 37 of the EWF in Jamaica to function in London as a sub-Local of Local 37 (Adams 2002, 35). Significantly, in 1972, Local 33 of the EWF was formally established in England, and the brethren of sub-Local 37, including Ascento Foxe who had been instrumental in this, became prominent members. After a degree of agitation and negotiation with the Ethiopian Orthodox Church, on a visit to Jamaica in 1972, the brethren were able to have the Ethiopian Orthodox Church established in England (Adams 2002).

Arguably, it was in 1983 that Ascento Foxe dramatically asserted his influence on the Rastafari movement, when after forging strong ties with Crown Prince Asfa Woosen and the Ethiopian Crown Council that was in exile at the time because of the Ethiopian coup of 1974, Foxe broke away from the EWF and established a rival organization, the Imperial Ethiopian World Federation (IEWF), primarily because he was unhappy with the direction that the EWF was taking at the time. Importantly, because his organization was endorsed by Haile Selassie's first son, who was at that time the President of the Ethiopian Crown Council, the IEWF had a certain degree of legitimacy that made it a strong influential mansion of Rastafari in its own right. Ascento Foxe's IEWF would later come to worldwide attention when it contested the Jamaican national elections both in 1997 and 2002.

Ascento Foxe then went on to found the Church of Haile Selassie in 1987, with branches in New York, London, Trinidad and Barbados, and Jamaica as the headquarters (www.himchurch.org). One of Foxe's objectives was to secure a level of official recognition for Rastafari that is accorded to most churches by nation states. After founding the church he formally took on the mantle of Abuna. In October 2013, he was successful in this goal, when the Jamaican parliament enacted a bill that conveyed official status to Foxe's Church of Haile Selassie I, making it the first mansion of Rastafari to be formally recognized by the government. Importantly, as a consequence the Church of Haile Selassie now has the right to hold property in its name (as an official entity) and to officiate important ceremonies such as marriages and funerals (*Jamaica Observer*, 30 October 2013).

Ascento Foxe, through the strong ties that he maintained with the Ethiopian Crown Council, played a notable supporting role along with me and my Rastafari 50th Anniversary of the Visit of Haile Selassie I to Jamaica Commemorative Committee in ensuring that the visit of Prince Ermias Sahle-Selassie (the present president of the Ethiopian Crown Council) to Jamaica in April 2016 went smoothly.

Ascento Foxe sadly passed on 20 April 2020 after ailing for a few months in New York. His body was flown to Jamaica and is presently in Kingston at the time of writing. Negotiations are presently underway between the current members of the Church of Haile Selassie I and the Jamaican Government for a burial at National Heroes Park. It remains to be seen how this mansion will fare without the charismatic leadership of Abuna Ascento Foxe.

Priest Dermot Fagan – Third-Generation Rastafari Leader

Dermot Fagan is clearly a third-generation leader, having founded his very own house of Rastafari, known as the "School of Vision", in 1997. His house is notably affiliated with the Nyahbinghi Mansion, but there are some notable differences in terms of the teachings of this mansion, largely because of the particular ideological perspectives of its leader and founder, Priest Dermot Fagan.

For one thing, for this mansion, "Zion" is actually Jerusalem in Israel and not Ethiopia, Africa. According to Priest Fagan in an interview with this author (July 2007), a correct reading of the Bible indicates clearly that Zion, the promised land, is actually Jerusalem in Israel. "This is what the scripture reveals", argued Priest Fagan emphatically when I conversed with him.

Priest Fagan's main ideological premise is that we are living in the "End Days", the time of widespread disaster and destruction prophesized in the book of Revelation. He argues that in the "End Days" the forces of Babylon (oppression) will look to brand people with "the mark of the beast". For him, "the mark of the beast" will be specifically a microchip implanted in people's hands or brains. At the time of judgement (what many theologians refer to as the Rapture), Priest Fagan predicts that Haile Selassie will reappear in the physical realm and come to save his followers from certain death and destruction with a fleet of flying saucers. Along these lines one can't help wondering if Priest Fagan has been distinctly influenced by the doctrine of the Nation of Islam that argues something similar when they lament on the End Days. Only in their theological vision it is Master Fard Muhammad (the founder of the Nation of Islam) who would come to save the chosen from Armageddon with a mother ship/spaceship as opposed to Haile Selassie I (Lieb 1998, 169).

Although a third-generation leader, Priest Dermot Fagan has shown himself to be steeped in the early traditions of the Rastafari movement, with his development of a successful, self- sustaining Rastafari commune up in the Blue Mountains above Irish Town and modelled along the lines of Pinnacle, the first-ever Rastafari commune, which was developed by Leonard Howell. Again Priest Fagan is another Rastafari leader who leads through charisma, and it remains to be seen how successfully this Rastafari organization would continue should anything happen to him.

The Routinization of Charisma According to Max Weber

A useful theoretical framework that we can utilize to provide a critical lens with which to analyze the leadership structures of the Rastafari movement is that of Max Weber's work on authority. For the renowned classical sociological theorist Max Weber there are fundamentally three different types of authority: Traditional, Charismatic and Rational-Legal (Ritzer 2003, 30–34). Traditional authority is based on the notion that certain people, based on their family, tribe or lineage, have the right to exercise authority (leadership) over their society or community. The leaders make their claim to leadership (and the followers buy into this of course) via bloodline and an age-old process of tradition. For Weber, traditional leadership structures are not rational and in fact impede the rationalization process. Because Weber associated modernity with the increased rationalization of society, for him traditional authority structures could only exist in non-modern, less developed societies. Rational-Legal authority is a type of authority that is based on accepted rules and procedures, which are legally constituted and instituted. The key stipulation here so far as leadership is concerned is that certain people have the right to exercise authority over others by virtue of holding a particular office or position, which has been legally vested with certain powers. For Weber, this type of authority (leadership) structure has its highest expression in the bureaucracies of the Western world. Charismatic authority is a type of authority that is based on the charisma of a leader. By charisma we mean extraordinary qualities possessed by a particular person. Of extreme importance is not whether the particular person or leader actually possesses extraordinary qualities or not, but that they are perceived to possess special qualities by their followers. Ultimately for Weber, the charismatic authority of an individual is legitimated by a belief by his/her followers in the exceptional heroism, sanctity or exemplary character of that individual. Weber recognized charismatic leadership as an extremely powerful revolutionary force. He concluded that charisma changes people's minds—it changes people from within—so that they adapt themselves to the vision of the charismatic leader and envisage the possibility of a different reality.

What becomes clear is that while traditional and rational-legal leadership are based on the established norms and values that exist in the society, charismatic leadership is based solely around the personality of the leader. The stronger their personalities, the stronger their ability to attract a following and to evoke loyalty. Weber, in his famous work *Economy and Society* (1978), argues that charisma in its purest form transforms all of society's values and breaks all of its norms. Thus charismatic leaders tend to march to a different drummer, so to speak, and their followers likewise follow suit, setting in motion a revolutionary force which can potentially overturn both traditional and rational-legal leadership structures.

However, there are some drawbacks with charismatic leadership so far as Weber is concerned (Ritzer 2003). For him, charismatic leadership is not rational; additionally, it is inherently unstable and temporary. Because it is not rational, it is ill-suited for carrying out mundane day-to-day tasks of administration. It is inherently unstable and temporary because the legitimization for leadership is centred around the charismatic leader, usually with little or no thought given to succession. If anything untoward should happen to the leader, it follows that his/her organization would meet its demise. Along these lines, Weber saw the remedy to the prospective dissolution of the organization to be what he termed the "routinization of charisma". This is where the followers seek to recast the nature of their organization such that while still maintaining some elements of the organization's "charismatic emergence", they tweak some aspects of its revolutionary and extraordinary nature so that it is able to handle mundane (but necessary) administrative tasks. Additionally, the issue of succession is addressed so that when the charismatic leader dies, the organization does not implode, explode or simply meet a quiet death.

Ennis Edmonds addresses the matter of the routinization of charisma and outlines six possible ways that Weber deems leadership succession can take place in the process of the routinization of charisma (Edmonds 2003, 15):

1) By special appointment on the basis of special charismatic qualities
2) By appointment through the use of oracles
3) The original Charismatic Leader designates a successor prior to their death
4) By appointment by an administrative board located within the organization, or by election by the membership of the organization
5) By succession according to heredity
6) By achievement of the qualifications for leadership through education or ordination

The result is that the authority of the leaders of the organization is no longer legitimated by their extraordinary capabilities, or their special relationship with God, but through established procedures and processes. This stabilizes the organization but leads to an extraordinary contradiction: the routinization of charisma leads to the erosion and in some cases the complete eradication of the charismatic essence that was part of the movement or organization in the first place. The organization thus starts to resemble a different authority structure, either traditional or rational-legal depending on how the succession proceeds. With this theoretical framework in mind, we will now squarely address the dynamics of leadership within the Jamaican Rastafari movement.

In an earlier work (Barnett 2012), I had noted that by the time we get to the dawn of the Ethiopian millennium (September 2007 on the Western [Gregorian] and 2000 on the Ethiopian [Julian] calendar), all the previously mentioned second-generation Rastafari leaders (not to mention the first-generation leaders) had passed away or "transitioned" in the Rastafari vernacular. For instance, Prince Emmanuel, the founder and leader of the Bobo Shanti, transitioned in 1994; Bongo Wato, the key patriarch for the Nyahbinghi Order, transitioned in 2000; and Prophet Gad, the founder and leader of the Twelve Tribes of Israel, transitioned in 2005. Additionally, if we consider the case of the other second-generation Rastafari leaders, we see that Rev. Claudius Henry transitioned in 1986, Ras Sam Brown in 1998, while Mortimo Planno transitioned in 2006. This has led to a present-day dilemma in terms of leadership in the Rastafari movement, especially so far as the major mansions of Rastafari are concerned.

In the case of the Bobo Shanti (EABIC) for instance, the founder and leader of the mansion, Prince Emmanuel, was also considered to be part of the divine Trinity. This is an indication of just how central he was to this particular mansion. In fact, because he was such a dominant force so far as the Bobo Shanti are concerned, it seems that the path for greatest stability of the mansion would have been for him to have publicly named a successor before he transitioned. As things presently stand, the Bobo Shanti Mansion in Jamaica has splintered into three groups and is no longer a unified entity.

In the case of the Twelve Tribes of Israel, Vernon Carrington was referred to by his membership as Prophet Gad and deemed to be just that—a prophet. So far as the membership is concerned, Prophet Gad had a special relationship with God. In this regard anything he commanded was deemed law. When he determined a course of action the membership would follow him unquestionably. There was no hesitation or indecision in regards to projects or policy to be undertaken by the mansion under Prophet Gad's watch.

This is no longer the case so far as this mansion is concerned, but the silver lining here is that Prophet Gad incorporated forty-eight executives into the Jamaican branch of the mansion, a "first" and "second" bench, constituted of twelve males and twelve females each, which thus constituted the main executive council. So while it was Prophet Gad who made the major decisions for the organization as a whole, he would sit in with his executive council and allow them to give input. This effectively served as leadership training for when he would no longer be around, and to some extent it has reaped dividends. While it may take a while for the Twelve Tribes mansion to determine a particular course of action in some instances, there is at least a leadership structure in place and decisions are made eventually. One key issue however is that the mansion is now bereft of charisma and has now become perhaps too bureaucratic with its decidedly rational-legal authoritarian orientation.

In the case of the Nyahbinghi Order, Bongo Wato when he was alive acted as a very influential force within the Council of Elders and was effectively (in my opinion at least) the captain of the figurative ship, steering the mansion in a particular direction and keeping it on a particular course. Presently within the Nyahbinghi Order/Mansion in Jamaica, the Council of Eldership system that used to run relatively effectively has broken down, and what we now have are several leading and competing personalities each trying to pull the mansion in a different direction. As a result, the mansion lacks the cohesiveness and stability that would make it a viable force in the movement. In the case of this mansion, the Council of Elders (post-Bongo Wato era) did not adhere rigidly to the Nyahbinghi guidelines pertaining to administration of the house that had been carefully formulated during the early years of the Nyahbinghi Order, thus allowing charismatic personalities from outside the mansion to effectively usurp their leadership. Because none of the charismatic persons who vied for leadership were able to win over the loyalty of the followers from the entire mansion, this has led to the Nyahbinghi Order/Mansion in Jamaica splintering into different factions with various differing perspectives on who should lead the mansion. Emblematic of this is that in July 2019, the customary Nyahbinghi celebration of Haile Selassie's Birthday that is usually held at the Scott's Pass Nyahbinghi Centre in Clarendon was celebrated at two different Nyahbinghi centres on the island simultaneously—the Pitfour Nyahbinghi Centre in Montego Bay as well as at the Scott's Pass Centre in Clarendon. This open rivalry within the Nyahbinghi Mansion in Jamaica is unheralded, having never occurred during the mansion's existence. Even some of the seemingly most mundane matters in the mansion, such as how many nights a particular Nyahbinghi ceremony will be kept for, can lead to disagreements and tension among the various factions.

Herein then lies a conundrum in terms of the leadership structure of the various Rastafari mansions and houses. Historically the Rastafari leaders of the various mansions and houses (both first generation and second generation) have been of the charismatic vein. Thus when the leader dies, the particular mansion or house suffers. To compound this, planned leadership succession has been a distinct problem for the Rastafari movement, and this is what has led to the current leadership vacuum that currently exists for most of the major Rastafari mansions. Effective routinization of charisma has not taken place within the various mansions arguably (except for the Twelve Tribes of Israel), and this needs to be addressed in the case of the major mansions of Rastafari as well as the various houses of Rastafari.

In conclusion, I propose that if all the Rastafari mansions and organizations discussed above willingly embrace a model of democratically elected councils to head up and direct them, as opposed to the charismatic leadership model of old, they will all gain greater stability (even if it is at the expense of the much celebrated charisma that African oriented organizations like to be associated with).

Notes

1   Leonard Howell died in 1981, Joseph Hibbert in 1986 and Robert Hinds in 1950.

2   The Bonogees were the followers of Ras Boanerges aka Bongo Wato.

3   Arthur and Pan-Handle were some of the leading figures or personalities in the Youth Black Faith movement along with Bongo Wato.

4   The Nazarite vow is a vow taken by a person who decides voluntarily to become a Nazarite, for which the rules of conduct are governed by Numbers 6:1–21 in the Old Testament. For instance, Numbers 6:5 reads: "All the days of the vow of his separation there shall no razor come upon his head: until the days be fulfilled, in which he separateth himself unto the Lord, he shall be holy and shall let the locks of the hair of his head grow". This part of the Nazarite vow then is seen by some Rastafari as the basis of growing their hair into dreadlocks and not cutting or combing it. In this regard, being Rastafari is synonymous with being a Nazarite.

References

Adams, Norman. 2002. *A Historical Report: The Rastafari Movement in England.* London: GWA Works.

Barnett, Michael A. 2012. "Rastafari in the New Millennium: Rastafari at the Dawn of the Fifth Epoch". In *Rastafari in the New Millennium: A Rastafari Reader*, edited by M. Barnett, 1–10. NY: Syracuse University Press.

_____. 2015. "Interrogating Leonard Howell as the First Rasta". In *Leonard Percival Howell and the Genesis of Rastafari*, edited by C. Hutton, M. Barnett, J. Niaah, and D. Dunkley, 53–68. Kingston, Jamaica: UWI Press.

_____. 2018. *The Rastafari Movement: A North American and Caribbean Perspective.* Abingdon, Oxon, UK: Routledge.

Barrett, Leonard E. 1997. *The Rastafarians.* Boston, MA: Beacon Press.

Bishton, Derek. 1983. "Meeting Joseph Nathaniel Hibbert 23 July 1983". https://derek-bishton.wordpress.com/2013/03/11/meeting-joseph-nathaniel-hibbert-july-23-1983/

Chevannes, Barry. 1994. *Rastafari: Roots and Ideology.* NY: Syracuse University Press.

_____. 1999. "Between the Living and the Dead: The Apotheosis of Rastafari Heroes". In *Religion, Diaspora and Cultural Identity: A Reader on the Anglophone Caribbean,* edited by John Pulis, 337–356. Amsterdam: Gordon and Breach Publishers.

Edmonds, Ennis. 2003. *Rastafari: From Outcasts to Culture Bearers.* NY: Oxford University Press.

Erskine, Noel. 2005. *From Garvey to Marley: Rastafari Theology.* Gainesville, FL: University Press of Florida.

Fagan, Dermot. 2007. Interview with author (14 July).

Hill, Robert. 2001. *Dread History: Leonard P. Howell and Millenarian Visions in the Early Rastafarian Religion.* Chicago, IL and Kingston, Jamaica: Frontline Distribution International Inc. and Miguel Lorne Publishers.

Hutton, Clinton. 2015. "Announcing God: The Conditions that Gave Birth to Rastafari in Jamaica". In *Leonard Percival Howell and the Genesis of Rastafari,* edited by C. Hutton, M. Barnett, J. Niaah, and D. Dunkley, 9–52. Kingston, Jamaica: The UWI Press.

Jamaica Observer. 2013. "Church of Haile Selassie I Gets Legal Status". (30 October).

Lee, Helen. 2003. *The First Rasta: Leonard Howell and the Rise of Rastafarianism.* Chicago, IL: Lawrence Books.

Leib, Michael. 1998. *Children of Ezekiel.* Durham, North Carolina: Duke University Press.

Lewis, Rupert. 1998. "Marcus Garvey and the Early Rastafarians: Continuity and Discontinuity". In *Chanting Down Babylon: The Rastafari Reader,* edited by N.S. Murrell, W.D. Spencer, and A.A. McFarlane, 145–158. Philadelphia: Temple University Press.

McPherson, E.S.P., ed. 1993. *The Culture-History and Universal Spread of Rastafari: Two Essays.* Clarendon, Jamaica: Black International Iyahbinghi.

Paul, Annie. 2012. "A Visit to Rev Claudius Henry's Church, Sandy Bay, Jamaica". https://anniepaul.net/2012/08/19/a-visit-to-rev-claudius-henrys-church-sandy-bay-jamaica/

Planno, Mortimo. 2003. Interview with author. University of the West Indies, Mona Campus, Jamaica (18 July).

Ritzer, George. 2003. *Contemporary Sociological Theory and Its Classical Roots: The Basics.* New York, NY: McGraw Hill.

Simpson, George E. 1955. "The Ras Tafari Movement in Jamaica: A Study of Race and Class Conflict". Social Forces 34 (2): 167–171.

Smith, Michael G., Roy Augier, and Rex Nettleford. 1988. *The Ras Tafari Movement in Kingston, Jamaica.* Reprint. Kingston, Jamaica, University of the West Indies: Department of Extra-Mural Studies.

The Church of Haile Selassi I, and IEWF Inc. 2020. "CHSI Sabbath Worship Scriptures". http://www.himchurch.org (Accessed 29 June 2020) .

The Gleaner. 1934. "Chief Justice Denounces Leonard Howell as a Fraud". (17 March).

Waters, Anita. 1985. *Race, Class and Political Symbols: Rastafari and Reggae in Jamaican Politics.* New Brunswick, NJ: Transaction Press.

Weber, Max. 1978. *Economy and Society: An Outline of Interpretive Sociology.* California: University of California Press.

A RASTAFARI CULTURAL INSTITUTION: HERB CAMPS IN THE CITY

Jahlani Niaah

Abstract   Ganja is widely dispensed and consumed across Jamaica in "discreetly obvious" ways, and its points of sale can be potentially likened to Dawn Scott's (1985) reading of "A Cultural Object". This is being applied to speak of yet another spatial marker, Rastafari and ganja. As much as there is a well established connection between Rastafari and ganja, a herb described generally as a sacrament for the movement, there is very limited research focused specifically on the milieu of cannabis within the community. Except for the work of Carole Yawney, Dennis Forsythe and Barry Chevannes, little has been published in this sphere. The data here are developed from a mapping and ongoing study of more than thirty ganja points of sale in Kingston and its environs. Building on an analytical framework which interrogates Rastafari leadership and patriarchy, this chapter provides a reading of a grassroots construct, presented by way of select case studies based on ethnographic research highlighting herb camps in Kingston as a long-standing "cultural institution", a hybrid Rastafari space of liberation, pedagogy and community therapy.

Keywords • Sacrament school • herb camp • Rastafari • ganja • community therapy • ritual • cultural studies

INTRODUCTION

The city of Kingston became a stronghold for the Rastafari brethren in the 1950s, especially after the destruction of Pinnacle as an encampment space. Dispersal of the movement occurred across the island, but the inner city of Kingston became a hotbed for various pockets of the leaders, who from their residences in many instances, established what is here described as "camps". This refers to the space—the physical site for congregating and consumption of the herb. Such spaces conform usually to the Rastafari aesthetic framework in their inner logic and operation, being primarily urban innovations for access to the ganja, considered a sacrament or a sacred offering.

Ganja, the preferred local term for cannabis, occupies a well-known sphere not just physically, but also psychosocially and is widely dispensed and consumed across Jamaica in "discreetly obvious" ways. Its points of sale can be potentially likened to Dawn Scott's (1985) reading of "A Cultural Object".[1] In this piece, an early demonstration of installation art, three-dimensional constructs, Scott makes a comment about slum dwellings, zinc fences, cardboard walls, metallic debris and our framings assembled for the "squatter's" inhabitation. Her installation at the National Gallery of Jamaica was often taken for a piss-pot (or so some viewers of the work treated it). She was a pioneer in her artistic representation of slum dwelling, recognizing this as a cultural object which has begotten a type of social institution. This bit of contemporary art mirrors the space that many urban Rastafari have historically encamped, taking refuge from their enemies. One of the camps encountered in my survey had the poignant words painted on the gate, "Lord protect me from my friends, I will protect myself from my enemies". This friend and enemy contrast from a Rastafari standpoint can be translated also as Zion/Ethiopia and Hell/Babylon/European hegemony. The camps offer a threshold to navigate these worlds.

Patrick Leigh Fermor (1951) provides an early account of his encounter with Rastafari in the Dungle:

> The Rastafari live in a patch of waste land by the railway in the western slums of Kingston known as the Dunghill . . . a collection of huts built of the same flimsy materials as the hovels of San Juan de Puerto Rico. Some of the slightly more luxurious dwellings are composed of the rusting bodies of old motor-cars from which the wheels have been removed . . . the glassless window space is filled in with paper; holes cut in the hood service as chimneys. The other houses are constructed throughout of cardboard and paper. From flagpoles above these hovels flutter the red, yellow and green tricolour flags of Abyssinia; and noticeboards bear messages in clumsily formed letters which say, 'Long live Abyssinia' or 'We are Ethiopians' (348–349).

Fermor further describes the Dungle, one of the earliest urban abodes of Rastafari, as a "pseudo-Ethiopian wilderness", and he takes us inside one of these spaces, a six-foot-square rough camp, fashioned from makeshift paper walls, plank bed and their marker of faith, a picture of the Negus, the Ethiopian Emperor Haile Selassie I. His encounter with ganja in this space is also noteworthy:

> I noticed that the boy [about 18] on the end of the bed was smoking a home-made cigarette as blunt and as unwieldy as an ice-cream cone. He smiled as my eyes fell on it and waved it in the air. 'It's the wisdom weed, boss,' he said. 'This is what makes us see everything so clear . . .' He hospitably rolled me one and handed it down the bed. I asked him how he got the stuff—didn't the police put a stop to it. They all laughed and pointed to a clump of weeds outside the door that turned out to be, on closer inspection, hemp. 'They can't take that away from us,' Paul said. 'The police don't come here. We smoke it all day.' The Dungle, apparently, is a fanatics' lair, like the refuge of the Old Man of the Mountains and his Hashasheens, in some senses more than one.

The youth in the above extract makes a statement about an understood "moral economy", or a system communally established with an overstanding founded on a common notion of what is good, just and connected to customary rights. The habitus in which he is situated is within a Rastafari threshold, and ganja in this context would become a part of a subsistence and community survival regime recognized at the level of a moral right. This is decidedly opposite to the developing moral order that had this as a harmful practice, and thus outlawed. This speaks to the ethos of Rastafari dwelling places in general, and especially the public space of a herb yard, a veritable camp of Ethiopian refugees, who inhabit a specific boundary, a liminal margin, oftentimes in foreboding garrison-type slums.

Erna Brodber's *A Study of Yards in the City Kingston* (1975) is something of a precursor to this study, though admittedly she is focused on "Yards" within its historical context of the "negro yard", tracing its evolution to becoming a unique Jamaican urban typology and cultural institution. She is also admittedly focused on residential spaces primarily and the way matrifocal family and community are produced and reproduced. In Brodber's schema of "Yard", she doesn't engage explicitly the space of Rastafari as a unique version of the yard phenomenon. Perhaps due to the matriarchal character of the Jamaican urban yard, the spaces of the movement are not featured in her groundbreaking study. Notwithstanding this, Brodber presents a compelling account of the domain of the working-class woman and her family, and how she navigates security, social elevation, children supervision, cooking, employment, sexual partners and overall respectability through the organization and operation of the yard. Yards are therefore somewhat similar but different from the herb camp, which is more akin to a male *public sphere*, explicitly straddling the purview of business, temporary reprieve/transitional dwelling space, sanctuary, lounge and continuing educational area. Building on analytical frameworks that interrogate Rastafari patriarchy (Owens 1976; Homiak 1998; Lake 1998; Tafari-Ama 1998; Price 2009), this chapter presents the general phenomenon of the camp—its history and contemporary expression by way of insights drawn from case studies based on ethnographic research. The documentation of patriarchy within Rastafari has largely placed emphasis on gender inequity in ways consistent with feminist theoretical critiques. Some updating is necessary of the related research, particularly as the "lioness" has been on the rise internationally as a major operative within the community (Niaah 2016). Here my interest is to uncover the phenomenon, structure and inner logic of what is still a relatively unknown fraternity. This is in keeping with what I have elsewhere described as sensitive scholarship (Niaah 2005), to mean focused on issues arising from empathy and interiority. I have thus built a framework which seeks to honour an institution and its builders as well as provide exposure to the system they have constructed, illustrating its contribution and function.

RASTAFARI AND GANJA EVERY DAY

The activities surrounding the chalice[2] (or "cup") are perhaps among the most important and intimate day-to-day ritualistic practices observable within Rastafari. It entails the sharing of the water-pipe, the ritual vessel, which is passed among the individuals, the objective being to share the sacrament being burnt in this "cup" by way of pulling the smoke into one's mouth through a channel or pipe that has been filtered through water. This vessel is then passed to the person sitting to the left, usually in a circle. Chalice smoking is the approach most immediately recognized as a communion ritual even though it is not the only way communing occurs.

Ganja points of sale/consumption can range from roadside kiosks to fully devoted structures of varying sizes holding provisions for relaxed in-house dispensing and consumption. These are historically referred to as herb camps and such spaces can be traced to the mid-eighteenth century when the East Indian indentured servants arrived at places where workers gathered for relaxation and recovery, engaging in the smoking of ganja while invoking reverence to Kali the Hindu goddess of destruction (Bilby 2000). Through the late nineteenth and into the early twentieth century, the African population became more imbedded in the use of the herb, until it ultimately became associated with labourers in general (Dreher 1982) and the camps more linked to points of cultivation, curing and bulk sale. The first Rastafari leader Leonard Howell's Pinnacle in the 1940s and 1950s had developed this profile, and it was this leader who helped to situate the association of Rastafari and ganja and the ritualistic usage of the herb. Leaders who emerged after Howell, such as Mortimo Planno, attest to visiting Pinnacle to purchase the herb and to partake in the related activities. As legislative penalties were strengthened, a major one of which was the destruction of Pinnacle, cultivation of ganja became more dispersed and discreet across the island as did the associated camps. But at the same time, within the environs of Kingston the Rastafari community was becoming more embedded and with this came the urban versioning of the points of sale, the "cultural institution", the "herb camps" here under scrutiny. Within this survey there are camps which date their origins back to the 1950s, usually as a residential or meeting place for key foundation leaders such as Bongo Rocky, Ras Historian, Prophet Gad and Mortimo Planno. Some of these were ephemeral, and some mobile— reconstituted wherever or whenever key brethren gather. Camps inevitably are ranked and in this ranking is held the context for its success and longevity as a business venture. This has everything to do with the host or operation's leader and the quality of clients and herb he is able to garner, as well as his ability to secure those who come into his space from the law officials or other undesirables. The most settled camps brought into focus by this survey have been existing for nearly forty years or more in the same locations and have demonstrated the ability to put in train legatee. This often might mean the ability to pass down a skill/trade (for example, tiling, tailoring, auto mechanics or carpentry), as well as to groom a successor for managing the camp. It was at one time thought that the usage of chalices had subsided if not disappeared, particularly during the 1980s as there was a rise in the police harassment of individuals who used herbs or were found in possession of chalice paraphernalia generally and those found in these spaces in particular. Presently there is increased usage of the chalice; this no doubt is also linked to the prevailing liberal atmosphere surrounding decriminalization and medicinal cannabis, and the steam and smoke pipes as premium delivery options for ganja therapeutic extraction. Steam-pipes, and its practice of "steaming" ganja, provides for extraction of ganja's medicinal vapours without directly burning the herb (the method of the conventionally popular chalice which produces smoke), but instead passing heated air though the buds and "sipping" the gentle flavours released.

Ganja Community:

Camps are primarily masculine community-based enterprises[3] and halfway homes (for wellness), if they were to be situated within the community therapy framework. They serve as points for ganja management, distribution and control as well as spaces for consumption and community development. They provide supportive services (financial, psychological and care nurture), thus where they exist they serve immeasurably in maintaining tranquility in such communities, especially in easing day-to-day stress and "pressures" of life (for related discussion of pressure and stress see Hickling 2012, 2016; Yawney 1985). Generally, camps occur in close proximity to residential spaces and thus maintain a level of safety for clients to walk to and from, avoiding issues of getting home after hours if fatigued or in any way impaired. Where individuals come from greater distances and may experience transport problems in getting home—the "camp" is a certain option for sleeping rough overnight, sometimes extended into a few days or more, especially for its members who may have housing and or domestic challenges.

These "herb ends" (as camps are sometimes called) also have to secure their approval from the surrounding community which serves as a watchful buffer zone for the camps. They are a critical navigation point between those from the street and those assisted into camps by way of their assessment of the inquiries made in locating the space. This facility within the community is achieved largely through the charisma of the host in building solidarity in the community, which often requires a level of broader service to the neighbourhood which is appreciated. To this extent, camps are expected to be points of refuge with a give back/community building image and are relied on for a sense of defence and security, financial trust, as well as for demonstrating hardcore morally upright teachings and conduct, an expectation of

Rastafari foundations. They are regarded by the youth in particular as spaces of culture, congregations of serious Rastafari elders and points of spiritual and moral upliftment. Further, the establishment of the camp is a type of signifier in communities of oases of Rastafari ritual livity and civic control, suggesting a level of social success that is able to command respect among a varied network of people who variously support the business. The premises or "gates" at which the camps operate when functioning at the optimum capacity in a real sense have a resonance of the biblical king Solomon's court—a royal host, notwithstanding their modest resources, there is always a sense of benevolence from "camp masters" or hosts, and irrespective of how impoverished such spaces might be, there is a feeling of sharing, comfort and relaxation.

The Chalice Camp:

One of the most often expressed views about ganja by Rastafari is that it is a sacrament for the healing of the nation, a redemptive postcolonial curative and within the community its ritual of consumption is akin to prayer,[4] requiring the reverencing of the Most High Father of Creation throughout its engagement. This invocation is generally expressed through references to Jah, Jah Rastafari and Emperor Haile Selassie I, all of these terms being standard in ganja congregations even when not explicitly Rastafari managed as they still operate as sanctuaries for fellowship and honour the related protocols. In such spaces, circles of smoking organically and peacefully take place. The chalice circle has a propensity for commensality, and thus harmony within the gathering is necessary to optimize the elevation in atmosphere expected to pervade from the smoking ritual. Arising from this, the chalice space and the related implements help to produce deeper insights as to the performance of community at the more subtle day-to-day levels of "way of life" or *livity* as performed from its interior most visible (and still yet invisible by way of privacy and the need perhaps for initiation) way through moment-by-moment interaction among communities of brethren. Rastafari pedagogical development and masculinity are performed as rites in an anticolonial pan-African context in urban working-class communities especially. Among the teachings are new ways of praying, new ways of viewing and being in the world.

The camp facilitates networks of males (and occasionally a few females) straddling many different capacities, educational, occupational and skills training, as well as personalities, highlighting issues encountered within male survival challenges. The genesis of the interactions stem from and are sustained by herb-related relations. Money as well as goods and services are exchanged within this context which keep members afloat as well as ad hoc money ventures, such as betting on horse racing, playing lotto, natural juices and roots winemaking, cooking sales, and other passing schemes and innovations for earning. I will now provide some details of one iconic herb camp in Kingston, known by the moniker "Herb for the Poor".

CASE STUDY

Herb for the Poor is located in the Papine area of Kingston. Over the past decade this camp has distinguished itself as a cutting-edge Rastafari herb space. Its name is derived from the principle of providing the ganja sacrament to all its clients regardless of their economic circumstances. This means that all needs are catered to as best as possible, including the ability to arrange credit or obtain cannabis of every quality and related prices within the budget of its clients. The space is a secure Rastafari property, which places this sacramental space more securely in relation to its tenure. The core area for chalice smoking is a well ventilated annex offering a 24-hour service through smoking vigils from sunrise to sunrise, as well as self-service possibilities. This space, unlike most other such establishments, has proper gating, and the inner boundaries are defensively supported by dogs—making membership even more exclusive to those who have developed relationships with these animals. Indeed, moving through this camp can be likened to entering into a genuine "lion's den", as an individual's fearlessness is tested and demonstrated through their ability to enter the gates and comfortably operate among the dogs.

Rituals of setting up and maintaining camp are evident—with the daily preparation of congregation spaces, sweeping, raking, watering ganja seedlings and plants, and garbage disposal all constituting a daily maintenance regime. This is undertaken by various individuals who pitch in to assist with cleaning the ritual vessel, cutting up and packaging ganja and "grabba" (tobacco), refilling water bottles and providing supplies of spring water, fruits and other food provisions. Nowhere else in Rastafari spheres of operation is there this casual but organized devotional work ethic. This code of conduct is understood and recognized as an essential means of preserving civility among brethren because their well-being and economy depend on this space.

With regard to the provision of cannabis, this camp is akin to a herb emporium, attracting various traders and growers seeking to offload or juggle herbs they have secured. There are also set suppliers, and herb at this point becomes available in various weights and quantities as well as product quality. The operational practice of this space is that of catering to the services that converge around this institution, camp members, suppliers, diehard clients, as well as ordinary customers and their various needs, opening and closing according to the flow of such individuals.

Decor/Vernacular Archives:

The space has resources developed through materials that are purchased, donated and repurposed scraps as well as found objects and refuse from houses (bed springs, executive chairs, pallets, slightly damaged fixtures, odds and ends). These are complemented by appropriated signage, promotional decals, paintings and pictures. There are three paintings which feature on the main wall: a portrait of the Emperor Haile Selassie I, a framed print of a lion sitting poised with a lion cub in close attention, and a painting of Bob Marley, king of reggae. The parts of this visual narrative of the Emperor, lions, and reggae's most famous teacher, Bob Marley, become themselves real signifiers for the conduct and energy and atmosphere of the camp. This space also has a range of provisions and equipment: TV, DVDs and player, radio, WiFi, tablet, speaker boxes, dominoes table, device chargers, fan, stove and refrigerator.

The host is a multitalented businessman who is supported by co-hosts as required. These co-hosts/attendants potentially operate on a shift basis within the idea of a relief attendant who is not only reliably scheduled, but also a main point of stability for the camp. This person is usually drawn from the immediate community. The camp's location effectively serves clients within a two- or three-mile radius (but at times much further) with the key walk-in customers coming from the immediate vicinity. Most camps rely as much on walk-in as on devoted members who see the space as the location where they would primarily participate in smoking. The facility further serves as a space for after-work unwinding and is thus likely to see peak membership in the after-work periods. Sometimes this is facilitated by a DJ selector (at times, professionals are invited) and there is further provision of a liquid "sip" or a vegetarian soup.

Fathers Honouring Fathers:

This is a gathering primarily of fathers (and grandfathers). Many of these lions, as Rastafari males are often called, occasionally take their cubs. This is a striking feature perhaps accentuated by the fact that there are at least two youths under twelve years of age who live in the space (offspring of the host and a tenant). This proximity affords these youth a high level of group supervision from the committed clients with an emphasis on academic support as well as mentoring within a patriarchal tradition.

Fathering and its attendant responsibilities are much celebrated by Rastafari, conforming to the ideal of procreative proclivity. On Father's Day, in honour of fatherhood, a feature of this camp and other camps is the celebration of fathers by fathers and the exclusion of the "geldings"— those who are not literal fathers.[5] Fatherhood in Jamaica is often demeaned due to the high incidence of absenteeism, but here at Herb for the Poor and other camps it is reinterpreted, elevated and seen as a premium status, which not only acknowledges the confidence and affinity bestowed by the mothers of the children, but further potentially identifies the security of personal legacy, financial and social responsibility of such individuals. It is understood as a serious measure of one's manly purpose and capacity, and quality of paternal input and the attainments, achievements and challenges of their offspring are shared, and at times help is given with managing situations. Men past middle age without children are perceived as "wasting time" in securing their name and family lineage. Fatherhood is thus not only a highly elevated signifier, but it is also an index for how individuals are treated (respected) and the support they receive in the chalice space. Perhaps one of the most amazing disclosures I have heard in this space is that of camp master host Fata, who indicated that he so admired the devotion towards fatherhood shown by one of the brethren (Shut) that he avowed that he would entrust him with the responsibility of helping to raise his son (one of the youths mentioned above)—Shut thus becoming something of a literal godfather of this child. Perhaps because of these elements, Herb for the Poor holds a consistently scholastic atmosphere with educational arguments and investigations as dominant parts of the discussions. This imbues the space with a feeling of Rastafari teachers converged to facilitate and inspire youth with ambition and educational zeal, encouraging and steering the younger ones towards ambition and intellectual thirst.

The Communing:

There are common key themes explored by such spaces, among which are the day-to-day camp updates, personal issues, community and local news, herb/ganja matters as well as ideas surrounding God and the universe, Rastafari celebration, and conversations about health, curatives and physical strength and fitness. There are also predictable discussions about mystic and/or unusual occurrences—perhaps best captured within the idea of "rakes", denoting fortuitous guiding signs, and the synchronicity of things which are unfolding as the evidence of the Almighty Father at work. This is often especially applied to the small gambling schemes which abound and are often taken very seriously for their potential for the day's earnings. The winning lotto numbers are thus often recorded for public scrutiny and horse races at times collectively viewed. Generally, males in this space are likely to share their strategies for economic survival, including interests in migration prospects or other types of hustling, as well as fairly personal issues concerning their domestic pressures or confrontations with their women. Often there is frank discussion of mothers—baby-mothers as well as their birth moms—and the space does not escape the tendency to brag about past glories with women.

The space is particularly honorific in recognizing Earthdays (Rastafari lexicon for birthdays) and other significant moments for the members such as the celebration of anniversaries, visiting with shut-in members, nine-night and funeral honouring (including taking the chalice practice to the celebration of the life of deceased members and even burying the chalice with the body after the celebration is completed). The local news of violence/criminality is always subject to deeper analysis. It is not unusual for "male" movies (i.e., more action-oriented flicks) to be collectively viewed and discussed, or at times for musical selections to be played for hours, sometimes accompanied by discussions of the artistes and their songs, often enriched by intergenerational gatherings spanning ages thirty-five to seventy-five years. There are also regular cannabis deliberations, related to quality/grade, acquisition and trade. Consciously or otherwise, there are membership updates and status checks, discussion of children's progress in school and life in general. It was noted by a camp host that outside of such spaces, few of the men had "stable" family lives in the nuclear sense, where mother, father and children are together. This was more the exception than the norm, of course reflecting the generally known high instance of absentee fathering in Jamaica, while highlighting access points for this group. But within the Herb for the Poor space this is noticeably different: three of the Rastafari elders were single parents responsible for several offspring from their infancy. In such cases the wider group would show their support, empathy, respect and open admiration for these fathers, for the time and financial responsibilty they undertook, as well as their sense of commitment and devotion in being good fathers.

GENERAL COMMENTS ON CASES SURVEYED

Membership, Inclusion and Exclusion:

Membership is contingent on a system of referral or introductions generally. It is unusual for this to just occur without a recommendation of some type, even if not accompanied at the time of the first visit. That means that individuals are immediately able to identify the source of their direction to the camp, by so doing providing a secure context for the engagement and interaction with new participants. The usual way this occurs is to arrange a link-up at a camp, or at times to be literally taken, and at other times still it could be that individuals are sent directly to an individual in the camp with phone calls supporting the arrival as well as verifying the context for the visit and specific service.

At times in some spaces there are the formations of subgroups related to specific thematic moments—private reasonings are one such case, or moments of separation as accorded by tasks one might be engaged in. Generally spliff smokers, Italist[6]/avoiders of grabba, women, defiled categories, children, and clients under certain medications and prescriptions usually opt to keep their distance when in the presence of the chalice.

Normally, as is the case with most Rastafari spaces, there is a practice of self-inclusion and exclusion. This means that the boundaries are usually established not by physical force but by the word, and those words create the vibrations which require conformity or dissent. Words can also be sent through someone else to summon or to expel in absentia. Dissidents or dissenting individuals are rarely physically expelled, but depending on the situation or reason for expulsion, again the word sound can be the source of removal of an individual from membership. For example, there have been instances where personalities develop animosity towards others—usually over some statements and at times over actions. As much as there is space and time for contending views to work themselves out, there is generally an attempt to quash issues and to focus on the peaceful vibration. The seasoned members give camp a "cool out" until tempers calm themselves; there are also instances which give rise to more permanent disconnections, with persons avowing never to return. Real members however stay the course, sometimes through thick and thin, and thus the connectivity becomes like a life-giving family charge, crucial for their recreation, fellowship and well-being, as the personalities go through cycles of ebb and flow.

Magnets:

No camp can succeed without the presence of a charismatic personality to facilitate the pull of a regular gathering. This is a real skill, and in some instances the host straddles a role akin to a magnet for counselling, advising, teaching as well as potentially psychiatric assessments and evaluation (all issues taken into consideration in his dispensing of the herb). Charisma in this sense is not only confined to the carrying of the word and its resultant appeal to others, but more generally is concerned with the capacity to convincingly run a business that requires diplomacy, security, compassion and trust in administering this illicit product. This means a consistent and satisfactory supply of herbs and related paraphernalia, but most importantly the ability to provide a welcoming space for congenial gathering. A host who balances the ability to maintain a professional stance on financial matters while still permitting the necessary indebtedness/availability of credit lines to keep the spirits up is thus ideal.

In addition to the host's abilities, the clients/participants also provide attractive energies for gatherings. The quality of the reasoning that specific individuals afford, or their sensitivity to the dynamic of the communing in general will also provide attractiveness. The Energy Gods also include those with herbs in abundance, especially high-grade cannabis connoisseurs—or more appropriately "cannaseurs". The financially well resourced are generous with the sacrament, while at the same time some individuals will proudly stay away from this category in keeping with what Rastafari would say in chants, "it is neither your gold nor your silver brought I here", while proudly providing for themselves.

CONCLUSION: A TRUE SANCTUARY

Ganja camps are a unique hybrid creation of Rastafari—of increased significance in a decriminalized, medicinal cannabis environment—as they represent years of cultural practice. Given the imbedded facility that herb camps have provided for local community therapy and point of sale distribution as well as their demographic spread making them a penetrative network and connected system of standardized control, whether through duress or a sense of understanding and responsibility, herb camps have tremendous importance to the city of Kingston. Demonstrated by their historical presence, their endurance notwithstanding their liminal civil position with respect to the reaction from the communities they are located within as well as the civility accorded to them by the police, who routinely "don't come here", in recognition of the space as a house of peace.

Rastafari elder Frank-I Francis defines this herb camp space as one of marronage, or better "petit marronage", to refer to the "socially unacceptable" reprieve, the momentary running away from "officialdom" created by the Rastafari camp, a space of safety established by rituals and codes of respect. These camps are predominantly Rastafari holdings, though admittedly the centrality of the faith is not always the visible characteristic. A herb camp is the quintessential marker of resistance continuously, a makeshift (sometimes ephemeral) "cardboard, old sign and advertisements boards, zinc composed hut" boundary, on the ground among Rastafari on a daily basis. They are of significance because they have allowed Rastafari to navigate all the conceivable barriers to the access of the herb over the past century while also responsibly advancing an industry. They permeate the city, particularly the areas considered "no man's land", like oases in an otherwise desert land for herb celebrants. They can be likened to a "house of prayer" and are perhaps not dissimilar from that which is described in Isaiah: as a holy mountain place where friends gather to be made joyful through the sharing of burnt offerings and sacrifice upon the altar (Isaiah 56:7). In this way the experience of Isaiah's mountaintop "house of prayer" becomes a dispersed local convenience made more localized around the city, and the camp thus provides a channel into a liminal transcendence of the often pressurized urban space, without the trouble of a pilgrimage to a far place.

The herb camp provides this type of space for a restitution of spiritual heights and the achievement of "balancing", as it is often described. This "balance" is multileveled. It refers to a moment of complete sovereignty or freedom and control over mind and body, and the ability to have oneself excused from the pressures of the mundane. It becomes an important breakfast, pre-work meditation and a perfect nightcap at the end of a day. These camps are a vital part of the cultural landscape and function as alternative centres, helping to provide a balancing force to life and acting as a predominantly Rastafari male social service for maintaining optimal health and well-being. This conforms to basic embedded practice within Rastafari to collectively deal with prayer rituals, domestic and even economic matters through separation of gender. As the legal and related social attitudes towards ganja (and Rastafari) become less restricted, this is no doubt impacting women's visibility as users of the herb with the need for access and interaction within camps. Growing numbers of the younger women and some males are actively rejecting these ideas of separation taboos or perceived gender discrimination, voicing fewer ideas about exclusion of women but instead conversations about feminine balance as missing or necessary. Notwithstanding that trend, in contrast to the female-centric urban yards, the logic, structure and function of the herb camps are oriented and likely to endure in appeal, servicing primarily an otherwise peripheral brotherhood.

Notes

1   For a discussion of this work and the artist, see Poupeye (2016).

2   This is a term imported into Rastafari lexicon from Judeo-Christian practices to similarly refer to the vessel ritually used for communing when smoking cannabis.

3   It should be noted, however, it is not unusual for the spouse/wife of a camp's host to fill in on occasions where the host is absent to ensure that clientele has access. On a few occasions females are also employed as a type of unsuspecting person within the midst of the brethren.

4   Carole Yawney (1985); also Abuna Yesehaq of the Ethiopian Orthodox Church (EOC) in reference to the usage of the sacrament by Rastafari—information afforded by EOC congregant Oral "Gabre Medhin" Taylor in conversation with the author, 11 September 2017.

5   I was first made conscious of this term as a descriptor for adult males without children by one of the "geldings", who was highlighting his lack of mature manly status because he had not yet fathered any children (at age 28).

6   Ital is a Rastafari food system centred on natural plant-based nutrition, with minimal inputs from artificial chemical, processed or animal. In relation to the smoking ritual, "Italist" refers to individuals holding preference for cannabis without the additive of tobacco blend, a common practice.

References

Bilby, Kenneth M. 2000. "The Holy Herb: Notes on the Background of Cannabis in Jamaica". In *Rastafari (Caribbean Quarterly* Monograph), edited by Rex Nettleford, 82–95. Kingston: University of the West Indies.

Brodber, Erna. 1975. "A Study of Yards in the City of Kingston". Working Paper, 9. Kingston, University of the West Indies: ISER.

Chevannes, Barry. 2001. "Crime and Drug-Related Issues in Jamaica". *Souls* 3 (4): 32–38.

_____. 2004. "Criminalizing Cultural Practice: The Case of Ganja in Jamaica". In *Caribbean Drugs: From Criminalization to Harm Reduction,* edited by A. Klein, M. Day and A. Harriott, 67–81. New York, NY: Ian Randle/Zed Books.

Dreher, Melanie C. 1982. "Working Men and Ganja: Marijuana Use in Rural Jamaica". Institute for the Study of Human Issues, Inc., Philadelphia, Pennsylvania, USA.

Fermor, Patrick Leigh. 1951. *The Traveller's Tree: A Journey Through the Caribbean Islands*. London: John Murray.

Forsythe, Dennis. 1983. *Rastafari: For the Healing of the Nations*. New York: One Drop Books.

_____. 1993. *The Law Against Ganja in Jamaica*. Kingston, Jamaica: Zaika Publications.

Hickling, Frederick W. 2012. *Psychohistoriography: A Post-Colonial Psycho analytic and Psychotherapeutic Model*. 1st ed. London: Jessica Kingsley Publishers.

_____. 2016. *Owning Our Madness: Facing Reality in Post-Colonial Jamaica*. Kingston, Jamaica, UWI: Caribbean Institute of Mental Health and Substance Abuse (CARIMENSA).

Homiak, John. 1995. "Dub History: Soundings on Rastafari Livity and Language". In *Rastafari and Other African-Caribbean Worldviews*, edited by B. Chevannes, 127–181. London: Macmillan.

_____. 1999. "Movements of Jah People: From Soundscapes to Mediascape". In *Religion, Diaspora and Cultural Identity: A Reader in the Anglophone Caribbean*, edited by John Pulis, 87–124. London: Routledge.

Lake, Obiagele. 1998. *Rastafari Women: Subordination in the Midst of Liberation Theology*. Durham, NC: Carolina Academic Press.

Niaah, Jahlani. 2005. "Sensitive Scholarship: A Review of Rastafari Literature(s)". *Caribbean Quarterly* 51 (3&4): 11–34.

_____. 2016. "'I'd Rather See a Sermon than Hear One . . .': Africa/Heaven and Women of the Diaspora in Creating Global Futures and Transformation". *Africa Development* 41 (3): 1–24.

Owens, Joseph. 1976. *Dread: The Rastafarians of Jamaica*. Kingston, JA: Sangster.

Poupeye, Veerle. 2016. "Dawn Scott—A Cultural Object". Accessed 22 April 2020. https://veerlepoupeye.wordpress.com/2016/09/03/dawn-scott-a-cultural-object-1985/.

Price, Charles. 2009. *Becoming Rasta: Origins of Rastafari Identity in Jamaica*. New York: NYU Press.

Rubin, Vera D., and Lambros Comitas. 1976. *Ganja in Jamaica: The Effects of Marijuana Use*. Garden City, NY: Anchor Press.

Tafari-Ama, Imani. 1998. "Rastawoman as Rebel: Case Studies in Jamaica". In *Chanting Down Babylon: The Rastafari Reader,* edited by N. S. Murrell, W. D. Spencer, and A. A. McFarlane, 89–106. Philadelphia: Temple University Press.

Yawney, Carole D. 1985. "Strictly Ital: Rastafari Livity and Holistic Health". Paper presented at Annual Meeting of the Society for Caribbean Studies, Hertfordshire, UK. 2–4 July (Working draft, sourced from Smithsonian Institution).

BOB MARLEY, EMERGING RASTA 1966-1970

DEAN MACNEIL

Abstract   During his time recording and touring for Island Records from 1972 to 1980, Bob Marley became an international music superstar, the "King of Reggae" and Rastafari's global messenger. An examination of the transitional period from 1966 to 1970 sheds light on Marley's progression toward Rasta emissary. Three songs in particular foreshadow his later work while preserving early artistic elements that would remain constants throughout his career, including the influence of the Bible and theme of redemption. In "Freedom Time" (1966), Marley has already assumed the role of wisdom teacher, bringing a message of redemption to his "children". In his recording of Thomas A. Dorsey's "The Lord Will Make A Way" (1968), Marley honours the influence of gospel music on reggae and identifies with the song's message of trust in God. In "Man to Man" (1970), Marley is the consummate wisdom teacher of broad appeal, countering bleak circumstances with a hopeful message inspired by Paul (Romans 8:31). These early songs provide insight into Marley's realization of Rasta and are indicative of an artist who is true to himself and his mission.

Keywords • Bob Marley • Rastafari • Bible • resistance • redemption

IDEAZ—an interdisciplinary social science & humanities journal, vol. 15, 2020, pp.94-109

Bob Marley's impact on both popular music and the spread of Rastafari is impressive. *The New York Times* (2000) called Marley "the most influential musician of the second half of the 20th century". Researchers have documented Marley's influence on the globalization and acceptance of Rastafari (Barrett 1988, 213; van Dijk 1993, 24). His life represents a hero's journey: from humble village origin; through the trials of rejection, abandonment and survival in the ghetto; to international acclaim and stardom. But Marley is more than a rock star. His music has universal appeal and carries an aura of righteousness, expressed in themes of resistance and redemption, rooted in his personal experience and reading of Scripture. While these elements are evident in his earliest recorded works, they developed and grew as Rastafari played an increasing role in Marley's life.

In his time recording and touring for Island Records from 1972 to 1980, Marley became an international superstar and Rastafari's global messenger.[1] But the biblical Rasta rebel did not emerge fully formed in August 1972 when he, Bunny Wailer and Peter Tosh signed a recording agreement with Chris Blackwell in the London office of Island Records. Marley's career leading up to this period sheds light on the development of reggae and of Rastafari. Furthermore, Marley returned to many of his earlier songs to polish, rework and rerelease them at a later time, allowing us to trace the development of his songwriting and theology. In particular, songs from 1966–70 foreshadow the Island era and provide early indication that his art and thought would resonate well with Rastafari.

When the Wailers began recording in 1962, they had not yet sighted Rastafari, and the reggae artform was yet to evolve. Their means of resistance against the system was ska. In songs like "Simmer Down" (1963) and "Hooligan" (1965), their message to kindred rude boys in Trench Town was to remain calm and not resort to the violence that claimed so many young lives. Their songs were imbued with wisdom consciousness rooted in Scripture, from Marley's first recording in 1962, "Judge Not" (Matt 7:1, Luke 6:37), to the Wailers' "Good Good Rudie" (Matt 11:25, Luke 10:21, Psalm 8:2), recorded during their last session produced by Clement "Sir Coxone" Dodd in December 1965. At that time, the ska era was drawing to a close, and the Wailers would soon enter the transitional period of 1966–70.

Three songs from this period are studied below: "Freedom Time", "The Lord Will Make a Way Somehow" and "Man to Man". Marley later reworked them into "Crazy Baldhead", "I Know" and "Who the Cap Fit" respectively, while recording his breakthrough *Rastaman Vibration* album in August and September 1975. While they prefigure this time when Marley's role as Rasta emissary was coming to fruition, the original songs were recorded during the first four years of Marley's Rasta journey, which began after that of Tosh and Wailer, as evidenced by their first songs to espouse Rasta.

For most of 1966, Marley was working in Delaware factories and absorbing influences of the US Black Power movement that would later materialize in songs like "Black Progress" and "It's Alright", an early version of "Nightshift". Meanwhile, in Jamaica, Tosh and Wailer were moving the Wailers in a Rasta direction. Tosh recorded "Rasta Shook Them Up" shortly after Emperor Haile Selassie's historic visit to Jamaica on 21 April 1966, and Wailer recorded "I Stand Predominant", the first Wailers song to use the Rasta phrase "I and I", around August the same year.

Like Tosh and Wailer, Marley's wife Rita, whom he married 10 February 1966, was present for Haile Selassie's visit. In her oft-repeated account, reminiscent of the story of Thomas (John 20:24–29), she tells of her initial doubt being erased in a life-changing instant upon making eye contact with His Majesty and witnessing a nail print in the palm of his hand as he waved at her. She wrote excitedly of her experience in a letter to Marley, but his response was to advise Rita to focus her energy on her daughter Sharon, whom Marley adopted (Marley 2004, 42–43). Her fervour for Rastafari, however, would continue and make an impression on Marley (Salewicz 2009, 117; White 2006, 224).

While it is generally accepted that Marley began his path to Rasta upon his return from the United States in late 1966 (Davis 1994, 68; Goldman

2006, 43; Marre 2000, chap. 4; White 2006, 224), his first Rasta-themed song was not recorded until 1968. After attending his first Groundation ceremony on 21 April of that year (White 2006, 255), Marley recorded "Selassie Is the Chapel" on 8 June. Interestingly, he neither wrote the song nor intended it for commercial release. It was a reworking of Artie Glenn's "Crying in the Chapel", popularized by several artistes, most contemporaneously Elvis Presley, with lyrics penned by Rasta elder Mortimo Planno, who had become Marley's spiritual advisor and business manager. Music journalist Chris Salewicz notes that for a period of time, Marley was "unwilling to speak to anyone other than Rita or Planno" (2009, 122–123), pointing to their importance during this formative period.

Marley's first Rasta song intended for commercial release was "Jah Is Mighty", recorded in December 1970. During the same studio session, the Wailers recorded a more secular version of the song entitled "Corner Stone", which was released on the *Soul Rebels* album. Whereas previously he used the word "Lord" in songs like "One Love" (1965) and "Thank You Lord" (1967), here he uses the word "Jah", signaling his embrace of Rasta.[2] It would remain his preferred word for God throughout the 1970s, evident in songs such as "So Jah Seh" (1974), "Exodus" (1977), and "One Drop" (1979). Midway through this golden period of roots rock reggae came the *Rastaman Vibration* recording sessions, during which he reworked songs from 1966–70.

In many ways, "Freedom Time" is the quintessential song from this period. It marks the end of the Studio One ska era and beginning of the rock steady phase that led to reggae. It comes at the start of Marley's Rasta journey, foreshadows themes from his landmark *Exodus* album of 1977, and highlights his signature theme of redemption that was a constant throughout his career.

Marley had recently returned from his stint in the United States when he and the Wailers recorded "Freedom Time" in November 1966. After years of recording hits for Kingston record producers without proper compensation, the Wailers decided to launch their own label, Wail N Soul M. Although Dodd was a major culprit in underpaying the Wailers, Marley wanted to give him another chance. The Wailers therefore recorded their first self-produced single, "Bend Down Low", backed by "Freedom Time", at Dodd's studio, and secured limited distribution through Dodd's company. The single was a hit for the new record label; however, the distribution deal generated financial tensions, and as a result, this marked the last time the Wailers would work with Dodd.

In the song's opening couplet, Marley learns good news of freedom from a "whispering tree". As with the "Three Little Birds" who would later preach to Marley in his song by that name from *Exodus*, a message of divine truth is revealed via the Creator's natural world. Because the tree is whispering, one must listen carefully, that is, be attuned to creation and exhibit a wisdom consciousness (MacNeil 2013, 46). This is reminiscent of "Natural Mystic" from *Exodus*, and a sign of the creation theology Marley shares with the sages who wrote Proverbs and many of the Psalms: divine truths are revealed through God's creation. Here, Marley distinguishes himself from other reggae artistes and Rasta lyricists with the profound influence of wisdom literature on his work. But Marley goes further than the traditional sages by linking creation theology with redemption, as do the later biblical writers of Sirach and Wisdom of Solomon (MacNeil 2013, 83).

The second couplet expands the message of freedom by proclaiming the end of futile burden and the recoupment of losses. The phrase "in vain" applied to "burden" foreshadows "Waiting in Vain" from *Exodus*, highlighting Marley's perpetual concern with fruitless activity, be it work, waiting on a lover, or otherwise. Here it signifies work without remuneration, hinting at the Wailers' monetary issues with Dodd, exploitation and even the historical context of slavery. But the verse ends with the hope of redemption: all that has been lost will be regained. Marley sings with conviction, summarizing expansive themes in a single verse of four lines.

The reason for this conviction is clear in the chorus that follows: at this early stage in his career, Marley has already assumed the role of wisdom teacher. Echoing the parental sentiment of the biblical sages (Ps 34:11; Prov 4:1, 8:32), he addresses his audience as "children". He would continue to do so throughout his career in such songs as "Wisdom" (1970), "Natty Dread" (1974), "Jah Live" (1975) and "We and Dem" (1980). As befitting his role of teacher, Marley keeps the message simple and clear, and uses triple repetition when he urges his listeners to "Get ready". The phrase echoes Curtis Mayfield's gospel-influenced song, "People Get Ready", which Marley had previously incorporated into his 1965 ska anthem, "One Love", later rerecorded for *Exodus*. If Marley alludes to Mayfield here, it is appropriate, as Mayfield's song uses the traditional imagery of a train to freedom. However, Marley too was aware of the spirituals and gospel that inspired Mayfield.

The influence of spirituals on Marley's music can be seen as early as 1963, when the Wailers recorded "I Am Going Home", quoting lines from "Swing Low, Sweet Chariot", a traditional freedom song associated with the Underground Railroad. The Wailers would go on to record numerous spirituals and gospel songs including "Amen", "Wings of a Dove" and "Nobody Knows the Trouble I've Seen" in 1964, and "This Train", "Let the Lord Be Seen in You" and "Just in Time" in 1965. Indeed, this phase lasted until May 1970 when the Wailers recorded "Go Tell It on the Mountain".

Continuing in the mode of teacher, Marley asks three rhetorical questions in verse two of "Freedom Time" that situate the song within the historical context of slavery. The communal "I" links Marley with his ancestors, whom he calls "my people before me", who, while enslaved, were building cabins and planting corn. Years later, these lines would become the first verse of "Crazy Baldhead".

In verse three, Marley progresses from building a cabin to building a sermon. He sings that his sermon "was built for freedom". One thinks of the sermons preached by Paul Bogle, leader of the Morant Bay Rebellion of 1865, of whom Marley sings in "So Much Things to Say" from *Exodus*. Former enslavement and unjust toil will be left behind, because Marley is clear that a message of freedom has come directly from the "good Lord". Moreover, in Marley's take on the idiom "if you're going to talk the talk, you've got to walk the walk", he indicates that words will lead to action. He will practise what he preaches in his freedom sermon, his redemption song. Marley is a messenger and a catalyst. He will not merely spread the message of freedom, but enact it. This emphasis on action would intensify when Marley reworked "Freedom Time" nearly nine years later.

Marley modulates from redemption to resistance in "Crazy Baldhead", recorded in September 1975. He is now fully the Rasta rebel, well on his way to musical stardom, and recording the album that would spread Rasta to the masses. Whereas "Freedom Time" started with a verse and alternated to the chorus four times before a closing verse, here Marley begins emphatically with the chorus, alternating to verses three times before closing with the chorus. The tempo is now a deliberate, pulse-like skank of 63 beats per minute (BPM), versus 102 BPM of its rock steady precursor. More importantly, "Crazy Baldhead" starts with a war cry, Marley's inimitable vocal trill, setting the tone for the call to eradicate "crazy baldheads"—those without wisdom consciousness, those who serve to divide rather than unite, who repay hatred for love—from the town.

As noted above, the first verse is based on verse two of "Freedom Time". It is here that we see the emergence of Rastafari when Marley switches the pronoun "I" to the Rasta phrase "I and I". Whereas in "Freedom Time" he addressed his "children", that is his flock or his students, here Marley addresses his adversaries. He changes the first two rhetorical questions into statements and adds a final couplet to the verse that addresses those who look upon him with "scorn" before devouring his "corn", the fruit of his labours. In doing so, he moves from a declaration of freedom to one of resistance. Furthermore, he exhibits confidence and determination by distancing himself from the larger Babylonian culture, as seen in the next verse.

In verse two, Marley continues addressing his adversaries. Expanding the earlier reference to the building of cabins, here he sings of building "your penitentiaries" and "your schools". The labour is for a system to which Marley and his Idren do not conform. It is a system that attempts to "brainwash" and subjugate people. Marley uses the word "your" twice again in the verse, further distancing himself from the Babylonian system he denounces. He sings that "hatred" is "your reward", offered in exchange for the "love" and toil in building up the infrastructure of the country. Furthermore, while being subjected to this hatred, Marley sings that his people are told about "your God above"; that is, they are being offered a pie-in-the-sky theology. Here, Marley is giving voice to the marginalized and calling out motivating factors in the rise of Rastafari: the legacy of slavery and the church's implication in it. He sings of a system that promises heavenly reward from a God above, while effectuating an earthly reward of hatred to a loving people who were willing to hear the message. This system failed the people and in response a new movement arose, rooted in Scripture, revealing Haile Selassie as redeemer and Africa as promised land. But there would be continuing interplay with the broader culture, as we shall see in the next song.

1968 is a pivotal year for Jamaican music in general and Marley specifically. Ska, which had included Rastas like Count Ossie and Don Drummond among its leading practitioners, completed its transformation via rock steady into reggae, characterized by its heartbeat tempo and deliberate infusion of Rasta spirituality. Marley would later call it the "King's music", associating it with Haile Selassie. Sociologist Anita Waters notes that many young people began growing dreadlocks in 1968, whereas they previously kept their hair short to avoid persecution (1989, 71–72). Thus began the Rasta method of what Barry Chevannes calls "symbolic confrontation" through "hair, language, dress, and several other modes" (1998, 66). Music and biblical interpretation must be counted among these modes. Prior to his Rasta immersion, Marley was already well versed in the Bible, deriving from it the dual strands of his music's message: resistance and redemption. From late 1966 onward, the message became more pronounced. In April 1968, the Wailers recorded "Fire Fire", their scathing condemnation of Babylon and first song to mention it by name. The same month, Marley attended his first Groundation, as noted earlier. The Wailers at this time were firmly onboard the Rasta movement, but interestingly, that did not diminish their recording of gospel.

In April 1968, two years into their Rasta journey, the Wailers recorded "The Lord Will Make a Way Somehow", an important and overlooked song in Marley's canon, and released it on their Wail N Soul M label. Rich in biblical imagery, its theme is trust in God. Thomas A. Dorsey (1899–1993), the father of gospel music, originally wrote and published the song in 1943. That the Wailers recorded spirituals and gospel virtually from their inception until 1970 demonstrates the Christian and gospel roots of Rastafari and reggae. Leonard Barrett, who conducted field studies of the Rastafari movement in the 1960s and early 1970s, states that approximately 90 per cent of his interviewees were former Christians (1988, 3). Joseph Owens, who lived and worked with members of the Kingston Rastafari community in the early 1970s, concurs (1976, 22–23). The growth of Rastafari from Christian roots is mirrored in the progression of Marley's music. To fully grasp Marley's message, then, one must understand Rastafari in context with Christianity.

In some ways it is not surprising that the father of gospel influenced the king of reggae. Both men came from rural upbringings and transitioned to the city where they pursued music. They were well acquainted with the Bible, overcame obstacles through trust in God, and fashioned their experiences and religious insights into works of art, often blurring the distinction between secular and sacred music.

The adversities Dorsey had overcome include suffering two nervous breakdowns and years of depression. He persevered to become an acclaimed jazz and blues pianist, leading the band for Gertrude "Ma" Rainey, known as the mother of the blues, for whom he wrote the classic "Stormy Sea Blues", and performing with slide guitarist Tampa Red (Hudson Whittaker), with whom he wrote the 1928 smash hit "It's Tight Like That". But Dorsey, who grew up discussing the Bible at the dinner table with his preacher father and church organist mother (Harris 1992, 18), was determined to write music that was not only popular, but spiritually uplifting as well. The greatest test of his life came in 1932 with the deaths of his wife Nettie, and within days, their newborn baby boy. Dorsey's response to the overwhelming tragedy and grief was to write one of his most beloved testaments of faith, "Precious Lord, Take My Hand", and to turn exclusively to the pioneering, performing and promoting of gospel. His songs offered a message of hope during the Great Depression and World War II, gaining acceptance in churches across the United States and eventually the world. "Precious Lord, Take My Hand" would go on to be translated into over forty languages (McNeil 2005, 107).

Marley was exposed to Dorsey's music in church as a boy (Steffens 1998, 254). The song's message of overcoming obstacles through trust in God appealed to Marley to such an extent that "The Lord Will Make a Way Somehow" became a motif in Marley's life.[3] He recorded the song in 1968, used it as the lyrical basis for "I Know", recorded in 1975, and directed that "I Know" be remixed and released as a single while undergoing cancer treatment in Germany in 1981 (Davis 1994, 254; White 2006, 334). Released shortly after his death, "I Know" would become Marley's farewell message to his fans.

Marley's version of "The Lord Will Make a Way Somehow" is condensed. He drops an entire verse of eight lines, uses only two lines from the last verse, and shortens the chorus. However, he preserves the biblical allusions and message of hope that characterized this and many other Dorsey compositions. Lyrically, the first verse is nearly a verbatim reading of Dorsey's original:

> Like a ship that's toss'd and driven
> Battered by an angry sea
> When the storms of life are raging
> And their fury falls on me (Warren 1997, 152–153)

When Dorsey penned the first two lines in 1943, he was paying homage to Charles A. Tindley (1851–1933), a son of slaves and self-taught preacher and composer, whose hymns of overcoming adversity greatly influenced Dorsey, and later, the civil rights movement of the 1960s. Witness the similarity of Tindley's "Stand By Me" from 1905: "When the world is tossing me / Like a ship upon the sea; / Thou who rules wind and sea, / Stand by me" (Warren 1997, 171). The biblical imagery evokes Psalm 107:23–32, a hymn of thanksgiving for being saved from danger at sea, as well as the Gospel story of Jesus calming the storm on the Sea of Galilee (Matt 8:23–27, Mark 4:35–41, Luke 8:22–25). In Marley's rendition, he changes Dorsey's "storms" in line three to "tide". He thereby likens the vicissitudes of life to the changing sea as he does in "High Tide or Low Tide", an out-take from the Wailers' first Island Records release, *Catch a Fire* (1973). Marley would later use all four lines as the fourth verse of "I Know".

Dorsey's use of biblical imagery continues in the next lines, this time evoking the Pauline athletic metaphor of pressing forward in a race towards the goal of salvation (1 Cor 9:24–27; Phil 3:13–14; cf. 2 Tim 4:7–8):

> I wonder what I have done
> That makes this race so hard to run
> Then I say to my soul take courage
> The Lord will make a way somehow (Warren 1997, 153)

Marley would later adapt these lines as the third verse of "I Know", in which he also employs the athletic imagery in verse one. The phrase "take courage" appears in several passages of the Bible (RSV). Notably, the Lord spoke these words to a beleaguered Paul in Acts 23:11, which resonates nicely with the Pauline theme of this verse. The phrase clearly appealed to Marley. Whereas Dorsey changes "take courage" to "be patient" and "don't worry" in successive verses, Marley repeats the line with "take courage" in each verse in his version of the song.

Marley preserves the first part of Dorsey's chorus nearly verbatim: "The Lord will make a way somehow / When beneath the cross I bow / He will take away each sorrow" (Warren 1997, 153). However, note that he substitutes the word "stars" for "cross" in line two. Here one sees the transitional nature of the recording. It contains the word "Lord", but no cross. This is not to diminish the salvific aspect of the cross, but to accentuate the creational aspect of God. For Marley, the answers to life's yearnings can be found in God's creation. By substituting "stars" for "cross", Marley also mitigates any possible misreading of redemptive suffering into the song's message. His focus is more on the cosmic realm than on earthly burdens and suffering. Thus, when shortening Dorsey's chorus from eight lines to four, he removes the lines about handing over one's burdens to the Lord (cf. Matt 11:28–30) and adds the line, "There will be no sad tomorrows".

As noted earlier, Marley repeats the phrase "take courage". Specifically, he appends it to lines from Dorsey's last verse, "So many nights I toss in pain, / Wondering what the day will bring", to create the third and fourth verses in his rendition of the song. By repeating these lines, Marley emphasizes the analogy between the person tossing at night and the ship tossed and driven in the song's opening line. The response to such distress advised by Dorsey and accentuated by Marley is to "take courage / The Lord will make a way somehow". Marley would revisit the message to take courage several years later when recording "I Know", and again many years after that when deciding to finally release the song.

Like its predecessor, "I Know" is styled as a soulful ballad. But aside from the shared lyrics, "I Know" bears little resemblance to "The Lord Will Make a Way Somehow", and no other commentators have noted the song's lineage. It is an uncharacteristic song that did not make it onto any of Marley's albums during his lifetime, regardless of when it was actually recorded. The general consensus is that it was recorded in 1975 during the *Rastaman Vibration* sessions (Davis 1994, 254; Steffens and Pierson 2005, 87; White 2006, 333–334), rather than after his July 1977 cancer diagnosis as some have suspected. These sessions also yielded material for *Exodus* (Goldman 2006, 198; Steffens and Pierson 2005, 89, 96), which is noteworthy because it and *Rastaman Vibration* are the only albums of the Island era that contain direct quotations of Paul. They constitute Marley's Pauline phase, recorded and released during a period of heightened political violence in Jamaica that included Marley himself being shot in an attempted assassination two days prior to his heroic performance at the Smile Jamaica Concert on 5 December 1976. This brush with mortality only strengthened Marley's resolve, but he moved his base of operation for nearly a year and a half to London, where he completed his masterpiece, *Exodus*, and began an internationalization of his work that Chevannes has astutely likened to "Paul's decision to preach to gentiles" (1994, 270).

The fact that Marley adapts Dorsey's lines containing Paul's metaphor of the athletic race in the first and third verses of "I Know" provides further evidence that the song was indeed recorded during Marley's Pauline phase. Perhaps Marley, an avid runner and football (aka soccer) player, identified with the athletic metaphor. But more importantly, he may have identified with Paul during this period. And while his Paul-like sense of mission was on the rise, his signature theme of resistance against the system was also coming to the fore.

In the second verse of "I Know", Marley sings that "the system" and people will "let you down", but that Jah "will be there to see you through". The message is clear: Put your trust in God, not in men. Marley was offering a message of hope amid considerable political unrest in Jamaica. In an undated statement, Marley noted that "politics are just things to keep people divided and foolish and to put your trust in men" (Lowney

1991, chap. 18). He saw politics as diametrically opposed to the Rasta ideals of unity, wisdom and trust in Jah. Recall that in "Crazy Baldhead", Marley denounces the systemic "brainwash education" meant to keep people ignorant and without hope. The remedy is trust in God, a theme that resonates well with Dorsey's words that Marley incorporates into "I Know".

As noted above, the fourth verse of "I Know" is comprised of the first four lines of Dorsey's composition, which in turn borrow from Tindley. Commenting on this verse, critic Kwame Dawes notes the triteness of the battered ship simile (2007, 332). However, it is important to consider that it is quoted directly from the original gospel hymn and evocative of the apostles on the Sea of Galilee—a timeless and universal message of hope. Moreover, it is fitting that Marley's lines trace back through Dorsey to Tindley's historical context of slavery and testimony that no matter the pain and suffering, or scale of atrocity, putting one's trust in God is not only possible, but a proven means of perseverance. This is a hard teaching, and one that is particularly poignant given that Marley intended his fans to interpret "I Know" in light of his battle with cancer when he decided to release the song in 1981.

In the chorus of "I Know", however, Marley departs somewhat from Dorsey's influence. Whereas Dorsey emphasizes the Lord making a way in this life for people enduring hardships, Marley seems to suggest that the afterlife is the place where the wrongs of this life will be righted. The emergence of Rasta is evident in Marley switching from "the Lord" to "Jah". There is also a progression from the Lord making a way to Jah "waiting there". Here one finds the recurring image of the lover waiting for his love to be returned, which Marley also employs in "I'm Still Waiting" (1965) and "Waiting in Vain" (1977). He appears to shift the action from God to the people, who must complete their work in this life before encountering Jah who is awaiting them "there", and one may assume that "there" signifies a world beyond.

But what of the injustices in this world? In songs like "Get Up, Stand Up", "So Jah Seh" and "Johnny Was", Marley preaches the value of life, and that the promise of an afterlife must not be accepted in exchange for present injustice (MacNeil 2013, 44, 65, 112–113). While "I Know" may contain a rare allusion to the afterlife in Marley's oeuvre, it does not remove the temporal aspect. Jah is not merely waiting; he is "there to see you through". It is an active, guiding type of waiting. The inference is that Jah is there for us in this life throughout our hardships as much as he will be there through the transition to the next life. Moreover, it is important to note the typical Rasta emphasis on firsthand knowledge rather than mere belief. As Marley stated in 1975, "I don't believe . . . When you believe, you have doubts. You have to know" (McCann 1993, 50). He reiterated the exhortation to "know and not believe" in "Ride Natty Ride", released on *Survival* in 1979. Marley is attesting to the mystical knowledge learned in this world of Jah's saving powers. It is the same knowledge he professes in "One Drop" from *Survival* when he sings, "I know Jah would never let us down".

And yet the apparent reference to a world hereafter helps this song to be seen as Marley's last testament. As he fought end-stage cancer, he directed that "I Know" be remixed and released as a single. It would become Marley's first posthumous release and testament of his faith that the battle would be won and Jah would be there to greet the victors. And given the song's Pauline imagery, it takes on an aspect of the farewell speech in 2 Timothy, where Paul proclaims, "I have fought the good fight, I have finished the race, I have kept the faith. Henceforth there is laid up for me the crown of righteousness" (2 Tim 4:7–8a, RSV).

Marley's artistic and theological development is evident in the biblical imagery he adds to "I Know", complementing the nautical and athletic imagery inherited from Dorsey. In a bridge section following the first chorus, Marley sings that Jah is waiting throughout the seasons. The image of the lover awaiting his beloved throughout the seasons is present also in "Waiting in Vain" from *Exodus*. However, here the four seasons symbolize the all-encompassing temporal aspect of Jah's guiding care for those who know and love him. Marley then adds a directional aspect, borrowing from Isaiah 43, which is a key chapter for Rastafari (Smith 1967, 6, 18–19). The passage Marley has chosen points to this importance, for it tells of the redemption from Babylon, written during the exile by the prophet Second Isaiah. Specifically, Marley paraphrases Isaiah 43:6, amplifying his song's theme of trust in God. This is because the words Second Isaiah speaks are God's own words, which strengthens the inference that Jah is not merely waiting. Indeed, God is speaking, as he did in the beginning (Genesis 1), and he's gathering his people. Here one sees the spatial dimension of God's love in gathering his people from the corners of the earth. But there is also a hint of reading the Bible through the lens of Africa.

Marley specifies that the sons and daughters gathered from across the earth are tribes, presumably the dispersed tribes of Israel. However, this also alludes to the African diaspora, positioning current struggles in a biblical-historical framework. This African-focused reading of Scripture is a hallmark of the Rasta hermeneutic, suggesting Marley's deepening expression of Rasta from the time of recording "The Lord Will Make a Way Somehow" in 1968 to "I Know" in 1975. Furthermore, Marley puts Dorsey's "hard to run" race into his own sociopolitical context, and the Pauline race is now seen in light of the exile to be a race towards redemption from Babylon. Marley has masterfully juxtaposed God's New Testament promise of eternal life with his Old Testament promise of redemption from Babylon, an act of canonical exegesis that he also performs in "Johnny Was", recorded during the same sessions as "I Know", where he similarly pairs Paul with Second Isaiah (MacNeil 2013,

114–115). Note that Marley also calls out "the system" in "Johnny Was", which shows a remarkable consistency in his songwriting at the time and once again argues the case for "I Know" being recorded concurrent with the songs released on *Rastaman Vibration*.

In the outro of "I Know", Marley alludes to the story from Luke's Gospel of the prodigal son, who "was lost, and is found" (Luke 15:24), an enduring symbol of God's never-ending love. This resonates with the passage from Isaiah, for the son's return parallels the return of dispersed tribes. What was "lost and found" may not be readily apparent: the tribes, the prodigal son, Marley himself. The last lines are cryptic, as if Marley is receiving a message and passing it on. He alternates the phrases "Lost and found" and "Speak I give" in a chant-like pattern of ABAB–BAAB, as if reaching to find lost meaning, to reunite with one who speaks through Scripture and through song. Marley is reaching towards the ineffable, towards Jah.

1970 can be considered a pivotal year in Marley's Rasta journey. Recall that his last recording of spirituals and gospel was made in May, and his first Rasta recording for commercial release was made in December. "Man to Man", the third and final song of this study, was recorded in September, one month into a nine-month partnership with producer Lee "Scratch" Perry that yielded a critically acclaimed body of work. Music journalist Stephen Davis notes that prior to this fruitful phase, Marley spent considerable time in his home village of Nine Mile where he farmed, lived off the land, wrote music and studied the Bible (Davis 1994, 69). Photos from the time show that Marley's iconic dreadlocks were only just beginning to sprout, an outward sign of the wisdom consciousness he'd been cultivating for years.

In "Man to Man", Marley is the consummate wisdom teacher of broad appeal. Recall that in "Freedom Time", recorded in 1966, Marley referred to his listeners pedagogically as "children". He does that too in "Man to Man", and again when he reworked the song into "Who the Cap Fit" in 1975, thus marking a decade in the role of wisdom teacher. To this day, Marley's success in this role is evidenced by the fact that many anonymous wisdom quotations circulated via social media are attributed to him.

Marley's proverbial wisdom never seems trite because of its seemingly universal applicability to the lives of diverse listeners. As a case in point, when I experienced a time of triple heartbreak from divorce, loss of job and betrayal by a best friend, I listened to Marley's teaching from "Man to Man" that one's close friend could actually be an enemy, feigning love while harbouring malicious intent. I knew and understood this facet of the human condition all too well. Yet the bleak reality Marley lyrically paints turns masterfully on the adversative conjunction, "But", to a hopeful message inspired by Paul: "who God bless, no one curse" (Rom 8:31; cf. Numbers 22:12, 23:8). Moreover, like Paul (Phil 4:6; 1 Thess 5:16–18), Marley provides the wisdom to thank God, even during times of distress. As the adage says, "it could always be worse", and Marley provides the guidance to "Thank God we're past the worst". Things will get better, the worst is over, and Jah will not let us down. It is with this confidence that I was able to carry on, thanks to the musical messenger of Jah, Bob Marley.

Marley was always striving to improve upon his songs, often updating them with the latest in recording studio technology, and at first listen the progression from "Man to Man" to "Who the Cap Fit" appears to be a straightforward rerecording of the Perry-era classic. However, there are two key differences between the original and the remake that are instructive as to Marley's artistic and spiritual development. In the latter, Marley changes "God" to "Jah" in "who God bless, no one curse". The shift to Rasta vocabulary is similar to the change from "I" to "I and I" in "Crazy Baldhead" noted above.

The second notable change in "Who the Cap Fit" is the extended chorus, which contains an agricultural image that Marley uses to taunt the "hypocrites and parasites" portrayed in the song. Dawes has rightly noted Marley's combative stance: "There is a baiting going on here that . . . points to Marley's confidence that he will not be tricked by these hypocrites. It is a confidence that is not as obvious in the rest of the song. Indeed, without the 't'row me corn' proverb, the trickery, and the confidence associated with that trickery, would be lost" (2007, 167–168). It is tempting to view this as an addition arising from the confidence Marley felt at this stage in his career. However, the "throw me corn" proverb is already present in the rare, full-length version of "Man to Man", clearly articulated amid Perry's swirling dub echo effects two minutes and twenty-six seconds into the song.[4] What is interesting, though, is that it goes from somewhat of a throwaway line to an extension of the chorus, repeated in the beginning, middle and end of the song, at the forefront of the sound mix and the song's message. The agricultural image is reminiscent of "Crazy Baldhead", where Marley sings of planting corn, and points to Marley's background as a farmer, rooted in the earth.[5] His connection with the earth, with God's creation, contributed to his mystical outlook and view that the divine can be experienced here and now, and could provide an endless source of strength and inspiration.

The songs of 1966–70 are situated during a period of artistic and spiritual transformation heralded by Haile Selassie's visit to Jamaica in 1966. While Marley was not witness to this event, he embraced the movement upon his return from the United States in late 1966 and went on to become Rastafari's foremost ambassador. While the songs are testament to the transformation underway in Jamaican society, their significance is not limited to Jamaica, but reaches out to the world as Marley himself was eclectic and drew from US influences among others. They also speak to the development of Marley as a man, musician and mystic. Marley worked hard to perfect his art, pouring his heart and soul into it. The songs provide insight to Marley's maturation and artistic process—one not calculated for profit or brand recognition, but driven by revelation and affinity for righteousness. Marley today is a global icon, and may seem to the casual observer to be merely an actively managed brand. While Marley the brand continues to have economic impact, Marley the man and artiste sought nothing more than to spread a dual message of resistance and redemption to the corners of the earth. That the world responded to Marley's creativity and spirituality likely exceeded the expectations of the humble mystic and farmer, skilled with a Bible and guitar, who tirelessly honed his craft of Jah music.

As Paul was to Christianity, Marley was a second-generation Rasta, writing at a time when the movement was still taking shape. His nickname, "Tuff Gong", was a nod to Rasta founder Leonard "Gong" Howell. While carrying the message of the founders, Marley also expanded it for general, indeed global, consumption. And while Marley is a Rasta icon there is more to the picture. There are elements of Marley that preceded his embrace of Rasta and are constants throughout his career. In this larger view, Marley's trust in God is the same that spans the African diaspora, evident in Marley's inherent kinship with Dorsey, and Tindley before him.

We do not know what Rastafari will look like hundreds of years from now, but Marley's role representing and influencing Rasta livity would seem to be secure. The songs of 1966–70 provide insight to Marley's realization of Rasta. But what is perhaps most interesting is what they tell us about Marley as a person. He would revisit his early songs, proving their timeless validity and improving them with his latest understanding and recording technology. He was true to himself, his mission and his cause. He never forgot who he was, where he came from, and the realizations of his youth, alone in the ghetto, with a Bible and guitar.

Notes

1 Marley's mother Cedella Booker, biographer Vivien Goldman and friend King Sporty, among many, have called him a "messenger". The Grammy Museum in Los Angeles debuted an exhibit in 2011 called "Bob Marley, Messenger".

2 Note that the Idren avow they are Rastas "from ever since", or "from Creation" as Marley stated. It is an awakening to the truth that already exists.

3 The biblically inspired theme of trust in God is a constant throughout Marley's songwriting, evident in "Small Axe" (1973), "So Jah Seh" (1974), "Forever Loving Jah" (1980) and others.

4 See the *Soul Adventurer* album, released through JAD France in 2002.

5 Marley considered himself first and foremost a farmer (Davis 1994, 1; White 2006, 220).

Selected Timeline 1966–1976

Date	Event
10 February 1966	Marley marries Rita Anderson
February 1966 – October 1966	Marley resides in Wilmington, Delaware
21 April 1966	Emperor Haile Selassie I visits Jamaica
November 1966	Wailers record "Freedom Time", released as B side of "Bend Down Low" on their newly founded Wail N Soul M label
April 1968	Wailers record "Fire Fire", their first song to mention "Babylon" by name, and the gospel classic "The Lord Will Make a Way", both released on Wail N Soul M
21 April 1968	Marley attends his first Groundation
8 June 1968	Marley records "Selassie Is the Chapel"
August 1970 – April 1971	Wailers produced by Lee "Scratch" Perry
September 1970	Wailers record "Man to Man", released on Perry's Upsetter label
December 1970	Wailers record "Jah Is Mighty", their first song to use the Rasta word for God
25 August 1972	Wailers sign with Island Records
October 1972	Wailers record *Catch a Fire*
13 April 1973	*Catch a Fire* released on Island Records
19 October 1973	*Burnin'* released on Island Records
Late 1973 – early 1974	Breakup of the original Wailers
25 October 1974	*Natty Dread* released on Island Records
August – September 1975	*Rastaman Vibration* recording sessions, including "Crazy Baldhead" (reworking of "Freedom Time"), "I Know" (reworking of "The Lord Will Make a Way") and "Who the Cap Fit" (reworking of "Man to Man")
5 December 1975	*Live!* released on Island Records
30 April 1976	*Rastaman Vibration* released on Island Records
3 December 1976	Assassination attempt
5 December 1976	Smile Jamaica Concert
6 December 1976 – early January 1977	Exile in Nassau, Bahamas, before heading to London for 14 months

References

Barrett, Leonard E. 1988. *The Rastafarians: Sounds of Cultural Dissonance*, rev. ed. Boston: Beacon Press.

Chevannes, Barry. 1994. *Rastafari: Roots and Ideology.* Syracuse: Syracuse University Press.

_____. 1998. "Rastafari and the Exorcism of Racism and Classism in Jamaica". In *Chanting Down Babylon*, edited by Nathaniel S. Murrell, William D. Spencer, and Adrian A. McFarlane, 55–71. Philadelphia: Temple University Press.

Davis, Stephen. 1994. *Bob Marley: Conquering Lion of Reggae*. 2nd rev. ed. London: Plexus.

Dawes, Kwame. 2007. *Bob Marley: Lyrical Genius*. New York: Bobcat.

Goldman, Vivien. 2006. *The Book of Exodus: The Making and Meaning of Bob Marley and the Wailers' Album of the Century*. New York: Three Rivers Press.

Harris, Michael W. 1992. *The Rise of Gospel Blues: The Music of Thomas Andrew Dorsey in the Urban Church*. New York: Oxford University Press.

Lowney, Declan, dir. 1991. *Time Will Tell*. DVD. Island Visual Arts Ltd. Special Feature in *Legend: The Best of Bob Marley and the Wailers*. New York: The Island Def Jam Music Group, 2003.

MacNeil, Dean. 2013. *The Bible and Bob Marley: Half the Story Has Never Been Told*. Eugene, OR: Cascade Books.

Marley, Rita. 2004. *No Woman No Cry: My Life with Bob Marley*. New York: Hyperion.

Marre, Jeremy, dir. 2000. *Rebel Music: The Bob Marley Story*. DVD. New York: Antelope (UK) Ltd.

McCann, Ian. 1993. *Bob Marley in His Own Words*. New York: Omnibus Press.

McNeil, W.K., ed. 2005. *Encyclopedia of American Gospel Music*. New York: Routledge.

New York Times. 2000. "Critics' Choices; Albums as Mileposts in a Musical Century". 3 January.

Owens, Joseph. 1976. *Dread: The Rastafarians of Jamaica*. Kingston: Sangster's.

Salewicz, Chris. 2009. *Bob Marley: The Untold Story*. New York: Faber and Faber.

Smith, M.G., Roy Augier, and Rex Nettleford. 1967. "The Rastafari Movement in Kingston, Jamaica. Part 1". *Caribbean Quarterly* 13, no. 3 (Sept): 3–29.

Steffens, Roger. 1998. "Bob Marley: Rasta Warrior". In *Chanting Down Babylon*, edited by Nathaniel S. Murrell, W.D. Spencer, and A.A. McFarlane, 253–265. Philadelphia: Temple University Press.

Steffens, Roger, and Leroy J. Pierson. 2005. *Bob Marley and the Wailers: The Definitive Discography*. Cambridge: Rounder Books.

Van Dijk, Frank Jan. 1993. *Jahmaica: Rastafari and Jamaican Society, 1930–1990*. New York: One Drop.

Warren, Gwendolyn S. 1997. *Ev'ry Time I Feel the Spirit: 101 Best-Loved Psalms, Gospel Hymns, and Spiritual Songs of the African-American Church*. New York: Henry Holt and Company.

Waters, Anita M. 1989. *Race, Class, and Political Symbols: Rastafari and Reggae in Jamaican Politics*. New Brunswick: Transaction.

White, Timothy. 2006. *Catch a Fire: The Life of Bob Marley*. Rev. enl. ed. New York: Henry Holt and Company.

BLACK RACIAL IDENTITY THEORY, NIGRESCENCE, RASTAFARI
Propositions on Black and Rastafari Identity

CHARLES PRICE

Abstract   Becoming Rastafari involves an identity transformation wherein specific experiences urge a person to redefine and re-educate themselves while shifting their reference group and networks in ways that facilitate Rastafari identity. I use Black racial identity theory to advance four propositions about Rastafari identity: the identity is both racial and religious; becoming Rastafari involves an identity transformation; Rastafari identity is learned; Rastafari identity is sustained through social interaction. The chapter contributes to our comprehension of Rastafari and Black identity formation through the insights and claims of Black racial identity theory.

Keywords • Black racial identity theory • Nigrescence • Rastafari • identity transformation

IDEAZ—an interdisciplinary social science & humanities journal, vol. 15, 2020, pp. 110-133

Anthropologist George Simpson, one of the earliest scholars of Rastafari, reported the following exchange between a Rastafari speaker and his audience during the early 1950s in Kingston, Jamaica:

> "How did we get here [Jamaica]?" Chorus: "Slavery." "Who brought us from Ethiopia?" Chorus: "The white man." "The white man tells us we are inferior, but we are not inferior. We are superior [morally] and he is inferior. The time has come for us to go back home [Africa] . . . The English are criminals and the Black traitors [middle-class Jamaicans] are just as bad. Ministers are thieves . . . The black man who doesn't want to go back to Ethiopia doesn't want freedom. *There is no freedom in Jamaica* . . . Ras Tafari says 'Death to the white man!'" Chorus: "And to the black traitor!" (Simpson 1955b, 135)

This racially and morally framed discourse, recorded during an activist phase of Rastafari ethnogenesis during the 1950s, offers hints to the speaker's and the audience's grievances and their beliefs about race, oppression and their relationship to Jamaica. Their talk yells out things about their identity. However, such hints have rarely moved scholars to ask the Rastafari themselves, "Why are you a Rastafari?" "Why do you make such claims?" and "How did you arrive at such a standpoint?" and then interpret the answers to such questions.

Nearly seventy years after Simpson's publications, we still barely grasp why and how people become Rastafari. Many of the first and second-generation Rastafari were strident, radical and assertive in elevating Black identity, Black history and Black culture at a time when such beliefs and behaviour were interpreted as so ridiculous that their sanity could be questioned. This meant that they were marked as abnormal, threatening and dangerous. What historically has been "normal" for African-descended (Black) people in the West has been the stereotypical "traditional Negro": submissive, deracinated, miseducated and lacking interest in Black identity, history and culture. The institutions informed by colonialism and White supremacy required the traditional Negro to perpetuate its own mythos about the world and European-descended people's dominant place in it.

Simpson, and many after him, suggested that the identity and behaviour of the Rastafari was a defence geared towards exorcising the hopelessness, stigma and low status associated with being poverty-stricken Black Jamaicans (for example, Barrett 1967; Coltri 2015). Said crudely, Rastafari identity involved fantasies where the downtrodden nominated themselves as superior beings who would soon be redeemed and uplifted by the divine intervention of an African monarch, Emperor Haile Selassie I. Such interpretations influenced scholarly conceptions of the Rastafari for more than two decades.

By the late 1970s, new explanations for Rastafari emerged, such as emphasis on Rastafari as a way of life, a form of Black nationalism or as a type of social movement. These new explanations, however, continued to neglect Rastafari identity formation and the historical, social and personal factors that influence why and how people became Rastafari. Becoming Rastafari involves an identity transformation wherein specific experiences urge a person to redefine and re-educate themselves while shifting their reference group and networks in ways that facilitate Rastafari identity. Our grasp of this identity transformation—and race, racial identity, racialization and faith as a part of the process—remains underdeveloped.

I will use and extend some of the major frames of Black Racial Identity Theory (BRIT) to advance four propositions about Rastafari identity. By propositions, I mean suggestions for consideration—proposals—that are open to extension or revision. The propositions are: 1) Rastafari is a morally framed racial *and* religious identification; 2) becoming Rastafari is typically (but not always) a person's reworking of their self-concept to make Rastafari identity salient; 3) Rastafari identity is learned through observation, study and practice; and 4) Rastafari identity is internalized and sustained through social interactions that affirm and nurture the identification. Central to Rastafari personal and collective identity are exaltation of Emperor Haile Selassie I as divine and the valorization of Blackness. This view is perhaps most applicable to the first two generations of Rastafari in Jamaica, whom I shall call "foundation" Rastafari. Nevertheless, I suggest that the propositions are relevant to contextualizing

Rastafari beyond the foundation Rastafari as well as Rastafari communities outside of Jamaica. Finally, I offer a suggestion slightly different from the preceding propositions: life narrative methodologies offer an empirical strategy for discerning Rastafari identity.

This article contributes to our comprehension of Rastafari and Black identity formation through the insights and claims of BRITs, focusing on Nigrescence Theory (also known as the psychology of becoming Black). Why and how do people redefine their existing identity, making Rastafari and Blackness central? What are some of the purposes of valorizing Blackness and Rastafari identity? How are such identifications sustained over time? Rastafari identity, a unique expression of Blackness, pushes us past the BRITs to address the intersection of the categorical identifications of both race and religion. I address the above propositions by 1) briefly reflecting on Rastafari identity and scholarship; 2) presenting a modified Nigrescence Theory that incorporates lessons from religious conversion theory and that informs the propositions; and 3) articulating the propositions. I should note that I do not address in this article any potential gendered differences in becoming Rastafari. This is a topic sorely in need of empirical attention.

RASTAFARI SCHOLARSHIP
AND THE NEGLECT OF IDENTITY

On 2 November 1930, King Ras Tafari was crowned Emperor of Ethiopia and assumed the name and title Emperor Haile Selassie I (might of the Trinity). By late 1933, Jamaican newspapers were reporting on the Black Jamaican Rastafari who pronounced allegiance to the African Emperor Selassie I. They anointed Selassie I as the Messiah who would redeem the subjugated Black people of the diaspora and the African continent. From the outset, Jamaican news media such as the *Daily Gleaner* depicted the Rastafari as racial lunatics who believed they could march "home" to Africa and dwell with their God and King, Emperor Selassie I. Why would someone valorize Ethiopia or Blackness? Why would someone pursue and revel in being a pariah, endure ostracization and risk violence and imprisonment for one's faith and identity? For four decades, such questions were barely broached.

There are many ways to define identity. Nevertheless, most readers will probably accept the following conception. Identity is about an awareness of oneself as a unique being who nevertheless shares cultural frameworks with other people and who conceives of oneself as possessing certain qualities that connects one to other people who also possess similar qualities (Burke 2003). For example, each Rastafari is unique, yet sees themselves connected to other unique Rastafari through their shared knowledge, cultural frames and relationships. Identity is about how people position and understand themselves in relationship to other people, places and times. It represents a storehouse of information about people's experience. Identity also involves creating notions of sameness and difference among the "members" and "non-members". Identity as experience is a dynamic and shifting phenomenon. Therefore, it is important to understand the dynamism, and relevant here, why and how people change their self-concept—say moving from Blackness as insignificant to significant, from not-Rastafari to Rastafari. Are there identifiable patterns of transformation and a systematic explanation for them? Yes.

Fernando Henriques (1953) offered one of the earliest academic references to the Rastafari in his book about family and colour in Jamaica. Henriques observed that Rastafari were scattered across the island of Jamaica, that they "neglected their physical appearances" and that they were of extreme poverty (1953, 68). Soon thereafter George Simpson (1955a; 1955b) described the "doctrines of the Ras Tafari".[1] Simpson did not elaborate upon the importance of Ethiopianism—an ideology of valorized Blackness—to Rastafari identity (though Simpson did invoke the "social psychological functions" of compensating for low status). Nevertheless, Simpson's account could affirm the then-dominant view of the Rastafari as vicious racists rather than as Black Jamaicans embracing a new religio-racial identification that valorized Blackness. Simpson was sympathetic but ambivalent, stating that "despite the fact that one of the main reasons for their movement is hatred of Whites, the writer's impression is that most Ras Tafarians will respond favorably to a white person who is friendly" (1955b, 134).

Rastafari Sam Brown (1966) rebutted such views that focused on racial animosity and cultism by offering an insider account of Rastafari doctrines, emphasizing Rastafari respect for all life forms. Brown hinted at the contours of Rastafari identity—why one is Rastafari and what is important to one as a Rastafari—without delving into detail.

The *Report on the Rastafari Movement in Kingston, Jamaica* (Smith, Augier & Nettleford 1960) was motivated by a need to quickly learn about the Rastafari and offer recommendations to the government on how to handle them. While the report presented a sympathetic account of the Rastafari by noted scholars, it cast very little light on questions of Rastafari identity, other than to tell us about their convictions. Its authors influenced analyses of the Rastafari for more than two decades.[2]

Between the mid-1970s and late 1990s, the trickle of publications on the Rastafari became a surge. Scholars were studying the Rastafari from varied perspectives that focused on Rastafari worldviews, Rastafari as gendered, Rastafari as anticapitalist or anticolonialist, Rastafari as cultural innovation, Rastafari as philosophy or faith, Rastafari as a social movement (revitalization, millenarian or messianic) and Rastafari beyond Jamaica. During the latter part of this period, the Rastafari themselves began to publish about their identity, faith and people.

Nevertheless, a scholarly focus on identity formation—becoming and being Rastafari—remained elusive. One could extrapolate why and how people became Rastafari through Rastafari insider accounts, or through academic publications. Examples include Douglas Mack's *From Babylon to Rastafari* (1999), which provided experiential details that one could glean for hints about becoming Rastafari, and Barry Chevannes' *Rastafari: Roots and Ideology* (1989; 1994), one of the first scholarly works to explain becoming Rastafari in terms of conversion, which implies that identity is relevant. Therefore, I was motivated to address this issue of identity from the perspective of Rastafari people and from a secular (but appropriate) theoretical standpoint (Price 2009), an approach in line with what Jahlani Niaah has dubbed Rastafari-"sensitive scholarship" (2005).

During the 2000s, scholars extended their focus on Rastafari in ways that help us better grasp the evolution of the Rastafari and their identity. For instance, scholars addressed artistic, philosophical, intellectual, linguistic, theological and legal concerns, as well as continuing to focus on historically documenting and contextualizing the development of the Rastafari people. Indeed, there is an emergent focus at the University of the West Indies at Mona, Jamaica, called "Rastafari Studies" (Niaah and MacLeod 2013). The list of publications on the development of Rastafari people and culture beyond Jamaica, the Caribbean, the United States and England continues to grow. William Hawkeswood was a trailblazer on the international front with his 1980s study of Rastafari in New Zealand (1983). Later, other works were published, for example, studies of Rastafari in Senegal (Savishinsky 1994), Mexico (Posadas 2010), Burkina Faso (Wittman 2011), Japan (Sterling 2010), Ethiopia (Minda 2004; MacLeod 2014; Bonacci 2015), Ghana (Middleton 2006), Cuba (Hansing 2006) and South Africa (Raphasha 2002). Most of this research, however, does not focus on identity formation.

RASTAFARI
AND CONTEMPORARY IDENTITY CONCERNS

The first two generations of Rastafari in Jamaica—"foundation" Rastafari— emphasized the divinity of Haile Selassie I, repatriation, Black redemption and the valorization of Black identity, history and culture. Subsequent generations of Rastafari in Jamaica and elsewhere are increasingly diverse in how they address these identity-relevant concerns. Why and how do people in places as disparate as New Zealand, Ethiopia, Japan, Mexico, Burkina Faso and Cuba become Rastafari? A focus on identity is important given the growth of Rastafari communities across the globe, and because with each new generation, wherever and whoever they are, we should expect change in how Rastafari is defined, embodied and enacted. (We shall sidestep the anthropological question of whether identity and a self-concept are universal or particular to modernity and western civilization.)

In the literature that *does* address Rastafari identity, there is evidence consistent with BRIT, indicating that specific experiences catalyse identity transformation and that challenges of transformation involve resocialization, internalization and acquisition of competence in the new identity. Drawing on BRIT, I argued that becoming and being Rastafari involved an identity transformation whereby a person had experiences that led them to emphasize being Rastafari and Black (Price 2009). The catalytic experience typically involved dreams, visions, observations or incidents that challenged people's self-comprehension and their comprehension of race, religion and history. For the foundation Rastafari, identity transformation involved noticeable phases, such as the search for Rastafari exemplars and motivation to learn about Scripture in relation to Black history and culture. Ultimately, many foundation Rastafari were interested in issues of morality, justice, truth, race and God that also allowed them to rectify miseducation, deracination and discrimination.

Of note, several of the recent studies of Rastafari that give significant attention to identity focus on communities beyond Jamaica. Glazier, for example, focused on becoming and being Rastafari among Trinidadians (2006). He argued that conversion (or transformation) to Rastafari must be understood in its individual, social and historical contexts (2006, 261). Sterling (2010) sought to use Rastafari identity to examine race, gender, ethnicity, class and nationality among Japanese Rastafari. Sterling contended that Japanese Rastafari "retool" the fundamental dimensions of Rastafari identity—race consciousness, redemption and critical moral discourse—for their Japanese cultural milieu (2010, 33). Posadas (2010) showed how people of Mexican ancestry reframed Rastafari into their own cultural idiom—"Azteca-Mexica" or "Razteca", while Hansing's (2006) interlocutors in Cuba developed their Rastafari identity in an environment in which information about the identity was severely limited. Common to such accounts of Rastafari identity is how foundation Rastafari beliefs are refashioned beyond Jamaica, yet also common across the accounts is how adherents resuscitate suppressed and oppressed identities and communities. Posadas notes, for example, how "Mexican-American Rastafari is a recontextualization of Jamaican cultural resources; however, it goes beyond the positive reconstruction of Blackness; it also aids in the positive reconstruction of Brown and Indigenous identities . . . . Rastafari provides a form of resistance against mainstream Mexican-American male archetypes, which offers little in the way of pious and righteous male figures" (2010, 7).

Makgompi Raphasha uses the case of Rastafari in South Africa to demonstrate how marginalization continues to accompany Rastafari identity and experience in the twenty-first century (2002). Raphasha (2002) argues that identity is the basis of being a member of a given society. In Raphasha's view, a key aspect of identity involves authenticity and recognition: an authentic identity is one that is the product of a person's desire and right to be recognized as who they believe they should be. However, authenticity is distorted by misrecognition or nonrecognition.

Of relevance here is the persisting existential condition of people refusing to acknowledge Rastafari as a "legitimate" faith, culture or identity. Paradoxically, Rastafari have acquired the status of paragons of Black identity and culture while simultaneously fighting to have their culture and practices recognized as legitimate (for example, repatriation to Africa; cannabis as sacrament; Nyahbinghi drumming and chanting as life force). Therefore, another continuity among the different generations of Rastafari and the different Rastafari communities is that they continue to strive for legitimacy and recognition in the face of people who deny their authenticity. Rastafari identity, then, cannot be separated from stigma and the identity work that buffers one against humiliation and discrimination. There is growing recognition that racial identity—Blackness for example—can serve as a buffer against racism (for example, Cross 2012).

Last, but not least, Rastafari people adhere to their own ethno-theory—a conversion narrative—of Rastafari identity formation called "inborn conception". An elder Rastafari, Bongo Duhaney, related the idea of inborn conception to anthropologist John Homiak:

> Feh a man to be Rasta him have to be an inborn man—but born without [being] 'taught', 'cause no one teaches us of what I-n-I [Rastafari] know. We's a cult 'inborn' within yuh [one]. It is an 'Order' . . . our faith is an Order of de Ras Nyabingi [a major and influential community of Rastafari]. But we now 'born' within such Order of de Nyabingi (1985, 157).

Inborn conception holds that the ability to become and be Rastafari is already within a person (Bongo Duhaney emphasizes "man" although the ability is not restricted to men). It suggests that humans harbour internal sensibilities, moral principles and the intellectual prowess conducive to the "livity" (life force and principled ethics) of Rastafari. Rastafari is activated and established through revelation. This ethno-theory of Rastafari identity is not totally inconsistent with the academic BRITs: both can identify what activates an identity (Rastafari) and what explains its development.

Rastafari people embrace at least two stigmatized identifications: Blackness and Rastafari; we could add others such as female. People are not born Rastafari. They become Rastafari. Becoming Rastafari involves people reworking their self-concept, reference groups and relationships (even for those who grow up Rastafari). They engage in re-education and resocialization attendant to the Rastafari identity. The Rastafari-in-the-making acquires new information that informs their identity repertoire, and likely, they will shift their social interaction in ways that privilege people and things associated with Rastafari identity. For some, transformation will entail trying to divorce oneself from previous relationships and practices associated with the identity-before-transformation. Gaining distance from the "old" identity can for some people be a formidable challenge. Nevertheless, we must also consider that for at least two generations it is not unusual for one to be born into a

Rastafari household or community and grow up as Rastafari from a young age rather than become Rastafari at some later point in one's life course.

Black Racial Identity Theory and Nigrescence Theory

For centuries, people of the African diaspora have grappled with identity challenges that involve deracination, miseducation and racism. The obstacles they have faced range from the erasure of African history and cultural practices to the submersion of African-descended people in Eurocentric teachings to outright discrimination against African and African-descended people based on the belief that they are inferior compared to Europeans and Asians (for example, Africans developed no civilizations; Africans and African-descended people are less intelligent than other "races"). At the heart of such identity issues is race.

Let me say a few things about race as used in this article. Most scholars will grant that race is socially constructed. However, we continue to lag in showing *how* race is socially constructed. Racial consciousness is not pure fantasy. Race is just as real and as socially constructed as Christianity or psychology. A defining characteristic of humans is their concern with organizing and making sense of their differences and similarities. Race, a construct of modernity, describes a categorical identification used to organize and make sense of human difference and similarity. Race has also been used to enforce exploitation, subordination and inequality. Racial identity describes how people give life to and live a racial category, while racialization describes the process by which people become racialized beings, sometimes in ways beyond their own control, such as through the workings of institutions, structures or media. Rather than dwell on whether race is real or imagined, good or bad, let us explain how it is conceived, created, utilized, practised and contested. This would allow us to show how race can be used in ways constructive or destructive while simultaneously demonstrating the range of how race is socially constructed.

An analytic framework that has something theoretically significant to say about race, racial identity and racialization is important to explaining Rastafari identity. BRITs can serve this purpose because they explain the development and functions of Black racial identity.

William Cross' theory of Nigrescence—the psychology of becoming Black—provides a conceptual structure for explaining why and how people valorize Blackness and make it central to their self-concept (for example, 1971; 1991; 1995). There are several codified and tested BRITs, Nigrescence Theory being among the most esteemed and empirically tested. Other major theorists of Black racial identity include Bailey Jackson (2012), Janet Helms (1990) and Robert Sellers and his colleagues (1998). While there are many other important contributors to BRIT, Cross, Jackson, Helms and Sellers (and colleagues) have been instrumental to developing and extending BRITs (see Price 2018a; 2018b for more on various BRITs).

The first academic publication on Nigrescence framed it as a conversion experience, a transition from "Negro-to-Black" (Cross 1971). Between the 1970s into the 2000s, Cross and a legion of scholars carried out research enriching our understanding of Black identity, not all of it under the coin of Nigrescence. Contemporary BRITs acknowledge the ephemeral nature of race, the remarkable variation in Black identifications and attitudes, the relations between age and identity and the multiple identifications that people embody and how they shift according to situation. In Cross' view (2012), several important functions of Black identity are: buffering (against racism); bonding (connections among Black people); and bridging (comfort with one's Blackness; the ability to reach out to diverse groups).

Nigrescence Theory explains valorization of Blackness as a means of dealing with racism, miseducation, deracination and the stigmatization of Blackness. Valorized Blackness offers a cultural antidote to the denigrating, discriminatory and racist treatment of Black people and Blackness. Many people, including those who identify as Black, lack a grasp of Black history and culture because so little about it is imparted through socialization or schooling. The deracination of African-descended people makes possible a quest to find out "who I am" and "who we are". The stigma of Blackness, ironically, can help contest deracination, miseducation and racism. Consider, for instance, the claim, "I am not ashamed to be Black. I am proud to be Black".

Developing a valorized Black identity entails questioning a view of Black people as inferior and "less than" and encourages searching for information that assists in creating such a valorized racial identity. Black identity transformation involves movement from a disengaged or devalued conception of Blackness to one invested in valorizing Blackness. The transformation entails active "identity work" that requires the involvement—positive and negative—of other people and attendant shifts in one's reference groups and worldview (Cross 1995; Price 2009).

Nigrescence Theory claims that a transformation towards making Blackness central to one's self concept involves four identifiable states (or phases) (Cross 1995; 2001). First, the identification that a person is socialized into is called the *pre-encounter* identity. Blackness, for a pre-encounter person, might hold little significance. For them, parenthood, politics, faith or career might be identifications more salient than race. Conceptually, pre-encounter acknowledges a vast variation in people's understanding of and attachment to Blackness.

Two pre-encounter Black attitudes that Cross identified during the early iterations of the Nigrescence model were "anti-Black Black" and "Blackness-as-burden". In later formulations Cross revised the pre-encounter attitudes, but they are worth mentioning because of their ideological relevance to pro-Black identifications. The anti-Black Black is a Black person who privileges Eurocentrism and Whiteness and denigrates Blackness and Black people. The impact of this attitude is significant because it speaks to the internalization of Black stigma and White hegemony by people of African descent. A Black Cuban Rastafari woman succinctly makes the point based on her observation of race relations in Cuba:

> Many black people here (in Cuba) feel inferior because of their skin colour . . . Everyone [Black] here wants to look like *La Gaviota* [a blonde, White female telenovela character, original italics] . . . I have never heard of anyone wanting to look like a black person, ever. Blackness is just not considered beautiful . . . The autodiscrimination is so bad, the people who have most criticized my locks have been other blacks. They feel that we are emphasizing our ugly black[ness] . . . There is this unquestioned conviction that white is better and more beautiful . . . Until I learned about Rastafari I thought this too (Hansing 2006, 189).

Blackness-as-burden describes people who self-identify as Black, but see their Blackness as a barrier and stigma. Blackness is signified as a heavy load to bear. Exemplars of the Blackness-as-burden attitude are those Black people of the Civil Rights movement generation and before. Many of them were race conscious, but dissatisfied with the travails that came with being Black. The rise of the Civil Rights and Black Power movements drew to Cross' attention how growing numbers of people viewed Blackness as positive and empowering (1991). Although Ethiopianism valorized Blackness long before the Civil Rights and Black Power movements, the latter increased the scale of valorized Blackness (Price 2003; 2014). Indeed, Cross and colleagues explain these movements as examples of collective Nigrescence (1998).

Second, a particular experience or series of experiences—*encounters*—is commonly a motivation for making Blackness an affirmative and central aspect of a person's self-concept and identity repertoire. Encounters are incidents that unsettle a person's understanding of "the way things work", and draws their attention to Blackness. Racialized exchanges are common for phenotypically Black people (for example, being singled out for scrutiny, mistreatment by police or remarks such as "you are different from other Black people"). Alone, a single racial exchange, even a negative one, is unlikely to move a person towards making Blackness a salient and positive dimension of their self-concept. A Nigrescence encounter, however, disrupts one's understanding of their world, stirring them to question society and their awareness of Blackness. A person repeatedly revisits their encounter. Encounters may involve a single incident or several incidents—either negative or positive—that occur over time, or that take culturally relevant forms such as dreams or visions. Encounters may involve oneself, observation of the experience of others or both. An encounter signals a potential mission to learn about Blackness—why it is maligned, disregarded and how it manifests positively in history and the present. For example, take Nyah Patrick. Nyah Patrick, born around 1929, told me that he was curious about Jamaican religious traditions such as Revival before becoming Rastafari. He said he was a "spiritual" person from the age of four. Nyah Patrick's encounter experiences involved being "shook" (shaken) during the 1940s by something he had never imagined: he heard Rastafari in the street pronouncing the ascendance of a Black God and King who heralded a new dispensation on Earth. By his late teens, he was spending time learning among Rasta people and by the 1950s had committed to Rastafari. After much thought, for Nyah Patrick it made sense that *his* God should be Black and that White people would promote a White God in their own image.

The fuel for Nigrescence, though, is the persistence of deracination and miseducation about Black history and culture among people of African descent. Encounters that I have investigated lead, eventually, to indignation about lack of awareness about Blackness, especially information about Blackness that is construed as positive and empowering.

Black identity transformation involves the pursuit of information about Blackness through study, observation and practice. There are two primary features of the third state: *immersion* and *emersion*. The embryonic convert *immerses* themselves in concern with historical and cultural information about Black people and pays attention to people who exhibit a positive embodiment of Blackness. Distinctive behaviours associated with immersion are militancy, defensiveness and zealousness. White people, for example, may be reckoned to be not only oppressive but evil. However, this conceit typically is only a phase. What is more likely to result is recognition that the denigration of Blackness and Black people is not a simple result of individual behaviour, but a product of systems (or institutions) that support inequality and injustice. It is more than a coincidence that Rastafari use the biblical *Babylon* to describe a historical system of suppression.

Nigrescence Theory assumes that a healthy Black-focused identity evolves beyond a state of frustration or anger. Eventually, a person becomes culturally competent in their new identity, and this is described as *emersion*. Emersion is a significant phase in Black identity transformation because the emergent identity is likely to become consistent across contexts and situations.

Emersion, nevertheless, does not signal the end of identity transformation. The new identity must be internalized, committed to and sustained over time. The fourth state identified by Nigrescence Theory is *internalization*. Ideally, the new identity becomes durable and enduring, even as a person evolves. Commitment to an amended self-concept and valorized Black identity is not a guaranteed outcome. Commitment requires identity work. A person might abandon the identity transformation process for various reasons, or might at a later point become an apostate (also deserving of study).

Nigrescence Theory's explanation of internalization is vague, though it shares this vagueness with the psychology of identity (the *Handbook of Self and Identity* dwells on internalization, for example, but does not clearly explain how it actually happens [Leary and Tangney 2005, 253–74]). From an anthropological perspective, internalization involves interior dialogue (what one tells oneself) and social activities that allow one to habituate the practices relevant to "performing" and living the identity. Internalization entails a person working to project an identification and assess how others respond to it. For example, being acknowledged as Rastafari by other Rastafari can validate the identity, as can, paradoxically, having the identity scorned. Another way to conceive of internalization is suggested by practice theory's notion of "habitus", and how people "internalize" the worlds that they inhabit (Bourdieu 1977). The learning, practice, reinforcement and challenge that occur within various social situations and social scenes are the makings of internalization.

BRITs alone, however, are insufficient to advance propositions about Rastafari identity. Rastafari identity concerns involve much more than race: Rastafari faith is inseparable from race. Rastafari are a Black, Chosen people (at least for the foundation Rastafari). BRIT must be extended to incorporate religiosity. Blackness can be inseparably intertwined with religion and ethical discourse that privileges Blackness as exceptional. Evident examples include Ethiopianism, the Nation of Islam, the racialization of Scripture and the Rastafari.

RELIGION AND BLACKNESS

One of the oldest models of positive Black identity, Ethiopianism, traces back at least to the era of the pre-revolutionary American colonies. Ethiopianism was informed by biblical narratives and history as well as collective remembrance of traumas such as enslavement and its impact on Africa, Africans and African descendants. (The term Ethiopia was used to describe the continent of Africa and its dark-skinned inhabitants into the early to mid 1800s.) There are different strands of Ethiopianist thought, but common to all are condemnation of enslavement and White supremacy, and exalted Blackness. One strand of Ethiopianism explicitly framed Africans and their descendants as modern Israelites awaiting redemption and arrival in a promised land. Rastafari thinking, especially the foundation Rastafari, was shaped by Ethiopianism.

The early incarnation of the Nation of Islam emphasized an Asiatic lineage, while Minister Louis Farrakhan's version emphasized Blackness (Austin 2006). In either case, racial identity was intertwined with religious belief. Like Ethiopianists, the Nation associated Whiteness with oppression and believed it doomed to suffer apocalyptic destruction.

Black members of the Civil Rights movement routinely approached racial justice and social justice with a spiritually infused Black consciousness. And even nominally religious Black people may explain their own situation or the condition of Black people as God's will. Hence, we must not neglect the influence of morality and the supernatural in Black and Rastafari identity formation.

One way to integrate a concern for the religious and the moral into BRITs like Nigrescence Theory is to integrate relevant constructs from religious conversion theory. The obvious difference between Nigrescence and religious conversion is, respectively, a focus on race and the supernatural. However, beyond the distinctions between race and religion, both categories allow people to revise how they identify—to convert—as it were, to revise their self-concept, social network(s), reference group(s) and meaning repertoire(s).[3]

Recent religious conversion scholarship considers a range of factors attendant to conversion, such as: individual dispositions; family and friends; sociocultural context; oppressor-oppressed relationships; faith-specific conversion narratives; community building; problem-solving; interest in a satisfying belief system; and traumatic experience, such as loss of a loved one or a catastrophic illness (for example, Gooren 2014; Jindra 2014; Premawardhana 2015; Rambo 1993). Religious converts, like racial converts, need the involvement of other people to perform their identity work. Social interaction and participation in ceremonies, rituals and organizations (or groups) are integral to learning and committing to the new faith and identity.

Limitations and Extension of Nigrescence Theory

There are limitations to Nigrescence Theory as an explanation for Black (and Rastafari) identity. One limitation is the reliance of Nigrescence Theory on the data drawn from the experience of African-American college students. However, Cha-Jua (1998), Price (2009) and Charles (2015) have shown that Nigrescence Theory is relevant beyond African Americans, applicable to African-descended people of the Caribbean (Christopher Charles used Nigrescence Theory to sketch a view of the "becoming Black" for a founding Rastafari, Leonard Howell [2015]). And recently, Worrell and MacFarlane determined through a survey of Jamaican attitudes that Nigrescence Theory is applicable to Jamaicans (2017).

Propositions on Rastafari Identity

We shall assume that Rastafari is a diverse collectivity, as attested to by the various Houses (groups or communities) of Rastafari of Jamaican provenance. Rastafari variation is even greater once we consider the international Rastafari communities. Therefore, the propositions suggest a baseline for explaining similarities and differences among Rastafari communities within and beyond Jamaica.

PROPOSITION 1: RASTAFARI IS A MORALLY FRAMED RACIAL AND RELIGIOUS IDENTIFICATION

Rastafari originated as a morally configured religio-racial community holding Emperor Haile Selassie I as divine and as Messiah. Rastafari people who have shared their life stories with me defined their self-concept—

who they are—within a racial and faith-oriented framework. They are Black *and* godly. Their identity as Rastafari is informed by a set of justice motifs—truth, righteousness and redemption—that provide a racial and moral schema for interpreting the world. The justice motifs are a means of staking out a moral ground; a means to foregrounding rights, justice and morality; and a means to critique systems and histories of exploitation that disadvantaged Africans and African-descended people: "English are criminals", "ministers are thieves" or middle-class Black Jamaicans are "traitors" (collaborators with a racially exploitative system). The justice motifs and critique are more than politico-juridical claims because people use them to guide their behaviour and pronounce their values.

Black redemption is central to foundation Rastafari identity: the view that oppressed Africans of the continent and diaspora shall be redeemed and exalted. Repatriation is a part of the configuration of Black redemption and takes form literally and symbolically. That is, some Rastafari seek to physically migrate to Africa, while others emphasize the symbolic value of the idea of repatriation. Therefore, in all Rastafari diversity, we must grasp how religion-faith, race and morality figure into Rastafari identity. We should expect variation on these themes, and understand that there is no perfect match between what people say and what they do. For example, some Rastafari in Japan and Mexico emphasize race, though their position vis-à-vis Blackness is oblique.

PROPOSITION 2: BECOMING AND BEING RASTAFARI TYPICALLY INVOLVES AN IDENTITY TRANSFORMATION

Becoming and being Rastafari involves a religio-racial identity transformation. People become Rastafari because of specific experiences or *encounters* that unsettle their extant belief systems and lead them to transform their self-concept.

My interviews of and reasonings with foundation Rastafari indicate that their encounters took three primary forms: dreams; visions; and tangible happenings (for example, personally experiencing an act of injustice or chancing upon a Rastafari who embodies charisma). Such culturally framed experiences challenge existing understandings of the world—"I never considered that the Messiah could be Black" or "I now recognize that some categories of people are consistently mistreated and I realize that I am a member of that category"—and motivate people to revise how they view themselves and the world. Rastafari identity is one resolution to the challenge.

An exception to an encounter as a path to becoming Rastafari is socialization into Rastafari from an early age. The numbers of Rastafari have grown since the 1970s, and it is possible that more people have an opportunity to grow up in a Rastafari household than during the first two generations.

However, socialization into Rastafari identity does not rule out a person having an encounter experience. Several foundation Rastafari have told me how their parents were Rastafari and involved in Marcus Garvey's United Negro Improvement Association (UNIA). The UNIA introduced the parents and their offspring to pride in Blackness. Ras J's parents, for example, were Garveyites. His mother was zealously active in a Kingston UNIA chapter during the 1950s. Ras J, born around the early 1940s, was a cobbler with his own shop in Kingston when I first met him during the late 1990s. Both of Ras J's parents manifested Rastafari during the 1950s. He recalls learning affirmative stories of Black history and culture from an early age, before he reached his teen years. Ras J said, "Through them, the head, me inna it too" (that is, Ras J followed their example and instruction). In talking about his growth as a Rastafari, Ras J did not harp on his own miseducation or deracination, but instead spoke to the miseducation and deracination of other Blacks in ways that made it his own concern. His awareness of the tangible effects of miseducation and deracination on Black people, such as Eurocentrism or anti-Blackness, strengthened his conviction in the power of Rastafari identity.

PROPOSITION 3: RASTAFARI IDENTITY IS LEARNED

All identities are socially constructed, and a person must learn what is expected of a given identification and how to enact it. While aspects of an identity might be widely recognized—preferring or shunning certain foods and drinks, wearing certain garments or practising certain occupations—there will always be unevenness and varying competence in how people grasp and enact a given identity.

Consider becoming and being Rastafari in Cuba. Because of the limited access to information about Rastafari and Black history and culture, Cuban Rastafari scour disparate sources like reggae music or publications—access to both in Cuba being limited—to patch together a conception of Rastafari (Hansing 2006). Some Cubans latch onto the philosophy of Blackness, for example, but do not grasp why Haile Selassie I should be treated as divine. From the perspective of some of the foundation Rastafari from Jamaica, such people are on the path to Rastafari—revelation is activated—but they have not yet fully "sighted up" (gained substantial competence) Emperor Haile Selassie I.

My point here is not to argue what or who constitutes authentic Rastafari, but to propose the different ways that Rastafari is constituted in different places under different conditions. The role of context should be incorporated into any BRIT analysis.

During immersion and emersion, nascent Rastafari engage in activities that assist in reorganizing their self-concept. Through observation, reflection, emulation and practice, they create a set of cultural lenses informed by race and Rastafari faith. The revised self-concept provides a different way to interpret life, history, culture and the mysteries of the world. The information and relationships informing the revised self-concept become a basis for combating miseducation, deracination and racism.

Yet the path towards the revised self-concept can be ambiguous and discomforting at times. My research and personal experience offer many examples of people mortified by not knowing what to expect or do during their identity transformation. Yet, what I see is that many people "figure it out". During 2011, I listened to a young self-identified Black woman in Durham, North Carolina, immersed in identity transformation ask rhetorically, "How am I supposed to know when I really am Rasta?" She was giving voice to her anxiety: ambiguity and insecurity about one's competence in the emergent identity accompanying transformation. A perhaps unsatisfying answer to the woman's question is that you are a Rastafari when you know it yourself and when others affirm your identity by acknowledging it—whether they confirm or disparage it.

PROPOSITION 4: COMMITMENT TO RASTAFARI IDENTITY IS SUSTAINED THROUGH SOCIAL INTERACTION

What supports the internalization of and enduring commitment to Rastafari identity? Telling oneself that one is Rastafari is insufficient. People must, at varying times, begin to grant acknowledgement to the person as a Rastafari. Rastafari and non-Rastafari will exert varied influence on Rastafari identity formation. Both are important to an emergent Rastafari. One signals a transition into "insider" status, such as when one Rastafari greets another as Rastafari. Non-Rastafari might say something like "I see you now are different from who you were" or "Oh, you are a Rasta!" Recognition is an important element of internalization and commitment.

Brother Yendis, born around 1940, and who manifested Rastafari during the early 1960s, pointed out how people who hailed him as Rastafari were in effect confirming his identification as Rastafari. Censure can have a similar effect, as when Ras Brenton (also born around 1940, and who manifested Rastafari during the 1960s) was forcibly lobbied by his mother's female friend to give up growing locks. The woman was anti-Rastafari, yet her opinion mattered to Ras Brenton. Ultimately, the woman's scorn for Rastafari led Ras Brenton to believe that living with scorn was part of being Rastafari, and it strengthened his conviction in Rastafari.

Stigmatized groups need commitment-support mechanisms such as close-knit communities, rituals and narratives that exalt or rationalize their position as stigmatized people and communities (Kanter 1972; McGuire 1992, 82; Toch 1965). Examples such as these remind us of how the social construction of identity relies on the engagement—real and imagined—of other people.

Peers, relatives and friends are of consequence in identity transformation. These are some of the people who deliver feedback—positive and negative—to the emergent about becoming Rastafari. These and other people contribute both through their affirmation and disapproval to the construction of the "new" identity as Rastafari.

An emergent Rastafari must participate in activities that affirm and deepen their competence in the identity. Rituals, ceremonies and quotidian interactions enlighten practice and sustain commitment. For instance, participation in reasoning sessions with other Rastafari or participation in ceremonies such as Nyahbinghi ceremonies ("Groundation" in Rastafari parlance) generate community, provide an ongoing source of fuel for Rastafari identity and affirm one's connection to a community. A Nyahbinghi ceremony is a commemoration of Rastafari faith, culture and community that involves communal chanting, praying and reasoning that lasts for a day or several days. This ceremony is a means to creating community, communitas and transcendence. It is a context for communion and engagement with all the symbolism, meaning and mysteries of being Rastafari. A beloved Rastafari chant (hymn) often sung at Rastafari ceremonies says, "Every time I chant Nyahbinghi, I want to go home a yard . . . too tired of the sufferation, I want [to] go home a yard". The act of chanting reminds one why one is Rastafari, what is important to Rastafari (going to a place [yard] called home [Africa]) and that going home is important (because a suppressive politico-economic system causes too much suffering and pain). The chant gives meaning and affect to Rastafari concern with repatriation. One must learn such chants, the many meanings of such chants and what is expected during a Nyahbinghi ceremony as a part of becoming Rastafari. "Reasoning", a culturally particular Rastafari practice of critical and reflective analysis and learning among two or more Rastafari, reinforces thinking and being Rastafari.

Apostasy does happen. For example, I-Three's vocalist Judy Mowatt shifted from Rastafari to Christianity later in her life. However, given what I have learned, the bottom line on commitment is that once a person has invested substantially in creating and maintaining a new identity, they are inclined to hold onto it.

ETHNOGRAPHIC LIFE NARRATIVE METHODOLOGY AS A METHODOLOGY FOR STUDYING IDENTITY

I will close with a suggestion which is not structurally equivalent to the preceding propositions but is important to empirically investigating them. One way to qualitatively comprehend a person's identity and various identifications is to have Rastafari people talk about their life course and to participate in their daily activities. A life narrative strategy allows one to discern Rastafari identity formation in terms of personal-individual subjectivity, in terms of social interaction and social structures and in terms of historical influences. Given the continued growth of Rastafari, we must better grasp why and how people continue to become Rastafari in conditions different from those of the foundation Rastafari of Jamaica.

Life narrative methodologies record a person's experience and memories through retrospective in-depth interviewing and participant observation.

This information can be triangulated with other data, such as personal documents, news stories, institutional records and other individuals' knowledge about the life being explored. An ethnographic life narrative strategy, for example, could tell us about a person's pre-encounter life and about their encounter and why it was unsettling. An ethnographic life narrative strategy would provide opportunity to fathom how one cultivates their Rastafari or other identities. Life narrative strategies allow us to identify specific events and experiences involved in identity transformation, the various ways the identity is enacted in different contexts, and how participation in ceremonies, rituals and organizations informs internalization, commitment and maintenance of the identity. We could, for instance, learn more about how those alleged "individualistic" Rastafari maintain their commitment to Rastafari identity. A life narrative strategy would be illuminating in explaining apostasy or fixation on anger.

Life narrative approaches encompass many frameworks: biography, autobiography, life story, life history and testimony, to list a few. All of these can convey a person's life trajectory, or how they explain, in their own language, who they are and how they came to be who they say they are. It can be made into Rastafari-"sensitive scholarship" (Niaah 2005). One life narrative approach is not superior to the other; each has its own merits and limitations. Primary differences between the life narrative genres involve the degree of authority granted to the narrator and author (if they are not the same); whether the emphasis is on historical truth (facts, verification), narrative truth (meaning, experience) or some combination thereof; and how much of a person's life is focused upon (for example, an entire life or part of a life) (see Maynes et al. 2008).

Historical truth calls us to explain how we situate and interpret the stories told to us. We need to show that what we report can be confirmed, that our analysis draws on recognized methods and data, and that we can at least suggest how one or a set of life narratives helps us understand something significant about humankind. However, if a person tells us that a mile-long phalanx of steam liners will arrive to Jamaica to ferry those Black Jamaicans who want to repatriate to Africa, as I have been told, the work then is to show why and how a person believes this and how it informs their identity and action, not to focus on whether their claim is empirically verifiable. Here, narrative truth is relevant, as it allows us to identify the salience and meaning people attribute to aspects of their identity such as race and religion.

Ethnographic life narrative methodologies that are used in ways respectful of accuracy and meaning that use information from multiple sources are a solid way to grasp a person's multiple identities, and in our case, how people transform their self-concept to privilege categorical identities such as Blackness and Rastafari.

SHIFTS IN RASTAFARI IDENTITY FORMATION

The four propositions and methodological suggestion ought to be useful in assessing why and how people become Rastafari in contexts different from those of the foundation Rastafari. There now are additional paths and motivations to become Rastafari as well as different conceptions of Rastafari. The changed identity-scape is primarily a result of globalization and new technologies. Ideas, images and believers now traverse the world more rapidly than ever before, facilitated by the internet, air travel and national governments that are less threatened by new faith communities (than in the past).

A significant new shift involves awareness ignited through reggae music and writings about the Rastafari. Foundation Rastafari were introduced to Rastafari through word-of-mouth, street preachers, news stories and observations of actual Rastafari. Textual media were utilized where they were accessible, but what little writing was available to them was about Black history and culture, not the Rastafari themselves (for example, the *Holy Piby, Promised Key*, and Garvey's publications like *Negro World*). The preponderance of writing about the Rastafari into the 1970s was published in Jamaican newspapers, and most of it was scandalous. Such shifts suggest the value of temporalizing identity formation in comparative and historical ways.

Sterling (2010), Posadas (2010) and Glazier (2006) identify reggae music as a significant factor attracting people to Rastafari. The people these scholars focus on became Rastafari post-1970, whereas Barrett (1967), Yawney (1978), Homiak (1985), Chevannes (1989; 1984) and Price (2009), for example, examined being Rastafari through the experience of foundation elders who became Rastafari before the early 1970s and the rise of reggae as an internationally popular music. Reggae music, originally Jamaican popular music and now world music, has communicated Rastafari knowledge and concerns such as criticism of injustice. In terms of reaching people, new sources of information about Rastafari like reggae music are readily available for consumption in ways more accessible than early textual media like the *Holy Piby* (which were suppressed by colonial authorities) and more efficiently broadcast than street preachers. For example, I met a group of twentyish-year-old Spanish-speaking Rastafari in Tampa, Florida, who hailed from Puerto Rico and Venezuela. They were inspired by reggae music. Their encounter involved the music of Bob Marley and the Wailers and other foundation Rastafari musicians, urging them to address their own miseducation and cultivate the identity Rastafari.[4]

The centrality of Blackness to Rastafari identity is shifting among new generations of Rastafari, including people who are not phenotypically or culturally designated as Black. Today, some Rastafari emphasize Blackness as central to their identity while others do not. For example, some African Rastafari emphasize being native Africans in addition to valorizing Black culture and history (Middleton 2006). In New Zealand, where valorized Blackness is a limited cultural resource, Maori people have determined to emphasize Blackness (Hawkeswood 1983). In Cuba, Blackness is salient, although details about it beyond Cuban experience are limited (Hansing 2006). Cuba has a tradition of valorized Blackness epitomized by the many UNIA chapters created there (Bonacci 2015; Castillo and Castillo 2000), though this tradition appears to have attenuated since the decline of Garveyism. Japanese Rastafari do not valorize Blackness. According to Sterling, Japanese Rastafari abstract Blackness from its "human referents" to use it in "rethinking one's life circumstance" (2010, 4–5). Race is not jettisoned but reframed into a Japanese idiom. Therefore, as Rastafari identity evolves, we must pay attention to the role of Blackness and conceptions of Emperor Selassie I in twenty-first century Rastafari identity transformation.

Another significant shift involves how Rastafari people conceive of Emperor Haile Selassie I. Foundation Rastafari expressed two predominant views. One view is the Emperor as Messiah and God Almighty, period. The other is that the Emperor is the Christ returned, not God writ large. New views emerged with subsequent generations of Rastafari, including one that does not mark Haile Selassie I as divine. Instead, Emperor Selassie I is treated as a revered figure but not divine (see Barnett 2005). Some African Rastafari find it difficult to divinize Emperor Selassie I because they see him as another African ruler with a questionable record (MacLeod 2014; Middleton 2006). Indisputably, the evolution of the Rastafari now involves shifts in why and how contemporary people become Rastafari. An issue at present and moving forward is identifying what are the pillars of Rastafari identity for various Rastafari communities in different places in the world.

CONCLUSION: ANOTHER WORLD IS POSSIBLE AND IT BEGINS WITH I

It is not uncommon to hear people express a desire for living in a "better world" or "another world". It is also not uncommon that people try to create another world by remaking themselves. Faith communities and social movements are instrumental in changing the world in the sense described here. Ultimately, change begins with oneself. When amplified by like-minded people, the material world, or at least parts of it, can as a result be changed. Beginning as a handful of misinterpreted and maligned people during the early 1930s, enough individuals found the idea of a Black African Messiah who signalled a new dispensation compelling enough to bear a cross in order to wear the crown of Rastafari. However, these individuals contributed to the growth of a collectivity that shifted the attitudes of Jamaicans and people of other nationalities in ways that valorized Black identity, history and culture. The Rastafari over four decades shifted from being pariahs to exemplars of Black identity and culture. Yet, for nearly seven decades, it was mainly Rasta people who knew the experience of becoming Rastafari. Scholars (and pundits) were interested in other things—cultism, dispossession, deprivation, racial fanaticism—and thus neglected the very thing, identity, that would help all make sense of both the Rastafari and Rastafari identity. To grasp why and how people become Rastafari, we must ask them and make sense of what they say in the context of their life course, relationships and environment.

We know enough about identity formation—racial and religious, for our purpose—to explain why and how people revise their self-concept to valorize Blackness and Rastafari identity. BRITs like Nigrescence Theory provide a frame for making sense of why and how people become Rastafari. I have suggested that BRITs, in the case of Rastafari identity, be revised to account for the intersection of race *and* faith.

Becoming Rastafari, especially among the foundation Rastafari, entails an identity transformation where Blackness and Rastafari—a morally configured religio-racial consciousness—become central to a person's revised self-concept. Like any identity, one must learn what the identity entails, and like any identity, much learning occurs through interaction with other people. The learning involves re-education and resocialization. Not only must an emergent Rastafari demonstrate their authenticity to others, they must generate and pursue situations and relationships that sustain Rastafari identity. The challenge for the emergent Rastafari is to look, talk, act and relate like a Rastafari—whatever that means in each place and given time. Arguments about authenticity imply both conceptions of ideal types of Rastafari and variation on the ideal types. The wider the range of actual variation, the greater the opportunity for new members to assume an identity as Rastafari, or to assume only parts of it. For example, wearing dreadlocks or Rastafari insignia, but not holding Haile Selassie I as divine.

Given that Rastafari as an identification persists and settles into new places and among new populations, we should feel a greater urge to explain the appeal, manifestation and function of Rastafari yesterday and today. I have offered some propositions about Rastafari identity that should function as a baseline or starting point for inquiry, not as an inflexible schema for ascribing authenticity or minimizing the complexities of identity formation/transformation.

Acknowledgments: I thank my research assistant Mary G. Krause for assisting with sources, formatting, and other matters, Robert Sauté for providing feedback on an early draft, and Michael Barnett for encouraging the line of thought I pursued.

Notes

1 The way that observers spell Rastafari has shifted over time. The prevailing convention now is one word, typically Rastafari and Rastafarian.

2 Some scholars have raised questions about the motivation for conducting the research in the first place: it was part of an intelligence operation to suss out Rastafari organization, leadership and activism (Hill 2013; Clarke 2016).

3 While people can revise-transform their self-concept, it can be a monumental challenge because one must deal with how others react to the change.

4 I met this group in 1991.

References

Austin, Algernon. 2006. *Achieving Blackness: Race, Black Nationalism, and Afrocentrism in the Twentieth Century*. New York: New York University Press.

Barnett, Michael. 2005. "The Many Faces of Rasta: Doctrinal Diversity within the Rastafari". *Caribbean Quarterly* 51 (2): 67–78.

Barrett, Leonard. 1967. "The Rastafarians: A Study in Messianic Cultism in Jamaica, West Indies". PhD diss., Temple University.

Bonacci, Giulia. 2015. *Exodus! Heirs and Pioneers, Rastafari Return to Ethiopia*. Kingston: The University of the West Indies Press.

Bourdieu, Pierre. 1977. *Outline of a Theory of Practice*. New York: Cambridge University Press.

Brown, Samuel. 1966. "Treatise on the Rastafarian Movement". *Caribbean Studies* 6 (1): 39–40.

Burke, Peter J. 2003. "Introduction". In *Advances in Identity Theory and Research*, edited by Peter J. Burke, Timothy J. Owens, Richard Serpe, and Peggy A. Thoits, 1–7. New York: Kluwer Academic/Plenum Publishers.

Castillo Bueno, María de, and Daisy Rubiera Castillo. 2000. *Reyita: The Life of a Black Cuban Woman in the Twentieth Century*. Durham, NC: Duke University Press.

Cha-Jua, Sundiata K. 1998. "C. L. R. James, Blackness, and the Making of a Neo-Marxist Diasporan Historiography". *Nature, Society, and Thought* 11 (1): 53–89.

Charles, Christopher. 2015. "The Process of Becoming Black: Leonard Howell and the Manifestation of Rastafari". In *Leonard Percival Howell and the Genesis of Rastafari*, edited by Clinton A. Hutton, Michael A. Barnett, D.A. Dunkley, and Jahlani A.H. Niaah, 155–171. Kingston: The University of the West Indies Press.

Chevannes, Barrington. 1989. "Social and Ideological Origins of the Rastafari Movement in Jamaica". PhD diss., Columbia University

_____. 1994. *Rastafari: Roots and Ideology*. New York: Syracuse University Press.

Clarke, Colin. 2016. *Race, Class, and the Politics of Decolonization: Jamaica Journals, 1961 and 1968*. Basingstoke: Palgrave Macmillan.

Coltri, Marzia Anna. 2015. *Beyond Rastafari: An Historical and Theological Introduction*. New York: Peter Lang/Internationaler Verlag der Wissenschaften.

Cross, William, Jr. 1971. "The Negro-to-Black Conversion Experience". *Black World* 20:13–27.

_____. 1995. "The Psychology of Nigrescence: Revising the Cross Model". In *Handbook of Multicultural Counseling*, edited by Joseph G. Ponterotto, J. Manuel Casas, Lisa A. Suzuki, and Charlene M. Alexander, 93–122. Thousand Oaks, CA: Sage Publications.

_____. 2001. "Encountering Nigrescence". In *Handbook of Multicultural Counseling*, edited by Joseph G. Ponterotto, J. Manuel Casas, Lisa A. Suzuki, and Charlene M. Alexander, 30–44. Thousand Oaks, CA: Sage Publications.

_____. 2012. "Enactment of Race and Other Social Identities during Everyday Transactions". In *New Perspectives on Racial Identity Development: Integrating Emerging Frameworks*, edited by Charmaine L. Wijeyesinghe and Bailey W. Jackson, 192–210. New York: New York University Press.

Cross, William E., Thomas A. Parham, and J.E. Helms. 1998. "Nigrescence Revisited: Theory and Research". In *African American Identity Development*, edited by R. L. Jones, 3–71. Hampton, VA: Cobb and Henry Publishers.

Glazier, Stephen. 2006. "Being and Becoming a Rastafarian: Notes on the Anthropology of Religious Conversion". In *Rastafari: A Universal Philosophy in the Third Millennium*, edited by Werner Zips, 256–281. Kingston, JA: Ian Randle Publishers.

Gooren, Henri. 2014. "Anthropology of Religious Conversion". In *The Oxford Handbook of Religious Conversion,* edited by Lewis R. Rambo and Charles E. Farhadian. New York: Oxford University Press.

Hansing, Katrin. 2006. *Rasta, Race and Revolution: The Emergence and Development of the Rastafari Movement in Socialist Cuba*. Münster, DE: LIT Verlag.

Hawkeswood, William E. 1983. "I'N'I Rastafari: Identity and the Rasta Movement in Auckland". MA thesis, University of Auckland.

Helms, Janet. 1990. "Introduction: Review of Racial Identity Terminology". In *Black and White Racial Identity: Theory, Research, and Practice*, edited by Janet Helms, 3–8. New York: Greenwood Press.

Henriques, Fernando. 1953. *Family and Colour in Jamaica*. London: MacGibbon and Kee.

Hill, Robert (with Annie Paul). 2013. "Our Man in Mona: A Conversation between Robert A. Hill and Annie Paul". https://anniepaul.net/our-man-in-mona-an-interview-by-robert-a-hill-with-annie-paul/.

Homiak, John P. 1985. "The 'Ancients of Days' Seated Black: Eldership, Oral Tradition, and Ritual in Rastafari Culture". PhD diss., Brandeis University.

_____. 1998. "Dub History: Soundings on Rastafari Livity and Language". In *Rastafari and Other African-Caribbean Worldviews*, edited by Barry Chevannes, 127–181. New Brunswick, NJ: Rutgers University Press.

Jackson, Bailey. 2012. "Black Identity Development: Influences of Culture and Social Oppression". In *New Perspectives on Racial Identity Development: Integrating Emerging Frameworks*, edited by C. Wijeyesinghe and B. Jackson, 33–50. New York: New York University Press.

Jindra, Ines W. 2014. *A New Model of Religious Conversion: Beyond Network Theory and Social Constructivism*. Leiden, NL: Brill.

Kanter, Rosabeth. 1972. *Commitment and Community: Communes and Utopians in Sociological Perspective*. Cambridge, MA: Harvard University Press.

Leary, Mark, and June Tangney. 2005. *Handbook of Self and Identity*. New York: Guilford Press.

Mack, Douglas R.A. 1999. *From Babylon to Rastafari: Origin and History of the Rastafari Movement*. Chicago, IL: Frontline Distribution International.

MacLeod, Erin C. 2014. *Visions of Zion: Ethiopians and Rastafari in the Search for the Promised Land*. New York: New York University Press.

Maynes, Mary J., Jennifer L. Pierce, and Barbara Laslett. 2008. *Telling Stories: The Use of Personal Narratives in the Social Sciences and History*. Ithaca, NY: Cornell University Press.

McGuire, Meredith. 1992. *Religion: The Social Context*. Belmont: Wadsworth Publishing.

Middleton, Darren. 2006. "As It Is in Zion: Seeking the Rastafari in Ghana, West Africa". *Black Theology: An International Journal* 4 (2): 151–172.

Minda, Ababu. 2004. "Rastafari in 'The Promised Land': A Change of Identity". *Africa Insight* 34 (4): 31–39.

Niaah, Jahlani. 2005. "Sensitive Scholarship: A Review of Rastafari Literature(s)". *Caribbean Quarterly* 51 (3/4): 11–34.

_____, and Erin MacLeod (eds.). 2013. *Let Us Start with Africa: Foundations of Rastafari Scholarship*. Mona, JM: University of the West Indies Press.

Posadas, Monique. 2010. "Reasoning Sessions with Irie Vatos: Mexican American Rastafari Identity". Unpublished manuscript.

Premawardhana, Shanta. 2015. *Religious Conversion: Religion Scholars Thinking Together*. West Sussex, UK: Wiley Blackwell.

Price, Charles. 2003. "'Cleave to the Black': Expressions of Ethiopianism in Jamaica". *New West Indian Guide* 77 (1 & 2): 31–64.

_____. 2009. *Becoming Rasta: Origins of Rastafari Identity in Jamaica*. New York: New York University Press.

_____. 2014. "The Cultural Production of a Black Messiah: Ethiopianism and the Rastafari". *Journal of Africana Religions* 2 (3): 418–433.

_____. 2018a: "A Meta-Ethnographic Analysis of Black Racial Identity Theory". In *The Cultural Construction of Identity: Meta-Ethnographies and Theory*, edited by Luis Urrieta and George Noblit. New York: Oxford University Press.

_____. 2018b: "Outlining a Strategy for Studying Race, Identity, and Acts of Political Significance: Black Racial Identity Theory and the Rastafari of Jamaica". In *Political Sentiments and Social Movements*, edited by Claudia Strauss and Jack Friedman. London: Palgrave Macmillan.

Rambo, Lewis. 1993. *Understanding Religious Conversion*. New Haven: Yale University Press.

Raphasha, Makgompi. 2002. "Misrecognition and Nonrecognition of Rastafarian Identity in South Africa: A Critique of 'Prince.'" MA thesis, University of Toronto.

Sellers, Robert M., Mia A. Smith, J. Nicole Shelton, Stephanie A.J. Rowley, and Tabbye M. Chavous. 1998. "Multidimensional Model of Racial Identity: A Reconceptualization of African American Racial Identity". *Personality and Social Psychology Review* 2 (1): 18–39.

Simpson, George Eaton. 1955a. "The Ras Tafari Movement in Jamaica: A Study of Race and Class Conflict". *Social Forces* 34 (2): 167–171.

_____ 1955b. "Political Cultism in West Kingston, Jamaica". *Social and Economic Studies* 4 (2): 133–149.

Smith, M.G., Roy Augier, and Rex Nettleford. 1960. *The Ras Tafari in Kingston, Jamaica*. Mona, JM: Institute of Social and Economic Research, University of the West Indies.

Sterling, Marvin. 2010. *Babylon East: Performing Dancehall, Roots Reggae, and Rastafari in Japan*. Durham, NC: Duke University Press.

Toch, Hans. 1965. *The Social Psychology of Social Movements*. Indianapolis, IN: Bobbs-Merrill.

Wittman, Frank. 2011. "The Global-Local Nexus: Popular Music Studies and the Rastafari in West Africa". *Critical Arts* 25 (2): 150–174.

Yawney, Carole D. 1978. "Lions in Babylon: the Rastafarians of Jamaica as a Visionary Movement". PhD diss., McGill University.

LIVITY AND LAW

RICHARD C. SALTER

Abstract   *Livity* is difficult to define because it is a moving target, manifesting itself in particular instances, but remaining hidden at a general level. *Livity* is always related to context. Among other things, the law is one force shaping the world in which *livity* emerges. This chapter presents four intrinsic features of Rastafari (newness, authority structure, tension with the world and symbols) that shape the relationship of *livity* and the law, plus four institutional contexts (work, courts, schools and prisons) where this relationship is tested in particularly interesting ways. *Livity* cannot be pinned down as a set of universal rules, but we can begin to understand how it works itself out if we focus on key elements of Rastafari and how those are tested in particular social contexts.

Keywords • Law • court • school • prison • religion

IDEAZ—an interdisciplinary social science & humanities journal, vol. 15, 2020, pp.134-149

The terms *livity* and law are both fuzzy because each encompasses so many different features. While it may be helpful to clarify what each means, we also have to be on guard against the kind of over-specification that would rob the terms of their dynamism. That is, we have to remain aware that *livity* is a practical relationship to the world, changing based not only on circumstances in the world, but also on the basis of a Rasta's own self-understanding. In this sense it resonates with the term "lived religion" as it is used in the work of scholars like David D. Hall and Robert Orsi. Hall (1997) might be paraphrased as conceiving of "lived religion" as the practice whereby what constitutes people's "religion" is worked out in everyday life. For Orsi (2010, xxxi), "lived religion" is "religious practice and imagination in ongoing, dynamic relation with the realities and structures of everyday life in particular times and places". These "realities and structures" include everything from the realities of power (e.g., in racism) to the specific structures of government, schools, the courts and the economy. Behind these thinkers one finds the broader "turn to practice" which has informed anthropology, sociology and history over the last fifty years, much of which has its roots in the early work on practice by Pierre Bourdieu.[1] Approaching *livity* not as a fixed doctrinal concept (a belief, a *doxa* or pre-accepted notion), but instead as practice, an ongoing relationship to the world, preserves the sense that *livity* is always being worked out anew in new circumstances. Additionally, it recognizes that *livity* does not exist subjectively in Rastas, nor objectively as a fixed tenet of Rastafari, but only in the relation to the world which is being enacted by actual Rastas living actual lives. This approach also seems faithful to Rasta self-understanding as a "way" of life with its rich organic and dynamic overtones. Thus, scholars who are interested in *livity* must also devote themselves to understanding not only Rastas as they live, but also the social, cultural and institutional structures within which *livity* occurs. This chapter follows the lived religion approach on a macro level by suggesting where future scholars might look and what questions they might ask as they examine how *livity* is worked out in relation to law.

Like *livity*, the word "law" uncovers a tangled morass, pointing at once to everything from the distinct criminal and civil laws in any jurisdiction's legal code, to general principles embedded in various constitutional laws, to notions of natural law, moral law, customary law and religious (and biblical) law that serve as a backdrop or foundation for the legal system. Disentangling the relationship of each of these to Rasta life would be a valuable but encyclopedic task. Instead, here I will use the terms *livity* and law broadly and ask the reader to keep in mind that the specific meaning of the term will vary. Indeed, it is the variation and movement in the relationship of *livity* and law that is so fascinating, for depending on context each may refer to different things.

Rastafari has developed rapidly in a short historical period that has itself been marked by massive social change. Having started in Jamaica in the 1930s and spread first to other Commonwealth countries, Rastafari was once an exclusively Black, poor and marginalized religion in white controlled, capitalist, Eurocentric, colonized countries; its concerns related to that context and focused on redemption of Black people from an unjust and corrupt system of oppression (*Babylon*). Although Rastafari remains intimately connected to those roots, it is now a religion of the world, including people of many racial and ethnic backgrounds, occupations and income levels; its concerns are now related to its new contexts, and though justice remains as much a focus as it ever was, the meaning of justice in these new contexts is still emerging.

We cannot know how *livity* and law will develop in the future, but we can begin to map out some of the general features of the terrain that will shape it and point to some further avenues for research. I propose four features that will be especially important as the movement *trods* on. First, social changes have set a wider context for the Rastafari relation to the law, facilitating its recognition as a religion (and of the rights it may have as a religious group) and expanding the range of reference groups with which it connects. Second, the broad ethos of respect for law in Rastafari will continue to bring Rastas to court, especially as they have the means and support to file cases, and will increase legal recognition of Rastafari as a religion. Nonetheless, and third, particular intrinsic features of Rastafari as a religion will continue to unsettle its relationship to the law. Consequently, and fourth, the specific institutional contexts in which Rastas live their relationship to the law will continue to raise civil rights, human rights and justice concerns *in particular rather than general ways*. How those concerns are worked through will not only affect Rastafari as it is lived in those contexts, but will also affect the nature of the movement more profoundly by requiring increased specificity and clarity in articulations about what Rastafari requires of Rastas. These statements in turn will produce a further rationalization and routinization of Rastafari, processes that may challenge Rastafari's radical prophetic and mystical dimensions.[2]

SOCIAL CHANGES: PLURALISM, HUMAN RIGHTS AND SECULARISM

The relationship of any religion and the law depends in part on the society that contains it. Rastafari has developed at a time when societies have become more pluralistic, concepts of human rights have expanded and been formalized, and the legal system has become more secular. These changes mean that the legal system no longer is meant to serve the interests of particular religions such as Christianity. Instead, the law is accountable to a broader concept of rights and must take into account a wider range of religions. At an impressionistic level it is conspicuous how frequently Rasta, Sikh and Muslim lawsuits over hair and head covering policies reference one another's faiths. Pluralization can both heighten the sense that one is being treated unfairly and heighten solidarity with others in a similar position.

Similarly, as concepts of human rights have expanded, Rastafari discourse about injustice can attach itself to and contribute to broader discussions of rights, thereby gaining a wider audience and automatically having a discursive framework in which to articulate its claims. Rastafari has always been a religion in motion physically (through work, migration, repatriation), and thus connected to a wider world, and the discussion of global human rights has provided another vehicle through which Rastas reach beyond the limits of their local context.

Even more important than pluralization and human rights, secularization has meant that, without a commitment to confessional religion, the legal criteria for what constitutes religion itself has changed. Perhaps the most illustrative case in the United States in this regard is *United States v. Ballard*, 322 US 78 (1944). In *Ballard* the US Supreme Court explicitly eliminates truth as a criterion for a religion, instead turning to the more subjective question of the quality of belief (e.g., is it deeply held and sincere). In recent years, even this latter consideration has been challenged as courts in various countries have been asked to rule on rights for believers in the International Church of Jediism or Pastafarianism (the latter an explicit parody of Intelligent Design), both of which call into question the seriousness of belief. Rulings on the recognition of these groups have been mixed, leading to the impression that the law is in a bind: on the one hand it protects the rights of religious groups, but on the other it seems unwilling (or, in the United States, constitutionally unable) to define exactly what religion is.

Nonetheless, as our canons about what constitutes religion have become less well defined, we have relied less on external and formal criteria of what constitutes religion and more on individual accounts of religiosity. By definition, the latter are idiosyncratic. Most concretely, the role of the law with regard to religion has changed from upholding historical religions and traditional definitions of religion to defending the value and right to individual choice in religion. This social development changes Rastafari's relationship to the law insofar as it adds plausibility to religious demands based in individual mystical revelation and interpretation—that is, claims that once might have been dismissed as individual rantings are taken at face value.

LAW IN RASTAFARI ETHOS

Social changes notwithstanding, where do we start exploring specifically Rastafari's relationship to the law? One approach in the past has been to explore the more salacious cases where Rastas have butted heads with the law or to fetishize the conflict with the law that is sometimes seen in cannabis cases. But an approach too focused on conflict foregrounds Rastafari's adversarial relationship with the law. Since the vast majority of Rastafari are *not* in conflict with the law, foregrounding conflict would be inaccurate. Let's start instead with a broader view of what we might call the place of the law in Rastafari ethos.[3]

Rastafari as a whole cultivates a profound respect and hope for the law, particularly as it serves as an instrument of justice. The stereotype of Rastafari in conflict with the law is actually a misreading of Rastafari tensions with an oppressive system (*Babylon*). Even when conflict with *Babylon* includes legal conflict, the conflict is with specific laws that are felt to target Rastas unfairly or unjust applications of the law that favour the powerful over the disadvantaged.

Rastafari typically includes a strong sense of codes and precepts by which to live—many of which, because of common biblical roots, overlap with typical Western positive attitudes towards the law. We now find Rasta lawyers, Rasta legislators, Rasta security guards, Rasta police officers and Rasta prison guards. Instead of exacerbating racial tensions, Rasta peace officers from the Haile Selassie Peace Foundation joined cooperatively with West Midlands police officers in joint neighborhood patrols in Birmingham, England. And in civil law, Rasta plaintiffs often seek just and peaceful resolution of problems *through* the courts. Cases in which Rastas have joined with others to sue for damages from the historical injustices of the trans-Atlantic slave trade show just how deep the faith in law extends.

Whether Rastas actually expect to win these suits is irrelevant; the point is going to court. Even Rasta parodies of the law express a deep hope for legal justice. The Prince Buster/Mutabaruka Judge Dread songs place slave society, Jamaican politics, "religion" and "denomination" on trial in a "People's Court" for their disregard of and "poly-tricks" on Black people.

Without a foundational hope for the law, such parodies do not make sense.[4]

At least at an aspirational level, Rastafari embraces law as a means to justice. As Rastas are increasingly in social positions which give them access to civil courts, we will see Rastas continue to use the law in pursuit of justice. One line of future research into *livity* and law will be to trace how Rastafari notions of law shift from more content-specific religious understandings (such as that found in Levitical law or in various biblically grounded versions of natural law) to more secular formal and procedural ideas of law as the courts become more accessible to Rastas. For example, insofar as different groups of Rastas have different levels of access to courts, will we see a divergence among different Rasta groups' understandings of law?

Intrinsic Features of Rastafari Structuring *Livity* and the Law

But if the ethos of Rastafari for the law is rooted in respect and hope, there are also several intrinsic features of Rastafari that complicate its relationship to the law. Among the most important of these are that it is a new religion, with an organizational structure that gives priority to the individual, that is often in tension with the world, but with symbols easily coopted by the world. Each one of these features of Rastafari has shaped its relationship with the law, but none of them is determinative.

Rastafari Is New

As a new religion, Rastafari has had to struggle for recognition and the rights that recognition might bring. In the contemporary West, where aesthetic styles and even religious beliefs are now generally considered a matter of individual conscience, it can be hard to understand just how earth-shattering it would have been for Rastas to say that a Black man is God, that beards are biblically mandated, that ("black", tightly curled, "nappy") hair should be uncombed and embraced in its natural form, or that people of African descent will be returned to Africa by a Black king. As individual preferences, these beliefs and practices may seem insignificant to us, but in the decades after Rastafari started, and even now in many places, they have been perceived as an assault on not only conventional religion, but on truth and decency itself, and therefore they were condemned with comments like, "They just don't want to comb their hair" or "They just want to smoke weed" or "They are a bunch of criminals". These comments should be recognized as not only comments specifically about hair or cannabis or relation to the law, but also as ways to undermine Rastafari challenges to broader social norms and to push Rastas further outside the boundaries of acceptable society.

Law formalizes social concepts of what is acceptable, so when Rastafari are labeled as deviant, a particular set of relationships with the law, ranging from intentional avoidance to outright persecution, is almost inevitable. Insofar as avoidance and persecution both make a group marginal, the law sometimes functions as a self-fulfilling prophecy, rendering marginal exactly what it seeks to guard against. A few examples from the history of Rastafari illustrate the process:

In the notorious 1959 Claudius Henry case, the son of a Rastafari leader, Claudius Henry, was found to be involved in a plot to overthrow the Jamaican government. The case was reported widely (and internationally), and as a result a link of Rastafari with treason and subversion was cemented in the minds of many Jamaicans and others. This link seemed to justify police persecution of Rastas, which had already been taking place for many years, and ultimately led to other notorious incidents of clearances of Rasta dwellings, mass arrests, forcible shavings/trimmings of hair and other persecutions. In Dominica, the so-called Dread Act, which permitted citizens to "shoot on sight" people with dreadlocks, legalized systematic violent persecution of Rastafari. The act was later amended into an antiterror act, but rather than ameliorate persecution of Rastafari, it simply associated them with the term "terrorism", again formalizing their position as unacceptable. And in the British Virgin Islands, legislation popularly known as the Rasta Law was passed that allowed immigration officials to deny entry to those with dreadlocks (and other forms of long hair). In this case, Rastafari had been associated popularly with drug use, stealing fruit, and sexual lasciviousness and a "hippie" subculture that was deemed undesirable.

When Rastas want legal rights as members of a religion, they must convince others that they should be recognized as such, a task that is more difficult when one is new or different from other religions. For Rastafari the task is made more difficult by their typical criticism of *Babylon*, since that criticism often includes a criticism or disavowal of "religion". In practice, this has meant that many Rastafari have denied that they are a "religion", instead opting for the label "way of life", "livity" or some other name. Outside of a legal context, Rastas often deny they are a "religion" because of the association they make between the word "religion" and the various historical organizations, denominations and ideologies ("-isms") associated with the word religion and the ways those ideologies have been implicated in slavery, colonization, racism and other injustices.

But there are no legal rights to a "way of life", so at other moments Rastafari must embrace its status as a religion. Over time courts have come to recognize Rastafari as having the formal attributes that would allow it to be classified as a religion in a legal sense. But as we will see below, such recognition can itself carry consequences.

Organization and Authority

Rastafari is recognized as a religion by many courts, but it is not always clear what exactly the courts are recognizing: there is no central organization that defines Rastafari orthodoxy, no universal creed accepted by all Rastas, and no hierarchy defining the relationship of individual practitioners to the religion. In fact, one of the hallmarks of Rastafari as a "way of life" is that it is up to the individual (the *I*) to see and embrace the truth—something done differently depending on each individual and where he or she is in the journey of seeing the world. In practice this means that individual Rastas may have deeply held but idiosyncratic beliefs that are perfectly in line with their Rastafari faith, but which are not shared by others who are also Rastas (e.g., whether to eat salt, degrees of vegetarianism, whether to wear shoes, how to wear/cover dreadlocks or not, on what to drum and other things).

It has often been remarked that Rastafari stress on the *I* gives it an acephalous or omnicephalous structure. There are important elders and others whose opinions carry great weight, and there are similarities among many Rasta beliefs and practices, but these develop differently in different locations (partly due to the relatively independent development of Rastafari in different locations), and the final arbiter is always the individual him or herself. For the uninformed, the emphasis on the individual can make it look like the only thing that unites Rastafari is the desire to do whatever they want to do.

Moreover, since Rastafari is more interested in how one lives than in what one believes, it blurs distinctions between "religion", "culture" and "politics". The key place of the *I* has led to an emphasis on reasoning practically about how to live, testing one's choices through experience, prayer and reasoning with others, instead of basing decisions on pre-existing doctrinal statements. One Rastafari criticism of mainstream religions has been that people are asked to follow them "blindly", opening up possibilities for deception.

Making matters more complicated, some larger Rastafari groups *are* well organized, with formal hierarchies, liturgies, creedal statements and rituals. Examples of these groups include the Nyahbinghi Order, the Bobo Shanti, the Twelve Tribes of Israel and the Church of Haile Selassie I (aka Ba Beta Kristiyan Haile Selassie I). As Rastafari becomes more well known and seeks institutional (and legal) recognition, some of these groups have also sought to define a Rastafari orthodoxy (for example, by affirming the theological principle that Haile Selassie is the Creator God, by affirming the liturgical principle that cannabis is a *sine qua non* of Rasta worship, by claiming the necessity of certain items in worship, or even by clarifying the historical relationship of Rastafari to Christianity). Is there an "elective affinity" of the legal system and other institutions towards those Rastafari organizations that best rationalize and systematize the faith, thereby providing criteria for what is necessary to the religion? If so, future research should detail the form it takes, how it varies depending on context, and what its effects are on Rastafari as a whole (for example, will the emphasis on the *I* diminish as Rastafari systematizes?).

Tension with the World

Rastas typically embrace the natural world, according great respect to and venerating the power of life that radiates through Creation. But Rastas are also in tension with the world insofar as they see that the world as it was created is not the world in which we live; we live in a world of injustice and corruption caused by people and the socio-historical structures people have created. The term *Babylon* not only condemns the existing unjust world order, but it also recognizes it as temporary and unnecessary. Rastafari criticisms of *Babylon* have been merciless in part because the end of *Babylon* has already been foretold and promised. Rastas do not think *Babylon* will fall—they know it.

At the same time, millenarian expectations about the fall of *Babylon* have softened over time, and as Rastafari has become more accepted and recognized, individual Rastas have also found greater integration and accommodation in the world. Whereas early Rastas may have expected the millennium to arrive any day, specifically in the form of ships that would transport Rastafari faithful back to Africa, the millennial expectations of most Rastas today are less precise. Ideas about redemption and repatriation remain central, but there is a sense that the fall of *Babylon* will not come suddenly. Contemporary Rastafari tension with the world is less about the impending millennium, and more about the limits imposed by society on individuals seeking to express or live out Rastafari. Interestingly, in what would have been unthinkable a generation ago, governments may even assist Rastas in their quest to live their lives according to conscience: the US Equal Opportunity Employment Commission webpage lists several suits it has brought under Title VII of the 1964 Civil Rights Act to defend the rights of Rastas to non-discrimination in the workplace and to wear religiously required head gear, hairstyles and facial hair.

One area where the limits of religious expression continue to be challenged has been in anti-drug legislation targeting cannabis. Rastafari has often valued cannabis for its ability to assist one to see beyond the veil of *Babylon*. In most places, until recently, cannabis has been criminally illegal, so Rastas who used cannabis have had to deal with laws that explicitly prohibit an important part of their practice. Yet, as Rastafari has become more well known and widely accepted in popular culture, especially through reggae music and the cooptation of Rastafari symbols as emblematic of a no-worry "island lifestyle", cannabis use has also become more socially accepted. A crucial question about *livity* and law is whether Rasta tension with the world will continue to soften as cannabis is legalized or decriminalized?

Rastafari Symbols and Counterculture

Finally, the relationship of Rastafari and the legal system is unsettled by the difficulty Rastafari has had in controlling its own image and identity.

Rastafari has given rise to and is closely linked to a set of cultural symbols and practices that are broadly appealing in non-religious ways to others.[5] As free-floating signifiers, these symbols can be used broadly to express everything from protest over injustice, to antinomian terrorists,[6] to Caribbean tourist destinations of easy living, relaxation and getting high. Because these symbols float relatively independently from Rastafari, people take up some parts of Rastafari without taking up other parts, blurring what it means to be part of the movement. One effect of such cherry-picking of ideas and practices is to minimize the historical complexity and seriousness of the religion, reducing it at times to what its critics say it is: a justification for a sophomoric rebellion against authority.

At the same time, as Rastafari images and symbols become more globally available, there have been some surprising attempts to control the image of Rastafari. Rapper Snoop Dogg famously changed his name to Snoop Lion after encountering Rastafari in Jamaica, but several prominent Rastas including Bunny Wailer and the Rastafari Millennium Council were not convinced of the sincerity of his experience, alleged that he used Rastafari symbols solely for personal gain, and then "excommunicated" him and threatened to sue him. Future research on *livity* and law should consider how the free-floating nature of Rastafari symbols shapes Rasta lawsuits. Could the legal system ultimately become a tool for protecting or maintaining Rastafari boundaries?

Institutional Contexts:
Work, Courts, Schools, Prisons

The Rastafari relationship to the law is contextualized by social changes, founded on an ethos of deep regard for law, and unsettled by intrinsic features of the movement. Four institutional contexts show how *livity* and law relate most publicly: work, courts, schools and prisons.

– Work

Although it is the broadest and, arguably, the most important context for Rastafari's relationship to the law, work (employment) situations are difficult to treat systematically because they are each so different. Where conflicts have arisen, they have often been related to questions of the degree to which owners and managers can impose particular conforming hairstyles and uniforms, the degree to which reasonable accommodations (including alternative styles or uniforms) can be made for the religious beliefs of Rasta employees, the degree to which private behaviours (such as using cannabis) impact work performance or violate workplace regulations, and even the degree to which hairstyle is protected depending on whether it is worn as a religious commitment, as a simple aesthetic style or as an embodiment of racial identity. These types of cases have been heard around the world, from a Rasta police officer in Baltimore, Maryland, requesting a hair exemption, to Rasta prison guards in South

Africa's Pollsmoor Prison refusing to cut their locks, to Rasta Jiffy Lube workers in Massachusetts alleging religious discrimination at only being allowed to work out of sight of customers because of a manager's fear of the impression dreadlocks would give. Major corporations including Disney, Greyhound and UPS have been cited in the suits and, as mentioned above, many of these suits have been filed through the US Equal Employment Opportunity Commission. Nonetheless, results have been mixed.

While Zimbabwe's Supreme Court had to consider twenty years ago whether a Rasta with dreadlocks could meet the job qualification of a "fit and proper person",[7] the more fundamental question of recognition as a religion now seems to have given way to questions about how to draw lines between religious rights and work obligations in specific cases. As Rastas participate in the daily work-a-day world, new cases will continue to arise, and many of them will be quite complicated. For example, in an online human resources and occupational safety forum, non-Rasta supervisors thoughtfully discussed questions about how to balance obligatory recognition of religious rights with obligations to safety laws: does a religious right to dreadlocks supersede occupational safety regulations for well-fitting hard hats on a construction site? In contrast to cases in which there has been direct discrimination against Rastas as Rastas (e.g., because of how Rastas look), if a case of this sort went to court it would represent a question about how the law balances different types of good. As Rastafari becomes more mainstream, we can expect these types of questions to increase.

– Courts[8]

Courts are interested in clarity, specificity and categories that are understandable and generalizable. In effect, this means that for the court to consider arguments about Rastafari as a religion, it has to understand Rastafari as a religion fitting alongside other religions *even if Rastafari does not always understand itself in this way*. Thus, what seems to be an inconsistency when Rastafari deny they are a religion on one hand and claim religious rights on the other is really a strategic decision based on what arguments have the best chance of success in court. When Mutabaruka's Judge Dread places "religion" on trial, it is meant as a true critique of "religion's" role in oppression; but when a litigant makes a "religious freedom" argument for the right to wear dreadlocks in school, the word "religion" is not used in the same way that Mutabaruka uses it. Nonetheless, from an outsider's perspective there is an ambiguity about whether Rastafari considers itself to be a religion or not. Courts are one context in which Rastafari has presented itself as a religion most clearly.

The court situation can also affect Rastafari's self-understanding. For example, in some court cases involving possession of cannabis (or cannabis-smoking paraphernalia), Rastas have tried to argue that they should be exempt from anti-cannabis laws because smoking cannabis is a sacrament, analogous to the Eucharist in Christianity, and thus smoking cannabis should be protected as a religious activity. Whether most Rastas would consider using cannabis to be a sacrament, whether it would be analogous to the Eucharist, or even whether there is a Rastafari conception of sacrament, are interesting theological questions, but it is not clear that they would have arisen as questions in the same way outside of the court context. In other words, the institutional context of the courts may unintentionally push Rastafari to new self-understandings and theological understandings that parallel or are even modelled on those of more established religions.

At the same time, we should remember that different courts serve different purposes, so while it may seem advantageous in a criminal court to argue that smoking cannabis is a *sine qua non* sacrament of Rastafari, the same claim may be disadvantageous in a family court that is trying to arrive at a decision about custody or visitation and wondering about the likelihood of the minor being exposed to cannabis. Future research on *livity* and law will have to attend to the way arguments in various courts may have affected theological concepts in Rastafari.

Courts also have an interest in specificity and clarity. For example, in seeking to explain what Rastafari is, reports and discovery materials can include lists of "tenets" even though many Rastas would say that their religion is not based on specific tenets. To put this another way, we might say that the legal system sometimes asks for a level of specificity and clarity about Rastafari that is not fitting to a religion that is often more oriented towards mystical experience. The effect of the courts on Rastafari in this case can be to reify the religion or falsely prioritize the systematicity of beliefs and practices over other aspects of the faith. If cases in which such clear and specific statements have been made are successful, they not only become precedents, but also become models of what Rastafari is. Strangely, then, the courts can sometimes create a kind of legitimacy for a certain kind of Rastafari, making it more likely for Rastafari to succeed in cases in which they present themselves in known or recognizable ways. Will future research bear out these impressions about legal engagement and formalization in Rastafari?

– Schools

Schools provide another institutional context for Rasta encounters with the law, especially as generational shifts bring more Rasta children to schools. Schools promote notions of order, conformity, aesthetics, citizenship and well-being. They also serve as "gatekeepers" by selectively distributing the credentials necessary for future access to work and other social goods. Rastafari challenges fundamental ideas of order, decorum and success embedded in schooling, thus some of the most important locations for *livity* with respect to law have been schools. The most common legal issues to arise between Rastas and schools have been those in which Rastafari children have been denied access to school for violating school codes: typically these codes pertain to hair, though there can also be standards regarding uniforms or personal accoutrements.

In many countries around the world, school children must follow a dress code that includes some restrictions about personal appearance, some of which reflect colonial norms. Hairstyles have been particularly controversial, and in countries as far ranging as Jamaica, Britain, South Africa, Malawi, Panama and various Eastern Caribbean island-nations, courts have heard complaints from parents whose children have been sent home from school over the question of hair and hair policy. The courts have generally found in favor of Rastas in these cases or, in some cases, the cases have been settled before going to court once it has been established that dreadlocks are religiously significant.

In addition to hair, a variety of personal accoutrements and symbols have also become matters of dispute in schools. When a Rasta student is suspended from school for distributing cannabis, even if he says it is for religious purposes or as self-expression of his faith, the interests of the state in legislating against cannabis take legal priority. Other cases are more difficult, such as when a student wants to be allowed to carry smoking paraphernalia (such as a pipe). Following the logic of a more accepted religion, the student might claim that the pipe is a sacramental and simply serves as a reminder of a centrally important religious ritual. Courts are no longer in a position to challenge these arguments, yet they may still find that the interests of the state take priority over the right to such a sacramental.

Other cases are even more complex. For example, in cultures where it is considered impolite for men to wear hats indoors, ought there to be an exception for Rastafari who want to wear tams/hats (*crowns*) or for Rastafari who want their children to wear hats in schools? Much depends on whether it is religiously required for Rastas to wear a hat. But because Rastafari is prophetically and mystically oriented, the issue is never fully decided: some Rastafari argue that *Babylon* has no right to see a Rasta's dreadlocks, and therefore it is a religious right to shield them from view. Others argue that dreadlocks function almost like antennae, picking up both good and bad vibrations from the world around Rastafari. In those cases, the question of whether to wear a hat or tam depends on the individual's perception of the vibrations at the moment. Still other Rastas argue that dreadlocks are emblematic of the religion and a statement of faith, and that they should therefore be worn openly as a proclamation and sign of faith. In those cases, it may actually be argued that keeping hair uncovered is a religious responsibility, and hats ought not to be worn.

Schools trying to establish standardized procedures are ill-equipped to deal with religious requirements that depend on personal interpretation, instead favoring policies based on published or otherwise known principles. Future research might explore the nuances of *livity* in the school context: do schools favor systematized accounts of Rastafari? Do other factors, such as gender norms, further muddy the waters when it comes to issues like hair-length codes or head gear? How does the school context affect Rasta decisions on legal strategies, such as whether to pursue religious rights or rights to free expression?

– Prisons

If schools are concerned with conformity and control as a way of enhancing education and creating citizens, prisons are more narrowly focused on conformity and control to maintain order and safety. But, with order, conformity and control at such a premium, inmates are correspondingly interested in the ways in which they can express individuality in prison. Thus, the prison context creates a different set of dynamics influencing *livity* and law. Let's be completely clear that a Rasta presence in prison *does not* point to a Rastafari predilection for crime or lawlessness (any more than a Christian presence in prison points to a Christian predilection for crime and lawlessness). At the same time, it is important to note that the Rastafari presence in prison does create circumstances that influence the way that Rastafari is lived (both in prison and out) because the institutional requirements of prison set the conditions for the development of Rastafari in prison and for those Rastas released from prison.

Numerous studies and statistics make obvious the ways in which systemic racism in the United States is reflected in a legal system that disproportionately incarcerates men of color. When combined with a War on Drugs that targeted cannabis and rigid minimum sentencing and "three strikes" laws that mandated life sentences in certain circumstances, it is not surprising that Rastas would be included in many prison populations, that Rastafari would be an attractive religion for inmates, and that Rastafari would be a recognizable religious community in many prisons.

Belonging to a Rastafari religious group can be appealing to inmates for several reasons (regardless of whether they entered prison as Rastas). First, Rastafari affirms Blackness in a world where Blackness is often denigrated or targeted. Second, Rastafari not only affirms the value of the individual in a context that is designed to impose conformity, but it values the individual as divine and grounds that value in a life-affirming metaphysics. Third, in some cases the Rastafari notion of *Babylon* may be helpful as a way of explaining the theodicy question about the injustice of incarceration. Fourth, Rastafari offers a form of discipline and self-care (e.g., *Ital* living and disavowal of violence) that is a healthy alternative in prisons. Fifth, Rastafari can be a vehicle for expressing an African and/or West Indian cultural heritage.

Outside of the prison context, Rastafari may gather both formally and informally to worship, to pray, to reason, to use cannabis, to drum or to otherwise celebrate their way of life, and it may or may not be advantageous for a group to seek recognition for itself as Rastafari. Prison changes the context for the practice of religion, and because of the rights that are associated with the practice of a religion in prison, there can be an incentive for inmates to join religious groups that are more formally recognized. In most correctional facilities inmates wear the same clothes and follow the same regulations regarding appearance and hygiene. Rastafari can be attractive simply because of the possibilities it presents for expressing individuality or difference. For example, in New York State prisons, Rastas (and members of other religions) have the opportunity to wear symbols (including pendants) associated with their faith. But again there is a complication: the number and form of symbols that can be worn are limited and (out of concern that such symbols will be used to express gang affiliations) must conform to a set of options approved by prison officials. It makes sense that prison officials, who are dealing with a wide range of religions in a correctional facility context, would approve symbols legitimized by formal Rasta organizations: for prison officials an image of Haile Selassie makes sense, but in an institution that incarcerates people for controlled substance offences, a ganja leaf does not.

Religious rights may also give the inmates a kind of weak power in relation to guards. For example, if dreadlocks are a recognized part of a religion, and if it violates someone's religious rights to have their dreadlocks touched by a non-Rastafari, then a Rasta can legitimately (if not always successfully) argue that a search of hair is a violation of the right to practice religion freely. Some states, and some individual prisons, have recognized that right, and policies have been changed not only to allow inmates to wear dreadlocks (so long as they are in keeping with established norms of hygiene and safety), but also to introduce less intrusive search methods where possible. For example, in some prisons in New York State, inmates who object to having their dreadlocks searched by a guard can ask for a different type of search in which they present their hair, slowly and in detail, to a guard. But states vary tremendously, and at the other extreme is the Commonwealth of Virginia, which kept ten Rastas in solitary confinement for a decade for refusing to cut their locks.

Although Rastafari may be a religion that is practiced somewhat idiosyncratically outside of prison, and which gives wide leeway to individual *livity*, the structural requirements of prison are even more demanding than work, court or school, and they require that Rastafari articulate and organize itself formally, systematically and in ways that are understandable to those who do not ordinarily participate in Rastafari. One important avenue for future research is whether participation in formal groups of Rastafari that starts in prisons continues upon release. Does the level of organization of Rastafari groups required in prison persist beyond the prison walls? Or, does the idiosyncratic nature of *livity* reassert itself upon release?

CONCLUSION

Livity's relationship to law will continue to unfold in new and unpredictable ways in the future, and throughout this chapter I have pointed to some of the directions for future research. But even without that research, we can predict some of the factors that will shape *livity* and law. While certain factors, such as the Rasta respect for law, will likely remain consistent, factors such as the legal recognition of Rastafari as a religion, or the degree to which Rastas are integrated into a range of employment situations, will continue to change. Symbols of Rastafari will continue to serve as free-floating signifiers and will cloud public perceptions of Rastafari, and Rastas themselves will be forced to articulate their beliefs and practices in more formal ways to garner legal recognition. The institutional contexts in which these articulations are made will also shape the form they take and the rights subsequently accorded to Rastas. One possible unintended consequence of these changes will be to shift Rastafari in a more formal direction and away from its prophetic and mystical roots.

Notes

1   Bourdieu's notions of *habitus* and *field* are instructive here because they provide one way of thinking about how practices, like *livity*, emerge in the interplay of subjectivity and objectivity. Individuals act through structured dispositions (*habitus*), which are both structured by and help structure a *field* of objective relations. This chapter is concerned with the broad contours of *livity* and law; one hopes that future scholarship might detail *livity* and law as it is worked out by specific Rastas in specific places and times. See Bourdieu (1977; 1990; 1998).

2   I am using the terms routinization and rationalization in a Weberian sense. Routinization refers to the process by which charismatic power or authority becomes transferable in more or less predictable ways. Religious rationalization refers to the process by which religious concepts are systematized and made self-consistent. See Kalberg (1980). This is one aspect of how Rastafari is changing. A recent book by Alexander Rocklin (2019) describes how "Hinduism" was made into a "religion" in Trinidad through the imposition of, and negotiation of, the category of "religion". The same process can be seen in Rastafari (and, indeed, many subaltern religions). The power dynamic of imposing and negotiating taxonomies of religion are endemic to the relationship of *livity* and law, as we will see in the sections on work, courts, schools and prisons.

3   I am using the word ethos to mean something like a comprehensive attitude. This is a simple version of how Geertz (1957) uses the term: "A people's ethos is the tone, character, and quality of their life, its moral and aesthetic style and mood; it is the underlying attitude toward themselves and their world that life reflects".

4   Thank you to an anonymous reviewer for pointing me in the direction of these three parody songs. They can be heard in various versions on YouTube.

5   On the movement of Rastafari "from outcasts to culture bearers", see Edmonds (2003).

6   Wikipedia lists a couple of Rasta disambiguations, including one for the Rasta militia, a terrorist group in Congo. See https://en.wikipedia.org/wiki/Rasta_militia.

7   See *In re Chikweche*, Case No CA 626/93, Zimbabwe: Supreme Court, 27 March 1995.

8   My observations here are based on my own experience as an expert witness in three particular cases, plus experience informally consulting via correspondence with two inmates at Sing Sing Correctional Facility. Two cases are covered by confidentiality agreements. The third was Shepherd v. Goord, No. 9:04-CV-655 (DNH) (N.D.N.Y. 8 June 2004).

References

Bourdieu, Pierre. 1977. *Outline of a Theory of Practice*. Trans. Richard Nice. New York: Cambridge University Press.

_____. 1990. *The Logic of Practice*. Trans. Richard Nice. Stanford, CA: Stanford University Press.

_____. 1998. *Practical Reason: On the Theory of Action*. Stanford, CA: Stanford University Press.

Edmonds, Ennis Barrington. 2003. *Rastafari: From Outcasts to Culture Bearers*. New York: Oxford University Press.

Geertz, Clifford. 1957. "Ethos, World-View and the Analysis of Sacred Symbols". *Antioch Review* 17 (4): 421. JSTOR: http://www.jstor.org/stable/4609997.

Hall, David D. 1997. *Lived Religion in America: Toward a History of Practice*. Princeton, NJ: Princeton University Press.

Kalberg, Stephen. 1980. "Max Weber's Types of Rationality: Cornerstones for the Analysis of Rationalization Processes in History". *American Journal of Sociology* 85 (5): 1145–1179. JSTOR: http://www.jstor.org/stable/2778894.

Orsi, Robert. 2010. *The Madonna of 115th Street: Faith and Community in Italian Harlem, 1880–1950*. 3rd edn. New Haven, CT: Yale University Press.

Rocklin, Alexander. 2019. *The Regulation of Religion and the Making of Hinduism in Colonial Trinidad*. Chapel Hill: University of North Carolina Press.

"THEY TOOK US BY BOAT AND WE'RE COMING BACK BY PLANE"[1]

An Assessment of Rastafari and Repatriation

GIULIA BONACCI

In loving memory of
Ras Mweya Masimba (Bradford 1964–Shashemene 2016)
Sister Welete Medhin (Kingston 1949–London 2019)
Sister Ijahnya Christian (Anguilla 1957–St Kitts 2020)

Abstract Repatriation to Africa represents a cornerstone of Rastafari faith and livity, a structuring paradigm of the movement's development, and an on-going physical mobility toward Africa. This paper proposes an assessment of the significance of Repatriation, which is still largely ignored in the literature on the Rastafari movement. The claim for the right to return to Africa ties Rastafari to the broader history of Black peoples in the Americas who have emphasized return as a redemptive mobility or as a political solution to their marginalized condition. Repatriation is a concept and a practice that raises many challenges and contradictions; and it endures in many different forms and places. Particular attention is given to repatriation to Ethiopia, but other African countries are addressed as well.

Keywords • Repatriation • reparation • Africa • Ethiopia • land grant

IDEAZ—an interdisciplinary social science & humanities journal, vol. 15, 2020, pp. 150-165

Since the inception of the Rastafari movement in the 1930s in Jamaica, repatriation to Africa has been prominent in the discourses produced by Rastafari. In fact, repatriation represents a cornerstone of Rastafari faith and livity, as well as a structuring paradigm of the movement's development, and an ongoing physical mobility towards the African continent. The significance of repatriation—here used interchangeably with return[2]—traverses the religious, the racial, the cultural and the political ethos of Rastafari, and as such represents one of its organizing principles. However, repatriation to Africa is often analysed as a utopia, a cultural trope or a theological motive, and rarely as a social process of mobility and integration in African societies. In the Jamaican context, repatriation remains often dismissed as mere underclass fantasy, and this is reflected in the paucity of scholarship focusing on repatriation. Some of the best references on Rastafari only allude to the actual, physical returns to Africa, despite Rastafari appearing as the main force claiming for repatriation to Africa since the 1940s until today (for example, Campbell 1994, 211–231; Chevannes 1998b, 30; Edmonds 2012, 78–79). This article proposes an assessment of the social and political significance of repatriation with a perspective that ties Rastafari with the wider world, and that faces the challenges and contradictions born in the wake of actual returns to Africa. It is based on almost twenty years of research in the archives and the press (in the United Kingdom, the United States, Jamaica and Ethiopia) and extensive fieldwork in the Caribbean, in Ethiopia, as well as in other African countries (in particular Ghana and South Africa). Aiming at summarizing and presenting the state of knowledge on the dynamics of Rastafari and repatriation, this paper does not discuss specific sources nor individuals' trajectories as they can be found in other publications.[3]

THE MANY CLAIMS TO RETURN

Repatriation, or the right to return to Africa, ties Rastafari to the broader history of Black peoples in the Americas who have emphasized return as a redemptive mobility or as a political solution to their marginalized condition. Since enslaved Africans were brought in ships to the Western plantations, there has always been a desire to return. This desire was expressed in ritual practices and in folk stories while memories of actual places and people in Africa were fading away in time and distance. The idea of return staged mythical images of Africa, and of a golden age toppled by slavery and colonialism, while the language of the biblical book of Exodus came to express the yearning for a place to belong for Black communities and congregations in the Americas. The archetype of the Hebrews, living in a land of bondage until Moses would lead them to the Promised Land, functioned as a metaphor for the fate of Black people in slave and post-slavery societies. Another archetype was at play there, as the Ethiopia mentioned in the Bible became synonymous with Blackness. Since the seventeenth century and the emergence of classical Ethiopianism, there are numerous occurrences of individuals, writers, travellers, communities or congregations who identify themselves as Ethiopian by virtue of their Black skin. It is only after the battle of Adwa, won by Ethiopians against Italians in 1896, that biblical Ethiopia became closely associated with political Ethiopia, a lone sovereign state in colonial Africa, thus launching what is known as modern Ethiopianism—of which Rastafari is a stalwart representative.[4]

Desire to return to Africa was fuelled by religious-based discourses on the prophetic destiny of Black people, supposed to contribute to the regeneration of Africa, and by political positions defending emigration against separation from or integration into mainstream society. In most cases, going to Africa was understood as an escape from the marginalized condition assigned to descendants of the enslaved Africans in the West and an exit from second-class citizenship. Early experiences of return to Sierra Leone and Liberia[5] involved philanthropist and paternalist practices as well as the reproduction of unequal relationships with natives while giving birth to early cosmopolitan societies on Africa's shores. It is significant to note that Caribbean people were over-represented in these projects (James 2004, 151–153). Engaged as they were in the development of modern education and media, they acted as forerunners to West African nationalism and to the pan-African idea of shared destiny between Africans and African-descended people.

A paradigmatic example in this regard is that of Marcus Garvey (1887–1940), the Jamaican printer and Black nationalist who founded the Universal Negro Improvement Association (UNIA) in 1914 in Kingston, Jamaica and inaugurated the New York Division in 1918. His programme of race primacy, economic self-empowerment, nation-building and return to Africa had a major impact on Black communities in the Americas and worldwide, in an age of increasing circulation of ideas and people. In particular, his project of a Black Star Liner that would enhance trade among Black communities and bring people to Africa had a social and popular impact much wider than what a few old ships bought with dues were actually able to offer. A charismatic and controversial leader, Marcus Garvey never reached Liberia where his program was unsettling the political elite and their Western partners in their exploitation of natural resources. Nonetheless, his impact on Caribbean popular culture and Black politics in the Americas, and his influence on early African leaders like Kwame Nkrumah and Jomo Kenyatta set him as the tutelary figure for return to Africa and for pan-Africanism in the twentieth century (Ewing 2014).

In Jamaica, claims for return predate the Rastafari movement. Indentured workers from Sierra Leone fought to get their right to return, and veterans of the First World War unable to survive decently in Jamaica pleaded for settlement in Africa. Local chapters of the UNIA drafted repatriation petitions and bills in the 1940s, while numerous other local civil society organizations (Afro-West Indian League, Afro-Caribbean League, etc.) mobilized their members towards establishing an African consciousness, in an effort to pulling Africa out of the shame it was usually associated with in Caribbean colonial societies. This broad social spectrum claiming some form of return is important as it evidences that Rastafari were not the first ones to claim return, and that Rastafari actually built their claim to repatriation on older discourses prevalent in the Americas.

RASTAFARI IN JAMAICA AND REPATRIATION

One of the specificities of Rastafari is to tie closely the claim to return with contemporary Ethiopia, where Emperor Haile Selassie I who they consider as the Living God was sitting on a throne priding biblical roots. Here three dimensions are intimately entangled: religious interpretations, political aims and framework, and self-development; these provide return with a unique significance for Rastafari, and function as a cornerstone to their faith and livity. In fact, repatriation is to be found at the heart of the cultural system developed by Rastafari. Return to Africa—and its synonyms, Ethiopia, Zion—is chanted in the Nyahbinghi repertoire of sacred music and in hundreds of roots reggae tunes, it is called upon in rituals and ceremonies, it influences participants' attitudes towards society, and its associated symbols adorn bodies, houses and community circles. The ubiquitous use by Rastafari of the call of prophet Isaiah (46:3), "I will say to the north, Give up; and to the south, Keep not back: bring my sons from far, and my daughters from the ends of the earth", acts as a signifier of this centrality. Repatriation is at the core of the discourses and the practices of Rastafari and is inseparable from the history of the movement.

Instead of following a chronological analysis of the many claims, hopes and failures of repatriation to Africa, I will focus here on a few significant aspects, keeping in mind that the distinction between the religious and the political is blurred more often than not. Rastafari claim repatriation as a prerequisite for redemption, which literally means "buying back" the Black bodies from slavery, an action that God only could conduct. Return and salvation are thus intimately related, and are often embedded in a form of social passivity. If one only need to wait upon "fireball" or upon "seven miles of Black Star Liner" to bring them back to Africa, no social or political action is deemed necessary.[6] The promises of imminent return made by Leonard P. Howell in 1934 or by Rev. Claudius Henry in 1959 led astray thousands of people who believed that life elsewhere was possible. These well-known events conceal other initiatives, like that of a number of individuals who in the 1940s addressed letters and petitions to the Colonial Secretary. These letters, framed in biblical terms, were early Rastafari addresses to the British Crown who was urged to take its responsibilities and carry back to Africa the descendants of those deported to the Caribbean. In 1958, as the Jamaican public opinion shivered when Rastafari took over Victoria Park in downtown Kingston for their first public convention, a letter written by charismatic Mortimo Planno was published in *African Opinion*, a pan-African journal produced in New York. Planno used the Universal Declaration of Human Rights publicized ten years earlier to legitimize the call for Rastafari's right of choosing another—Ethiopian—nationality, and the associated right of return to Africa. Rastafari claims climaxed in the late 1950s with the news that land was available for settlement in Ethiopia, and they felt reinforced in their harsh critique of the flourishing creole nationalism.

Beyond the mythology associated with return, and beyond the utopia it represents, repatriation is really a political critique of the state of the nation. A form of response to economic and social oppression, it addresses the current legacies of historical responsibilities. Colonial officials acknowledged very early the explosive potential of return. In 1933, colonial correspondence reveals the British were weighing the risk taken in entertaining the idea of return: it could potentially concern hundreds of thousands in the Americas. The colonial silence and repression of early Rastafari claims shaped a political response that remained roughly unchanged since then. The 1960s did start on another note though. The methods and objectives of the 1960 *Report on the Rastafarian Movement* remain debated among scholars, but it was the first occurrence when a putatively independent research team listed among its recommendations the need to study the feasibility of emigration to Africa (Smith et al. 1960). A government sponsored mission including Rastafari and other Black organizations visited five African countries in 1961, and was followed up by a technical mission the following year. However, with festivities for independence culminating in August 1962, all projects of facilitating repatriation were buried. As much as return threatened the British Empire, it did threaten as well independent Jamaica.

The strategy implemented since then by the Jamaican government relied heavily on the project of rehabilitating Rastafari, that is changing the social conditions of the Jamaican poor in order for the claim to repatriation to lose its social significance, and of co-opting Rastafari in order to exert some type of control over prominent representatives of the movement. In fact, by expressing allegiance to Ethiopia, identified as a Black sovereign state in Africa, Rastafari were opposing the nascent Jamaican nation and repelling the idea of a multicultural society. The insistence of Rastafari on the primacy of Blackness, on belonging to another country, and their despise of local politics formulated not so much their anti (Jamaican) nationalism but rather their alter-nationalism, that is their allegiance to another (Ethiopian) nation. The answer of the Jamaican State to this situation was clearly a repressive one: the massacre of Coral Gardens in 1963, the razing of Back O' Wall in 1966, the banning of Guyanese revolutionary historian Walter Rodney in 1968, as well as the numerous occurrences of police harassment and brutality against Rastafari that became a steady pattern of the 1960s. However, the 1966 State visit of Ethiopian Emperor Haile Selassie I in the Caribbean represented a turning point in the social relations at stake. The British and Jamaican governments had hoped that Haile Selassie I would deny the divinity attributed to him by Rastafari, and that this visit would put an end to the movement. But the opposite happened. The State visit was marked by massive popular fervour and enthusiasm, and it not only gave a prominent place to Rastafari in various official receptions, it signalled the spectacular growth of Rastafari and launched Rastafari departures to Africa. Vying for political influence in Jamaica, Prime Minister Hugh Shearer (JLP) visited Ethiopia in September 1969, and Michael Manley (PNP), then leader of the opposition, soon followed him. In the lead-up to the 1972 general elections that he won, Manley made extensive use of the "rod of correction" supposedly given to him by Haile Selassie I, thus illustrating the power of the discourse around repatriation to Ethiopia specifically. Local politicians largely instrumentalized symbols of Rastafari and repatriation, at a time when the voice of Rastafari in reggae music was beginning to have a massive impact locally and internationally (Waters 1985).

A lesser-known aspect of the significance of repatriation for Rastafari is located in its influence on the internal life of the movement. What research reveals is that the very issue of repatriation in part structured the politics of Rastafari (Bonacci 2015, 183–219). Rastafari is often considered an acephalous movement, and rightly so, as no single leader ever controlled or influenced the totality of its participants, and as individual sovereignty is deemed a primary step towards redemption. However, such an interpretation should not impede analysis of the many associations, organizations and institutions that are as well constitutive of Rastafari. Interestingly, claims to repatriation play a great part in the structuration of the movement. Suffice to give a closer look at the institutions of Rastafari to understand the significance of repatriation in the development of the movement. The Ethiopian World Federation (EWF), founded in New York in 1937 in the midst of the Italian-Ethiopian war, was first branched in Jamaica in 1939, but it was only in the 1950s that Rastafari invested in the pan-Ethiopian organization despite the reluctance of some of the US-based EWF leaders. This move happened really because, by then, it was public that EWF members were granted land in Ethiopia, and this fact acted as a magnet among Rastafari who became members in existing chapters or founded their own. While organizing return was not the primary aim of the EWF, return is the main reason why Rastafari joined. Along the years, very few EWF members from Jamaica left for Ethiopia, and the meagre resources available were channelled to the New York headquarters. Because of the inability of the EWF to mobilize effectively its members, some chapters decided to leave the historic organization and rely on themselves for funding effective return. The 1968 birth of a major Rastafari organization, the Twelve Tribes of Israel, is precisely located in this tension. The Twelve Tribes of Israel met with rapid growth in Jamaica and internationally, not least because its doctrine leaned towards Christianity, and accommodated members from the middle class, gave public positions to women, and rationalized non-Black membership. In addition, the Twelve Tribes of Israel largely contributed to the popularity of reggae music through its dances and its numerous artiste members. The centrality given to repatriation to Ethiopia represented a major fuel for the growth of the organization; it was built in the membership through various means: songs, weekly dues, personal identification to one of the Twelve Tribes of Israel, and a leadership structure focusing on Ethiopia. In fact, dozens of Twelve Tribes members have settled in and visited Ethiopia since the early 1970s. It was only later, in the 1990s, that other Rastafari mansions sent settlers to Ethiopia, namely the Nyahbinghi Order and the Ethiopia Africa Black International Congress.

INTERNATIONAL RASTAFARI AND REPATRIATION

Encouraged by the 1992 month-long celebration of the centenary of Haile Selassie I organized in Ethiopia by an international coalition of Rastafari, a number of individuals found their way to the East African country. They were coming from established mansions, as the EWF had been revitalized in the United Kingdom, and as the Twelve Tribes of Israel had expanded into numerous international branches, even though they did not "wait for their turn" as the blueprint of the organ recommended. The growth of the Rastafari movement in the United Kingdom appears as a major landmark both for the movement and for repatriation. A young generation of sons and daughters of Caribbean immigrants, fed up with the racism met in all strata of society, were at the forefront of the 1980s riots demanding social justice. Often radicalized by the very context they grew up in, they found no political relays, except for the support of a few MPs like Bernie Grant, from Guyana, who was elected for Tottenham in 1987 and a leader of the debates around repatriation and reparation during the 1990s. The dynamism and social relevance of Rastafari in the United Kingdom, and their ties with Jamaica and established mansions, gave a new breath to the movement that was then internationalizing quickly. In Trinidad, Rastafari has a long history, often shadowed by Jamaica, and can claim a major role in the development of the movement, its mansions, its livity and its practice of return. Other individuals and families returned as well, mainly Rastafari coming from places where no mansion was established, in particular from the Eastern Caribbean small islands and the French Caribbean. Despite the somehow minor position of Rastafari in the United States—compared with other Black-centred movements—Caribbean migrants and African-American Rastafari did return as well, the formers finding resources not available in the islands to facilitate their movement. As a reflection of the internationalization of Rastafari, a few Euro-American, British, Irish, Swedish, German, French, Austrian and even Italian Rastafari settled in Ethiopia, some for a few years and others for decades. Most of them legitimize their presence through a discourse on the African origins of humanity, thanks to their insertion into established mansions, or as a proof of the universality of their faith. While their presence is not without contradictions, and not without reluctance on behalf of some Caribbean or British-based Rastafari, they have become active participants in the community of returnees, and sometimes funders of community initiatives, which adds to the complexity of the local situation.

By the early 2000s, the Rastafari community in Ethiopia counted a few hundred people representing about twenty citizenships, thus reflecting the internationalization of Rastafari from Jamaica and the Caribbean to the world.[7] Of course, over the years many Rastafari never felt directly concerned by the tangible process of organizing themselves in order to leave. While repatriation has remained pervasive in Rastafari culture, in faith, music, rituals, media, public debates and sociably, a rationalization process did occur and was expressed in the distinction between a "physical" return and a "spiritual" return, which would legitimize remaining in "Babylon" within an Afro-centred personal and social position. Still, in the twenty-first century, return endures, in many different forms and places, and the international Rastafari movement remains a major actor of repatriation to Africa, a shared goal with other Black communities and congregations in the Americas, despite major changes in Jamaican and global discourses and political environments.

THE SHASHEMENE LAND GRANT

The Shashemene land grant, where an international Rastafari community lives today, has a central place in the discourses and social practices of repatriation (Bonacci 2015a; Christian 2011; MacLeod 2014; Niaah 2012). In fact, it is of particular significance in the history of return for a number of reasons. First, it ties directly the early Rastafari movement to the mobilization of a prior generation engaged in the defence of Ethiopia during the war with Italy (1935–1941). Second, it is the first gesture of invitation, in 1950, made by an African Head of State to members of the African Diaspora.[8] Third, Shashemene represents the symbolic centre of the contemporary international Rastafari movement. As such, the Shashemene settlement anchors return in an African society, it ties firmly the fate of Shashemene within a wider internationalist and pan-African history, and it evidences that the myth of return can actually survive to the vicissitudes of settlement in Africa.

Analysis of repatriation and settlement on the Shashemene land grant, located in the periphery of a southern Ethiopian market town, must articulate two distinct chronologies: a social chronology of arrivals in Ethiopia, and a political chronology of contemporary Ethiopia. The very first settlers to arrive on the Shashemene land grant in 1952 were Helen and James Piper, Black Jews and Garveyites from Montserrat, and they were followed by a handful of other people coming from the United States, the United Kingdom and Jamaica until the mid-1960s. In 1968, small groups of Jamaican Rastafari, unaffiliated or EWF members, started to arrive, followed after 1972 by Jamaican Rastafari members of the Twelve Tribes of Israel. This dynamic was slowed then halted by the revolution of September 1974 that took place in Ethiopia and dethroned Haile Selassie I. During the years of the military regime, with civil war raging and restrictions like food rations, mobility and curfew, some of the settlers left the land grant, and very few new settlers arrived. Some visitors made the journey, like Twelve Tribes international officers, and in

December 1978, Bob Marley who spent three weeks in Ethiopia. When borders reopened in 1991, a slow normalization took place in the country, and settlers came in, with peaks around 2000 and 2007, representing the Western and the Ethiopian millennia.[9] This chronology of arrivals, constrained in part by the political situation in Ethiopia, reflects the moving history of the Rastafari movement, of its mansions and of its international diffusion.

On arrival in Ethiopia, returnees met with the Ethiopian State that has a long tradition of authority and administration. Before 1974, the government helped those arriving in getting papers, work and access to land. The original land grant was of 200 hectares (or 5 *gasha*) in the periphery of Shashemene, and it was divided among twelve people in 1970. However, despite its pan-African motive, this land grant was nationalized in March 1975 like all rural land in the country. Returnees lost everything, their land, their houses, and the dream of return could have stopped there but for the determination of a few families who remained in Ethiopia during a difficult period. No constructions were allowed and primary materials were scarce, but following various petitions, eighteen lots of land were attributed in 1986 to eighteen families of returnees. These lots were situated within the borders of the original land grant, and are the last ones officially attributed to Rastafari families in the country. In the late 1990s, thanks to the ground-level involvement of some Rastafari turned middlemen, hundreds of lots were made available by the local peasant associations against retribution, thus allowing the settlement of numerous individuals and families. However, returnees have always lacked some kind of documentation regarding the land they settled. As in other African countries, land issues are central to the social fabric of society, and the Shashemene returnees were fragilized by their lack of land titles and their undocumented houses. Since the promulgation of the 1994 constitution of Ethiopia establishing a federal government, Shashemene is located in the federal state of Oromia, and returnees have faced the tortuous, and sometimes arbitrary, practices of local, regional and federal administrations.

Shashemene, a multi-ethnic underdeveloped town hosting migrants from the whole of Ethiopia, has developed quickly from six thousand inhabitants in the early 1950s to over 130,000 in the mid-2000s. As a consequence, the once rural land grant is now a very dense neighbourhood situated within town limits, which is identified as the "Jamaica *sefer*", the Jamaican neighbourhood. Living with the Ethiopian people has taken many forms, and collecting life histories of the returnees and their Ethiopian neighbours is the best way to document the family ties, the business initiatives, the trade relations and the everyday practices unfolding in and around Shashemene. Thanks to in-depth fieldwork, it is possible to understand how concern for local development (roads, water, health, schools, urban planning, agriculture) and for security remain central in the life of the community, in particular as burglary, rape and violent deaths have sadly landmarked the experience of repatriation. In a difficult environment typical of much of Ethiopia's secondary towns, the returnees have developed community sites, like the Twelve Tribes HQ, the EWF HQ and the Nyahbinghi Tabernacle, and community projects like the Ancient of Days Elders fund, Social Security services, involvement with the local police force, and a cemetery. Due to the cultural taboo around death within Rastafari, the cemetery still suffers from underfunding and lack of community support, even if it is a symbolically crucial issue, a marker of human dignity for Ethiopians, and a needed space as Rastafari who are not baptized in the Ethiopian Orthodox Church cannot be buried in Christian cemeteries. Various community organizations have strived, like the Jamaican Rastafari Development Community (JRDC), which runs a school in the neighbourhood. The major celebrations of Rastafari are held in the Nyahbinghi Tabernacle and in the Twelve Tribes HQ, and attract Ethiopian youths as well as international Rastafari. In addition, during the annual 23 July celebration of Haile Selassie's birth, a motorcade is always organized, involving a couple trucks crowded by drums, flags and Rastafari families dressed in white, who proudly parade in the centre of the town of Shashemene. Naturally, Rastafari are well known for their practice of reggae and sound-systems, and if they have to showcase in Addis Ababa to actually make a living of it, they do play in various community events in Shashemene as well. Some artistes like Sydney Salmon and the Imperial Majestic Band, as well as Ras Kawintseb and band Aethiofrika have played a critical role in teaching the practice of reggae to Ethiopian musicians and in developing musical collaborations (Aarons 2017).

The formal representation of the community has been plagued by rivalry and tensions between individuals and between mansions since the 1960s, and this has certainly contributed to the numerous setbacks faced by the community in order to be properly acknowledged by the Ethiopian government. However, the government announced in Spring 2017 that Rastafari will be granted formal recognition and national IDs, in line with the status of "Foreign Nationals of Ethiopian Origin" established in the early 2000s, which targets first of all the Ethiopian Diaspora, and gives them all rights except the right to vote and to get involved in the security services of the country. In fact, most members of the community were illegal residents in Ethiopia; they had expired visas and expired foreign passports, and because of their low resources many did not comply with the financial obligations of investors (Bonacci 2015b; Contreras 2018; MacLeod 2012). As a consequence, their mobility in and out of the country was extremely limited, and they risked arrest and deportation. This situation was particularly acute concerning the youths of the community born in Ethiopia of foreign parents as their lack of status impacted their schooling, their studies and their family life. On a few occasions over the past twenty years, the Ethiopian government has conducted surveys into the legal status of community members. The recent announcement was followed by implementation and by late 2019 a majority of Rastafari residents in the country had obtained residency permits. This represents a major evolution in the national insertion of the community, a very practical victory for returnees, and symbolically a great step in advancing the cause of repatriation to Africa.

The centrality of Shashemene in the international Rastafari movement is evident in the many ties between the community and the international associations dedicated to its support, like the Shashamane Foundation and IDOR in the United States, Sick Be Nourished and Rastafari The Majesty and the Movement in the United Kingdom, and international branches of Rastafari mansions as well as many other smaller associations. Because it is almost 70 years old by now, and has survived two violent changes of political regime, the settlement of returnees in Shashemene appears as a unique laboratory for the everyday practices of pan-Africanism.

RASTAFARI SETTLEMENTS IN OTHER AFRICAN COUNTRIES

Quite naturally, Rastafari have also settled in other African countries. What distinguishes Ethiopia from other countries, aside from the political will at the origin of the Shashemene land grant, is that it is almost only Rastafari returning there. Very few non-Rastafari go to live in Ethiopia, and they are often African-American educators. In other African countries, there is a wider diversity in the type of returnees, which include pan-Africanists, entrepreneurs, political activists, professionals, writers, and other religious congregations like the African Hebrew Israelites. This is due on the one hand to the difficulties of living in Ethiopia, a country that has restrictive laws with regards to foreigners, a very scarce use of the English language, and a specific culture that impregnates all aspects of everyday life (administration, calendar, religion, sociability, etc.). On the other hand, other African countries have something very important in common with the societies of the West, the Americas and the Caribbean: an experience of the convergence of racial policies and political violence, historically rooted in colonialism, and promoted by White supremacist regimes or by dictatorial regimes engaged in large-scale civil oppression.

The case of Ghana is probably best known as since its independence in 1957 President Kwame Nkrumah invited numerous African-American personalities, doctors and professionals: Trinidadian George Padmore was a member of his government and African-American W.E.B. Du Bois spent the last years of his life there. With this pan-Africanist orientation, and relatively peaceful changes of regimes, English-speaking Ghana acts as a magnet for would-be returnees. In 2014, thirty-five hundred returnees, including Rastafari, were counted in the country, even if many of them were without papers.[10] The Right of Abode, a specific status promulgated in 2000 that is designed for people of African descent in the Diaspora, is mobilized for members of the Ghanaian Diaspora rather than for returnees. Eventually in December 2016, thirty-four African-Caribbean Diasporans were granted citizenship by Ghana; and in 2019, coined the "Year of Return", the President of Ghana Nana Akufo-Addo granted citizenship to about 130 returnees. In Benin, the Famille Jah from Guadeloupe settled outside Ouidah with their four children in 1997. They have developed holistic agriculture, vegan restaurants and a school, and they are well known in the country and beyond thanks to the Cultural Embassy of the Diaspora and of Jah people they founded in 2001. They represent a major hub in the (French-speaking) African network of returnees. In Tanzania, the progressive politics of Julius Nyerere have facilitated the settlement of numerous people, including Black Panthers members and Rastafari (Bedasse 2017). There are reports of Rastafari settling in countries as varied as Zimbabwe, Malawi, Mali, Congo-Brazzaville and Niger. South Africa has a vibrant returnee community involved in numerous sectors including education, culture, entertainment, entrepreneurship and grassroots communities. However, there is yet no continental map or global numbers of returnees' settlement, and many of those initiatives remain little known, even by local politicians or specialists of these countries.

Quite interestingly, the phenomenon of return is intimately related to the growth of an African Rastafari movement. Highly visible in Accra or Johannesburg, it is much less detectable elsewhere, even if there is evidence of their communities in Abidjan, Bamako or Nairobi for example. Historical mansions of Rastafari are sometimes known on the continent, through the works of particular individuals, and the cultural identity of Rastafari is often adopted by African youths despite the reluctance of their relatives and their society. Rastafari is given new significance in Africa, and some African Rastafari have developed elaborate interpretations putting in line Rastafari thought with their own specific cultural background. This is prevalent in South Africa, where Rastafari has grown to become a major force in the national, social, cultural, political and religious landscape (Chawane 2012, 188). It is fascinating how quickly Rastafari has become an endogenous feature of South Africa. Rastafari have local and national social and ritual institutions; they have developed herbal knowledge based on traditional uses and lobbied successfully for the right to use ganja, or *dagga* as it is called. In new township neighbourhoods, the settlement of Rastafari families is encouraged in order to provide impartial referees in conflicts involving the local community (Ross quoted by Laplante 2012, 98). In Cape Town, Rastafari control a significant part of the greens and vegetables market; and despite the violence and the injustice still felt by a majority of the population twenty-five years after the fall of Apartheid, dreadlocks are widespread and worn by professionals and even police officers. Access to land, self-sustainable communities and villages, and music production appear as some of the areas of predilection for African Rastafari. In fact, the continent seems one of the places where Rastafari will undergo serious growth in the decades to come, which will in turn influence the very definition of what is Rastafari.

In November 2017, the All Africa Rastafari Gathering was held in Shashemene, Ethiopia. Born of the desire of returnee Ras Mweya Masimba to share continentally among Rastafari sustainable skills and trade, it was implemented thanks to the leadership of Sister Ijahnya Christian and the organizing committee based in Ethiopia. During a week, national representatives from Angola, Benin, Cameroon, Ghana, Ivory Coast, Kenya, Malawi, South Africa, South Sudan, Seychelles and Zimbabwe were hosted in Shashemene. They produced a formal declaration with delegates from the United States, the United Kingdom, Brazil and the Caribbean, a co-production illustrated by a few words mentioning the "examples of Haile Selassie I and Empress Menen, infused with the universal principle of Ubuntu".[11] Ubuntu is a word from Bantu languages widespread in central and southern Africa that defines humanity, or the bond of sharing that connects all humanity, and that acts now, in this particular context, as an African translation of the humanist aims of Rastafari. Under the auspices of the Nyahbinghi Order, participants joined in full nights of drumming and praise, an otherwise rare occurrence in Shashemene. The ubiquitous presence of dreadlocked Rastafari from all over Africa acted as a magnet to Ethiopian youths who observed and participated in the eventful week. Such an event while expanding Rastafari aesthetics in Ethiopia makes a powerful statement: history has been dividing African people for centuries, and now, the people have the power to create reunion and platforms uniting them in the name of Rastafari.[12]

On the threshold of the twenty-first century, repatriation finds a new breath with the debate on reparations, launched in the global arena at the occasion of the World Conference against Racism held by the United Nations in Durban in 2001. The significant political move of civil society and Caribbean states in particular towards getting reparations for slavery is unsettling European and African states, and intellectual communities, as they plead for revisiting the link between history and contemporary societies. Repatriation is among the ten-point plan pushed by CARICOM, the organization of Caribbean states, that is meeting a strong resistance and reluctance—to say the least—from many other states, including African states still dependent upon their good relations with their former colonizers (Beckles 2013). In fact, the role of African states is central in the unfolding of repatriation. The Diaspora Initiative developed by the African Union, the organization of African states since 2002, is supposed to give a place to the African Diaspora in the affairs of the continent. Despite numerous forums organized by the AU in the United States, the United Kingdom and the Caribbean, the main instrument of this initiative is an Institute of Remittances targeting the new African Diaspora, born of colonial and postcolonial migrations. And the definition of Diaspora proposed by the AU does not mention the returnees who did not wait on any African state to settle in Africa. These institutional shortcomings regarding return are not surprising, but it is interesting to see how Rastafari and repatriation occupy a place in the international pan-African arena, including in the recent and rival 8th Pan African Congresses, held in 2014 in Johannesburg, and in 2015 in Accra.

CONCLUSION

Repatriation to Africa is a cornerstone of Rastafari faith and livity, and, as well, it ties Rastafari with the broader experience of Black people in the Americas. It is simultaneously a very Jamaica-centred, Rastafari concern, and an internationalist issue located deep in the fabric of the pan-African idea. Return is a concept, a discursive space that gives ample room to political critique and mobilizes the imagination. At the same time, it is a practice, it is worked for, it is experienced, and it aims to overwrite the contours of historical geographies. While millions claimed return in the 1920s, only a handful of Rastafari settled in Africa, thanks to the organizations they built, and more recently, thanks to the determination of individuals and families. Repatriation is often still dismissed as a non-issue in Jamaican society in particular, but detailed studies do offer precious insights into the insertion of Rastafari into contemporary African societies and politics. Not to be assessed solely in terms of failure or success, return really talks about a certain idea of freedom, a freedom that no state, no government can hinder. This freedom is at the root of the pan-African project that historically ties Africa and the scattered Africans. Despite the many shortcomings of such a project, the returnees are some of its key actors, with Rastafari at the forefront, who contribute to redefining the central role of Africa in our contemporary world.

Notes

1   From interview of author with Brother Trika, Shashemene, October 2002.

2   The term repatriation is usually used in the social sciences to designate the return of a population to their country of origin. The term implies that it is a government-sponsored movement, or a movement backed by international agreements. Despite the overall absence of government support to the repatriation claimed by Rastafari and other descendants of Africans, it is used in this text in line with Rastafari's uses. It is here interchangeable with the term return, which opens a wider perspective on the same mobility (going back, going home, back and forth, etc.).

3   See for example some of my publications in English: Bonacci (2011; 2012; 2013; 2015a; 2015b; 2016; 2018).

4   Ethiopianism is an ideology that ties intimately racial, religious and political interpretations and that runs deep in time and space, as some of its occurrences can

be traced to the USA, the Caribbean, Brazil, as well as Western, Central and Southern Africa, and Ethiopia. For the USA, see for example William Scott (2004), and for an analysis of Ethiopianism vs. Egyptocentrism and Afrocentrism, see Bonacci (2019).

5   There are other classical examples of return, beyond the cases of Sierra Leone and Liberia. We can think in particular to the "return" of Afro-Brazilians to the Gold Coast after 1835; and to Haiti. Haiti, the first republic born in 1804 out of a successful slave revolt was hoped to become an alternative to Liberia, in particular by some pan-Africanist activists in the United States.

6   These terms are vernacular landmarks and refer to divine intervention (fireball) and to Marcus Garvey's project of a fleet (Black Star Line) that would connect and increase trade and exchanges between Africa and the Diaspora—brilliantly conveyed by Fred Locks in his reggae hit "Black Star Liner" (1976).

7   These numbers are taken from a 2003 survey on the Rastafari community undertaken by the Ethiopian government. In 2017, estimations are that about 800 Rastafari live in Shashemene, with about 400 more Rastafari settled in Addis Ababa and in Baher Dar, close to Lake Tana in the north of the country.

8   While oral tradition and vernacular history within Rastafari often quotes 1948 or 1955 as the year land was granted, archival research points to 1950. Future documentation from the Ethiopian archives might contribute to additional information regarding dates.

9   Ethiopian society and administration functions with the Julian calendar that is annually constituted by thirteen months, starts on 11 September, and is seven to eight years "behind" the Gregorian calendar in use in Western societies.

10 Sister Imahkush, a US returnee in Ghana, mentioned these figures at the occasion of the 8th Pan African Congress held in January 2014 in Johannesburg, Republic of South Africa.

11 This phrase is taken from the Shashemene Declaration, a text produced at the end of the All Africa Rastafari Gathering in 2017, and translated as well in French. For the full text, see http://rastaites.com/africa-rastafari-gathering- Shashemene-declaration/ (accessed 4 December 2017).

12 I want to thank Dr. Jahlani Niaah and Sister Berenice Morizeau for their kind sharing of the details of this week-long All Africa Rastafari Gathering held in Shashemene in 2017.

References

Aarons, David. 2017. "Chanting up Zion: Reggae as Productive Mechanism for Repatriated Rastafari in Ethiopia". PhD diss., University of Washington.

Beckles, Hilary. 2013. *Britain's Black Debt: Reparations for Slavery and Native Genocide*. Kingston, JA: The University of the West Indies Press.

Bedasse, Monique. 2017. *Jah Kingdom: Rastafarians, Tanzania, and Pan-Africanism in the Age of Decolonization*. Chapel Hill, NC: The University of North Carolina Press.

Bonacci, Giulia. 2011. "An Interview in Zion: The Life-History of a Jamaican Rastafarian in Shashemene, Ethiopia". *Callaloo* 34 (3):744–758.

_____. 2012. "Back to Ethiopia: African American and West Indian Returnees in Ethiopia (1896–2010)". In *Back to Africa*. Vol.II. *The Ideology and Practice of the African Returnee Phenomenon from the Caribbean and North America to Africa*, edited by Kwesi Kwaa Praah, 355–379. Cape Town: CASAS.

_____. 2013. "The Ethiopian World Federation: A Pan-African Organization among the Rastafari in Jamaica". *Caribbean Quarterly* 59 (2): 73–95.

_____. 2015a. *Exodus! Heirs and Pioneers, Rastafari Return to Ethiopia*. Kingston, JA: University of the West Indies Press.

_____. 2015b. "Mapping the Boundaries of Otherness. Naming Caribbean Settlers in Ethiopia". *African Diaspora* 8: 34–50.

_____. 2016. "The Return to Ethiopia of the Twelve Tribes of Israel". *New West Indian Guide* 90 (1&2): 1–27.

_____. 2018. "'It Would Have Pleased the Great Spirit of Mr. Garvey': Helen and James Piper and the Return to Ethiopia". *International Journal of African Historical Studies* 51 (2): 293–316.

_____. 2019. "Généalogies afrocentrées. Ethiopianisme et écriture de l'histoire". *Tumultes* 52:15–33.

Campbell, Horace. 1994. *Rasta and Resistance: From Marcus Garvey to Walter Rodney*. Trenton, NJ: Africa World Press.

Chawane, Midas. 2012. "The Rastafari Movement in South Africa: Before and After Apartheid". *New Contree* 65:163–188.

Chevannes, Barry. 1998. "New Approach to Rastafari". In *Rastafari and Other*

Christian, Ijahnya. 2011. "Return of the 6th Region: Rastafari Settlement in the Motherland Contributing to the African Renaissance". Paper presented at the General Assembly of CODESRIA, 5–9 December, Rabat, Morocco.

Contreras, Alberto Romero. 2018. "Etiopes en el extranjero ¿Ciudadanos en casa? La repatriación de la diáspora Rastafari a Shashemane, Etiopia". PhD diss., CIESAS, Mexico.

Edmonds, Ennis B. 2012. *Rastafari: A Very Short Introduction*. Oxford: Oxford University Press.

Ewing, Adam. 2014. *The Age of Garvey: How a Jamaican Activist Created a Mass Movement & Changed Global Black Politics*. Princeton: Princeton University Press.

James, Winston. 2004. "The Wings of Ethiopia: The Caribbean Diaspora and Pan-African Projects from John Brown Russwurm to George Padmore". In *African Diasporas in the New and Old Worlds: Consciousness and Imagination*, edited by G. Fabre and K. Benesh, 121–157. Amsterdam: Rodopi.

Laplante, Julie. 2012. "'Art de dire' Rastafari : Créativité musicale et *dagga*". *Drogues, Santé et Société* 11 (1): 91–106.

MacLeod, Erin. 2012. "Water Development Projects and Cultural Citizenship: Rastafari Engagement with the Oromo in Shashemene, Ethiopia". In *Rastafari in the New Millennium*, edited by Michael Barnett, 89–103. Syracuse: Syracuse University Press.

_____. 2014. *Visions of Zion: Ethiopians and Rastafari in the Search for the Promised Land*. New York: New York University Press.

Niaah, Jahlani. 2012. "The Rastafari Presence in Ethiopia: A Contemporary Perspective". In *Rastafari in the New Millennium*, edited by Michael Barnett, 66–88. Syracuse: Syracuse University Press.

Scott, William. 2004. "The Ethiopian Ethos in African American Thought". *International Journal of Ethiopian Studies* I (2): 40–57.

Smith M.G., Roy Augier, and Rex Nettleford. 1960. *Report on the Rastafari Movement in Jamaica*. Kingston: Institute of Social and Economic Research, University of the West Indies.

Waters, Anita M. 1985. *Race, Class, and Political Symbols: Rastafari and Reggae in Jamaican Politics*. New Brunswick, Oxford: Transaction Books.

RASTAFARI CITIZENSHIP STRATEGIES IN ETHIOPIA
Ethnic Existence, Diaspora Claims, Resident Identification

Erin C. MacLeod

For Professor Abraham Ford and Sister Ijahnya Christian[1]

Abstract   This paper describes the varying ways in which Rastafari repatriates engage with the notion of Ethiopian citizenship, recounting how Rastafari have grappled with the notion of what it means to be a repatriate and how to engage with official notions of citizenship and recognition. The paper accounts for a range of interventions on behalf of Rastafari and Ethiopia in terms of negotiating belonging through channels, official and otherwise. These include the Rastafari attempt to be recognized as an ethnic identity within Ethiopia, claims based on Diaspora categorization and the most recent classification as resident. The paper places each of these strategies in context.

Keywords • Citizenship • nationality • Ethiopia • ethnicity • belonging

INTRODUCTION

During the 2003 to 2014 period when I was engaged in research from which the book *Visions of Zion: Ethiopians and Rastafari in the Search for the Promised Land* eventually emerged, I listened to numerous discussions of the issue of citizenship and representation for Rastafari repatriates, both among Rastafari as well as Ethiopians. I'd be told how Rastafari should or should not be allowed to consider themselves as Ethiopian. Rastafari themselves would complain about not being accepted legally within the country, and many would say that they would keep fighting until full citizenship was granted. This particular paper represents a revisiting of these conversations in light of recent changes to Rastafari status in Ethiopia in 2017, which allowed for residency classification. The importance herein is the description of the differing strategies of connection to Ethiopian citizenship as made possible through long-term engagement with various defining possibilities through governing institutions in the country and in the wider world. From a historical perspective, this recounting provides an understanding of how Rastafari have grappled with the notion of what it means to be a repatriate and how to engage with official notions of citizenship and recognition.

Sister Ijahnya Christian, a more recent Rastafari repatriate to Ethiopia,

IDEAZ—an interdisciplinary social science & humanities journal, vol. 15, 2020, pp.166-179

who travelled between Ethiopia and her birth country of Anguilla and with whom I spoke in 2012, wrote that "governments need to understand and appreciate that whatever their views of Rastafari spirituality, the basis of the Rastafari demand for repatriation and reparations resonates in the United Nations principle of the Right of Return. They need to consider that their failure to act may impede the tide but will not diminish the Rastafari resolve to return home" (2012, 40). Regardless of discussion or circumstance, repatriation remains a must for Rastafari. Given this resolve, it is not surprising the desire for recognition in Ethiopia has been and still remains a long-term project. Though most of what I heard while involved in research related to future citizenship challenges, between 2003 and 2014 I was also privy to comments about possible legal changes allowing for alteration in status for repatriates living in Ethiopia. A number of questions arose: What could change? Could Rastafari claim status as a distinct ethnic minority? Is this strategy likely to work? This idea of lobbying the government as a specific ethnic group represented one possible strategy.

A second strategy took the form of engagement with a wider Diaspora policy as considered not just by Ethiopia, but by the wider pan-African world. In May 2012, the African Union, alongside the South African government and the pan-African Parliament, hosted the Global African Diaspora Summit. This was the first Diaspora summit ever held. The African Union as an organization and the governments of different African nations are actively encouraging Diaspora involvement in the continent. There has been much discussion in recent years of the value of the Diaspora in development—be it political or social. Development professionals, businesspeople, policymakers and academic researchers see the Diaspora as a resource (Agunias and Newland 2012; Ashworth and Nanji 2012; Brinkerhoff 2008; Hosein, Franklin & Joseph 2009; Ionescu 2006; Robertson 2008). Beyond the value of remittances from abroad, harnessing the skills and knowledge of the Diaspora for development seems an obvious result of today's transnational connections between countries. The Ethiopian Diaspora Association is one of many associations that attempt to connect Ethiopians in the Diaspora with the potential for involvement in their home country. Rastafari self-identify as members of the Diaspora and they wish to involve themselves in Africa; their settlement patterns as well as commitment to a range of projects in Ethiopia, and Shashemene specifically, demonstrate this. Repatriation is viewed as a must for Rastafari, and the earliest Rastafari did not have the resources to make this return possible or, as anthropologist Charles Price details, "sold all they possessed in order to leave for Africa" (2009, 218). Price has spoken of the shift in class among Rastafari; though many Rastafari are still economically deprived, there do exist "monied Rastafari" (ibid.). And it costs money to repatriate. Thus, the repatriate Rastafari in Shashemene, many of whom have economic resources that make not only repatriation but business development possible (see mentions of a hotel and tofu factory later in this essay), can contribute to the socio-economic growth and development of Ethiopia. Could Rastafari therefore leverage this Ethiopian national interest in the involvement of the African Diaspora to support the development of Africa?

Most recently, however, residency was provided to Rastafari repatriates in Ethiopia. Ethiopian Emperor Haile Selassie would have been 125 in 2017. Perhaps coincidentally—and indeed meaningfully for Rastafari—this same year the government of Ethiopia also announced a decision to issue identification cards to the repatriate population. According to Agence France-Presse, foreign ministry spokesperson Meles Alem discussed how this card would allow residence and many legal rights—such as the ability to come and go without a visa: "There were questions for them to recognize their presence in the country, so that is what the government did."[2] None, however, of these three approaches offer full citizenship, per se, but they all offer something, some element of acceptance within Ethiopia. These are all possibilities that could lead to eventual citizenship or perhaps some equal form of recognition—possibilities that seem to be more and more viable as time passes. The following will look at the various strategies as well as challenges.

RASTAFARI AS A NATION:
THE ETHNIC IDENTITY ARGUMENT

In a complete departure from previous Ethiopian regimes, the EPRDF government introduced a new constitution for the country back in 1995. This covered all aspects of the running of the state, including the provision of a new definition for the country. Ethiopia was now established formally as a country made up of "nations, nationalities and peoples". Article 39 of the 1995 Ethiopian constitution reads as follows:

The Right of Nations, Nationalities and Peoples

1. Every nation, nationality or people in Ethiopia shall have the unre-stricted right to self determination up to secession.

2. Every nation, nationality and people shall have the right to speak, write and develop its language and to promote its culture, help it grow and flourish, and preserve its historical heritage.

3. Every nation, nationality or people in Ethiopia shall have the unre-stricted right to administer itself; and this shall include the right to establish government institutions within the territory it inhabits and the right to fair representation in the federal and state governments (1995, 96).

Nations, nationalities and peoples are defined in the constitution as "a group of people who have or share a large measure of a common culture or similar customs, mutual intelligibility of language, belief in a common or related identities, a common psychological make-up and who inhabit an identifiable, predominantly contiguous territory" (97). This specific definition has led to arguments for nationhood from different groups within the country. Would it be possible for Rastafari to argue that they fit into this description and therefore should be declared one of the nations, nationalities or peoples?

At the 21 November 2007 Community Development forum in Shashemene, then mayor Demisse Shito commented on the trouble involved in having to represent Rastafari. The mayor said he was "working with community leaders. But found that he was asked to solve the problems of the EWF, Nyahbinghi, Twelve Tribe and not just 'Rasta people'. In [the municipality's] draft paper on Rasta people, if it included the terminology 'Rasta people', then the problem would be solved". This statement seems to validate the idea of Rastafari as a group—perhaps a "nation". The mayor wants to be able to see the Rastafari community as one entity rather than a collection of disparate groups. It is difficult, however, to refer to Rastafari by a single overarching umbrella term—the Jamaican Rastafari Development Community's use of "Jamaican" is problematic, given that Rastafari in Shashemene belong to numerous nationalities from British to Trinidadian and many in between, not to mention the fact that Rastafari, as a movement, is characterized by variation. As Michael Barnett explains, "the Rastafari movement is a multifaceted one, and not the uniform, homogenous movement many people conceive it to be" (2005, 77).

Though this multifaceted, multicultural reality of Rastafari is evident, I found through anecdotal discussions during my fieldwork from 2004 to 2014, and in conversations with Rastafari in general, that there has been some communication going on with the government about citizenship through identification as nation/ethnic group. In 2007, the owner of the Rift Valley Hotel informed me that the Rastafari community had been asked to petition the government as an ethnic group. This was reiterated by Joseph Smith at a tofu factory initiative located in Shashemene. Rastafari Priest Paul Phang, who in 2012 was sitting on the Shashemene city council, as a Rastafari municipal government representative, recounted how Rastafari had been invited to take part in a cultural event— the Ethiopian Nations, Nationalities and Peoples Day—in Awassa, the neighbouring town to Shashemene. At this celebration, Rastafari were hailed as yet another tribe among the many in Ethiopia. Giulia Bonacci provides a description of what was perhaps the same event, held in December 2010, and identified as the 5th Ethiopian Nations, Nationalities and Peoples' Day. She states that Rastafari were identified as the 83rd tribe (2015a, 28) at this event. In addition, when I asked about Rastafari applying to the Ethiopian government under Article 39, Priest Paul said, "We did that. The parliament advise us to do that. We made a petition on behalf of the Diaspora community and submit it to the Foreign Affairs Ministry, to the prime minister's office."[3] This petition was submitted in early 2012.

By claiming to belong in this manner Rastafari would be acting within a context of claims to ethnic identity made since the change to ethnic federalism under the Ethiopian People's Revolutionary Democratic Front (EPRDF). But they are not alone in contemplating a status claim under Article 39. This is not untrodden territory. As anthropologist Dereje Feyissa has argued, the new constitution of the late 1990s offered up a new opportunity and political space for many groups throughout Ethiopia, where differing ethnic groups "engage[d] in the intense politics of inclusion" (2010, 35; 2011, passim) made possible by the new regime's ethnic federalism. In research on the Anywaa and the Nuer ethnic groups in the Gambella People's National Regional State (GPNRS) region of Ethiopia, Feyissa has tracked the fraught nature of Ethiopian identity. He calls the new opportunity—or new political space—of the 1990s a "demographic strategy of ethnic entitlement" (2010, 35). This means that a group or groups that represent larger numbers can dominate the regional state.

In the GPNRS, one of the nine ethnic regions in the country, the Anywaa are dominant. Due to changes in the border between Ethiopia and Sudan, the Nuer are portrayed as "foreigners" by the Anywaa. During the time of the *Derg*, there were advantages to claiming Sudanese citizenship, but post-1991, the Nuer "sought to make use of the new opportunities that trickle down from Ethiopia's ethnic federalism" (Feyissa 2010, 34). It was more advantageous at that time to claim an Ethiopian connection. In response, the Anywaa have demanded that the Ethiopian state firmly establish the border between Sudan and Ethiopia, confirming their claim that the Nuer are foreigners in Ethiopia. This is not a "commitment to a national identity but rather a national framework within which ethnic interests are protected and renegotiated" (p. 43). It is not about appealing to a sense of belonging as an Ethiopian, but rather about making use of the rules and regulations under ethnic federalism so as to make claims that will "protect" a particular ethnic group. Both the Anywaa and the Nuer are working through a notion of Ethiopianness by appealing to the Ethiopian government's definitions of ethnic identity—the nations, nationalities and peoples of Ethiopia.

Anthropologist Sayuri Yoshida has discussed the claim of the Manjo people of southwest Ethiopia (2008; 2013). A socially discriminated minority[4] in the Kafa and Sheka zones of this part of the country, the Manjo have declared that they are an ethnic group and have petitioned the government, under Article 39, to be recognized as one of the nations, nationalities and peoples of Ethiopia. In 1997 and 1998 individual Manjo petitioned the government, but in 2001 and 2006 they repeated their petition as a group. Their claim was based on the historical and cultural background of the Manjo people and was lodged in the interest of increasing their stature and decreasing the discrimination they face. In 2008, however, the regional government rejected the petition, suggesting that the shared language and shared geography between the Manjo and the Kafa peoples means that the Manjo are not a separate nation, nationality or people. The government acknowledged the social discrimination, but suggested this was due to a lack of good policy and governance. Affirming Manjo as an ethnic group was not seen as a means of alleviating discrimination. Although the Manjo failed in their struggle for representation through the system of ethnic federalism, they did not accept the decision of the government and have continued their petitioning.[5] The Anywaa, Nuer and Manjo all presented their claims in terms of the framework created by the ethnic federalist government of the EPRDF. The 1995 constitution opened up new avenues for claiming representation in Ethiopia and each of these groups has been making use of this opportunity. The Rastafari claim to land on the basis of a land grant by the former Emperor Haile Selassie falls on deaf ears in post-imperial Ethiopia. This is especially true given that Shashemene lies in Oromia, the largest of Ethiopia's nine regions in terms of both area and population. Both Giulia Bonacci and I have written about the relationship between Oromo and Rastafari within Shashemene.[6] In discussions with a range of informants throughout my research, including a group of Oromo farmers living in the same area as many Rastafari, there was an underlying frustration with the Rastafari respect for Haile Selassie, given the Oromo perspective of the Emperor as colonizer. I was also told that Rastafari claim for land is problematic, but a lesser problem given the wider challenge of Oromo sovereignty within the wider Ethiopian state. With regard, however, to the particular Rastafari situation, the issue of colonization of the Oromo, with specific reference to the strategies of Haile Selassie, has also been discussed for a long period of time.[7] The reality as of 2019, however, is that Oromo groups have been actively protesting the government—and the Rastafari are included in the segment of the population that are being protested against.

Though the situation remains fraught with political uncertainty, it is important to note that this has opened up opportunities to renegotiate identity. In November 2019, the Sidama ethnic community voted with 98.5 per cent support to create a Sidama state, in accordance with the Ethiopian constitution. The results of this referendum remain to be seen.[8] In May 2020, an article in *Ethiopia Insight*[9] attributed to Sidama Human Rights Activists, stated that the results of the referendum were not being respected. As Ethiopia moves towards a 2020 election, this issue of the Sidama referendum will continue to be of import. Perhaps this ethnonationalist moment in Ethiopian history might allow Rastafari to succeed in making a claim to ethnic status in Ethiopia. Though the process is difficult and they might fail like the Manjo, Article 39 still holds out the possibility for recognition and acceptance.

PAN-AFRICAN IDENTITY: DIASPORA POSSIBILITY

The lack of cohesiveness in the Rastafari community—as well as the reality that some Rastafari wish to maintain other citizenship rights—does not mean that Rastafari have given up on returning home. Rastafari continue to come to Ethiopia in the hope of settling in Shashemene. Priest Paul underlines the narrative of Rastafari as members of the African Diaspora: "We realize not only our divine right to return home but our inherent responsibility to help in the development of Ethiopia/Africa as the slave trade hurt those at home and abroad. We do this for all the Africans of the world."[10]

In a subsequent interview with me, he spoke about the importance of seeing Rastafari as part of the African Diaspora as a strategy of belonging. "This conference was to stabilize our integration within the African society," he said. "Within the African Union and the African continent right now the agenda is the integration of the Diaspora. Because the Diaspora as they classify it are the Africans that live out of Africa." Although this is how he positions Rastafari, it is clear that the focus is on membership of the African Diaspora: "The conference that we organized in April [2012], it wasn't really a Rastafarian conference, it was a global Diaspora conference. Because I an I in the forefront it seemed like it was a Rasta thing." This was a conference to take Rastafari issues beyond the Rastafari community. Certainly, the goal of the seminar was to discuss issues of importance to the Rastafari community, but it was the issue of Diaspora that took precedence at the seminar and perhaps in the minds of the organizers. The press release refers to the organizers of the conference as the Shashemene African Diaspora Rastafarian Development Association. It is fitting that "Rastafarian" comes after "Diaspora" even here.

Priest Paul maintains that the event was "To show that we are here, why not work with us and we can work with you?" It could be argued that the very focus of the event suggests that Rastafari are looking for ways to work with the surrounding community—ways to fit in and leverage their membership in the wider African Diaspora community. Ethiopian citizenship is important, but engaging with the contemporary continent-wide focus on the historic, present and possible future contributions of the Diaspora is yet another way of figuring out how to work with the situation. Priest Paul described the feedback from the first-time visiting ambassadors as extremely positive. The event drew more than just the community. Significantly, Addis Ababa University Professor Abraham "Abiyi" Ford also attended. As the descendent of some of the first Black, yet non-Rastafari, settlers in Ethiopia, throughout his life, Ford connected with Rastafari through Diaspora. This focus allows Rastafari to access yet another type of cultural citizenship. Yes, they feel they have a divine right to return home to Ethiopia, here expressed by Priest Paul in the press release, but they are also willing to classify themselves alongside all other members of the African Diaspora. Addis Ababa-based Rastafari Desta Meghoo was also involved in the organization of the seminar and was the keynote speaker. In her address she spoke of the continued fight for legal recognition in Ethiopia on behalf of Rastafari as members of the African Diaspora.[11]

It was not until two years after the establishment of the African Union, headquartered in Addis Ababa, that the contribution of the African Diaspora was declared to be of significant import. According to amendments to the AU's constitutive act, the organization "invite[s] and encourage[s] the full participation of the African Diaspora as an important part of our Continent, in the building of the African Union" (2003, 2). The African Diaspora as a whole has been described at African Union gatherings as being the sixth region of the continent. Though this has not been established formally, it is certainly a mobilization platform. This Diaspora includes, as African-American founder of the Diaspora African Forum Mission in Ghana Erieka Bennett describes it, "two types of Diasporans—those of us taken during slavery and those who leave Africa to work in greener pastures" (Otas 2012). According to Bennett, it is the latter group that the AU is interested in at the moment. Given the launch of the Ethiopian Diaspora Association, an organization for those of Ethiopian heritage who have moved away from the country in relatively recent years, it is clear that Ethiopia's priorities are similar. Regardless, at the African Union's Diaspora affairs summit held in May 2012, Diaspora Engagement Affairs director general Mulugeta Kelil recalled Rastafari asking to be considered Diaspora. A Rastafari delegation did attend, but there were also other representatives, such as Bennett, who represented the pan-African community created by slavery. Though Ethiopia as a country may be focused on the more recent Diaspora as opposed to the one that developed as a result of forced removal during the trans-Atlantic slave trade, the AU definition of Diaspora is quite wide, "consisting of peoples of African origin living outside the continent, irrespective of their citizenship and nationality and who are willing to contribute to the development of the continent and the building of the African Union".[12] Thus, Rastafari could potentially leverage this definition as a means of engaging with Africa in general and Ethiopia in particular.

Desta Meghoo views the Rastafari argument for repatriation as members of the African Diaspora as a powerful means of connecting with Ethiopia. This, however, means focusing on a shared history, namely, that of being the descendants of those who were forcibly displaced: "We are talking about people who were displaced. Physically taken . . . That's the experience we are trying to address." The reality of Rastafari members of other races raises questions about Meghoo's framework—a framework that she and others presented to the government. Instead of claiming that Rastafari are an ethnic group, Meghoo's argument is that Rastafari— specifically Black Rastafari—are members of the African Diaspora, and that is the basis of the claim. The following quotation sheds light on Meghoo's explanation of this perspective and the context of her argument:

> It makes it very hard for us. Even the documents that we submitted having to do with reintegration we had to do as Black people. We had to take Rastafari out. Because if we submit a document to the government asking for citizenship for Rastafari, it's pink, blue, green, yellow orange. Locks, no locks, anyone can . . . Our reintegration and our claim to Africa is not based on our faith . . . Let me tell you what one of the immigration specialists said to us. He asked us, you Rastafarians come back and you are seeking immigration you are asking this, that, and the other. Now, if things are so bad in the west, how come you are bringing your colonialists with you? This is what the government wants to know. They're confused.
>
> We stay focused on the original aim: Black man redemption, liberation, repatriation. Whether you are a Black baldhead,[13] Black Rasta, this is what the movement was created for. Our elders never taught us that the movement was just for Rasta people. That's not what we were taught. We always knew that it was for Black people at home or abroad . . . If you are Black therefore and you can benefit from it, then, boom, here it is. We are going to lobby for you on your behalf . . . It used to be [in the] 60s and 70s that it was just understood that when you said Rasta you meant Black people. But that's not the case anymore.
>
> We are seeking legal remedies for these issues. And the first thing that we need to do is define the group . . . We are dealing with inheritance to the land of Ethiopia. The fact that you are Rastafari, that's wonderful, that's good, but it has gotten to the point that we have had to revert back to the African argument, to the African reasoning. That's the only protection we have and the only way to keep the vehicle driving. Otherwise we're going to be stuck in this quagmire.

Whereas the AU definition specifies the Diaspora as containing individuals of "African origin", Meghoo further clarifies the definition for Rastafari as she draws a line between Rastafari and the African Diaspora. All members of the African Diaspora can be Rastafari, but not all Rastafari are members of the African Diaspora. She defines ethnicity by historical connection to slavery and the experience of Blackness. This is not an all-inclusive picture. Though there are non-Black Rastafari, Meghoo is speaking only of Black Rastafari: "Whether you are a Black baldhead, Black Rasta, this is what the movement was created for". It also reflects other situations in which Rastafari have been granted residency in Africa—specifically in Ghana and Tanzania. Monique Bedasse writes of the Tanzanian offer of both residency and citizenship to Rastafari, but with racial specificity: "letters concerning land allotment for Rastafarians, repeatedly underscored that race was central to the pan-African negotiation that was taking place between Rastafarians and the Tanzanian state" (2017, 125). This strategy also reflects both the AU's focus on Diaspora as well as the Ethiopian government's ethnic federalist opportunities. Meghoo's claim, as she puts it, removes faith from the equation—it attempts to clarify the Rastafari position in Ethiopia, but by removing the belief system it removes a number of Rastafari faithful from the equation as well. Meghoo sees the community stuck in a "quagmire" and this is how she suggests it move forward.

Interestingly, by carving out the faith and focusing on the historical connection of Rastafari to Africa as well as an ethnic and historic connection to the Black experience, Meghoo is eliminating a large part of what disturbs so many Ethiopians about Rastafari—their belief system, which is associated with the view that Haile Selassie was divine. One might postulate that this approach is in keeping with the available means of integration. Much as Rastafari in Shashemene are attempting to work within the existing system in order to build cultural citizenship capital, in the same way this approach attempts to navigate the systems provided by the Ethiopian government and the African Union.

In 2011 a delegation of Rastafari sent a letter to the prime minister of Ethiopia discussing the history of the Rastafari community in Shashemene, the economic contribution of the repatriates, and the cultural make-up of the community (Christian 2012, 37). And then, about four weeks before Prime Minister Meles Zenawi passed away, arrangements were made for a delegation of Rastafari to meet with him. Meghoo explains:

> Interestingly enough . . . a meeting was arranged headed by Priest Paul, a delegation, myself, Sister Jasmine, Brother Moody, to go to the prime minister's chief of cabinet to discuss immigration issues . . . You've got these issues which have to be analyzed in context and in a legal framework because these are legal issues that we're talking about. Which we don't do. We usually bring our emotions to it and that just masks any solid talk so I was very pleased that we were able to present our proposal on reintegration and we had some ideas that addressed both citizenship and residency—both permanent and temporary. So that was under consideration, though since the prime minister passed, we have to get back on top of things.

One wonders how Meles Zenawi would have reacted. Would he have accepted a Rastafari petition as the 83rd nation of Ethiopia? Would he have preferred to encourage involvement in the country as members of the all-important African Diaspora? It is hard to tell. One thing is clear—the Ethiopian government was willing to listen to Rastafari. Over coffee at a restaurant in Addis Ababa in late 2012, some Ethiopian friends suggested that this meeting was a one-time window. There was no way the opportunity would recur. First, in a country of over eighty million adjusting to a new leader, the concerns of a group of a few hundred wouldn't be a great priority. But Meghoo understands this: "You have to be persistent, consistent, and follow up and so forth".

ANOTHER OPTION: WORKING WITH RESIDENCY

As a result of the persistence of Rastafari, the Ethiopian government moved a major step forward in 2017. It was reported that Rastafari repatriates, alongside both foreign contributors to the development of Ethiopia and Ethio-Israelis, were to be afforded residency in the country. Identification cards would provide legal legitimacy for Rastafari repatriates, but it was clear that this would not mean that Rastafari would be considered Ethiopian citizens: "Thousands of people who will be issued the new identity cards still cannot take part in elections or engage in the country's security and defense sectors" (Associated Press 2017). Given the research I had completed, this was a significant and perhaps somewhat stunning development. Here was a very specific, and legal, acknowledgement of Rastafari repatriation—but it still stopped short of the full acceptance as citizens, something that the previously described strategies still could potentially allow. It is also useful to note that documentation for Rastafari has not been unfamiliar during the years that Shashemene has acted as de facto Rastafari settlement in Ethiopia. Anthropologist Shelene Gomes documents a range of "local district identification cards or expired national identification cards . . . In a few cases, Rastafari and their children hold one-year or five-year renewable residence permits" (2018, 121). However, as both Gomes and I have noted, Rastafari, with few exceptions, do not possess Ethiopian passports and therefore citizenship.

In Mahlet Ayele Beyecha's master's thesis, the acquisition (or attempted acquisition) of resident identification is mentioned. Specifically, the struggle to gain residency status is mentioned in an interview conducted with Shashemene-based Bobo Ashanti *Qes*.[14] She identifies as being named Banduli:

> It has been like six months that they put up on the news that on the big media internationally . . . the Rastafari get legal status, but InI here same way and nothing has been done and it has been swept under the carpet and all this thing is wrong . . . the longer it take to get our residency, they have no respect for us (2018, 94).

It would seem that time will tell what the impact of the new access to residency actually will be. Alongside the ongoing conflict over ethnic sovereignty, this is an area that will require attention over the coming years.

Ethiopia is a large and varied country. There are indications that through the leadership of Prime Minister Abiy Ahmed, which began on 2 April 2018, the crisis in which Ethiopia found itself earlier in that year was apparently being resolved. But there are consistent reports of problems— for example, some social media reports from within the Rastafari community indicate that there has been fallout for repatriates. The reality of ethnic federalism and the multicultural nature of the country mean that Ethiopia and its citizens are grappling with the challenges of multiple narratives—multiple ways of conceiving of the future of Ethiopia. Rastafari, at the same time, are still grappling with integration into Ethiopia. But they will continue trying to make their narrative part of an Ethiopian narrative.

Note & Acknowledgment: Sections of this essay have been adapted from my *Visions of Zion: Ethiopians and Rastafari in the Search for the Promised Land* (2014). I also wish to thank the Canadian Social Sciences and Humanities Research Council for their kind support of my research.

Notes

1 I wish to add a note here to state that Professor Abraham Ford (affectionately known as *Gash* Abiyi), who is mentioned in this paper, was a tremendous support to me in my research. Also, Sister Ijahnya was such a welcoming presence in Shashemene, as well as a phenomenal teacher through her spoken and written words. Both joined the ancestors during the process of this publication coming to fruition. I believe it is important to commemorate those whose work has been so valuable and whose kindness is so appreciated. My understanding of the Rastafari movement and repatriation would be lesser would it have not been for *Gash* Abiyi and Sister Ijahnya, and for that reason this essay is livicated to them.

2 I discussed this in an article entitled "Encountering the Promised Land" for the website *Africa Is a Country* in 2017. See https://africasacountry.com/2017/08/encountering-the-promised-land-rastafari-in-ethiopia-and-shashemene.

3 Priest Paul (Wesley) Phang (Ethiopia Africa Black International Congress [EABIC]), interview, Shashemene, 14 June 2012.

4 Kafa and Sheka are located about four to five hundred kilometers southwest of Addis Ababa. Kafa is located partially in Oromia and partially in SNNPR. Sheka is located completely in SNNPR. Both areas are predominantly rural.

5 According to Leikola (2014), the Manjo are still considered as a minority within the wider Kafa ethnic group.

6 See Bonacci, "Mapping the Boundaries" (2015b) and some mention in *Exodus!* (2015a), and my "Water Development Projects" (2012).

7 A long message board post (and subsequent discussion) from 2003 is exemplary of this type of discussion that argues for the positionality of Oromo as colonized. See http://www.rastafarispeaks.com/repatriation/index.cgi?md=read;id=33029

8 I wish to thank Giulia Bonacci for bringing this to my attention. This event was covered by many international news services (BBC, Deutsche Welle, Al Jazeera, etc.). A particularly thorough treatment by Yonatan Fessha is "Standing Alone: Ethiopia's Sidama People Have Voted for Their Own State, a Turning Point for an Uncertain Federalism", *Quartz* (4 December 2019), https://qz.com/africa/1761079/ethiopias-sidama-people-voted-for-own-state-but-are-uncertain/

9 *Ethiopia Insight* is an online publication edited by British journalist and former Bloomberg Ethiopia correspondent William Davison. The piece I reference was published on 8 May 2020 as part of the "Verbatim" section of the website that allows for statements directly from organizations/groups such as Sidama Human Rights Activists. See "More Arrests in Sidama as Authorities Refuse to Hand Power to New Region", https://www.ethiopia-insight.com/2020/05/08/more-arrests-in-

sidama-as-authorities-refuse-to-hand-power-to-new-region/.

10 From the Returning Home Seminar in Shashemene, Ethiopia, press release that was published online in 2012 in a number of locations, including on Facebook at the following link: https://m.facebook.com/notes/rastafari-academy/returning-home-a-seminar-by-rastafari-for-african-ambassadors-in-shashemene-ethi/10151598237685241/

11 Desta Meghoo's keynote address was posted on SoundCloud on 8 May 2012, http://soundcloud.com/ethiopia-2

12 This definition can be found on the AU website. See here for further details: https://au.int/en/Diaspora-division

13 Meaning a Rastafari who does not wear his or her hair in dreadlocks.

14 It should be noted that *Qes* is "priest" in Amharic.

References

African Union. 2003. *Protocol on Amendments to the Constitutive Act of the African Union*. Adopted by the 1st Extraordinary Session of the Assembly of the Union in Addis Ababa, Ethiopia, on 3 February 2003 and by the 2nd Ordinary Session of the Assembly of the Union in Maputo, Mozambique, on 11 July 2003.

_____. 2013. Program of Events: 50th Anniversary of the OAU-AU. https://au.int/sites/default/files/newsevents/programmes/29101-pg-programm_of_africa_day_en…cairo_office.pdf.

Agence France-Presse. 2017. "Ethiopia to Issue IDs for Rastafarian Community". 30 July 2017. http:// www. jamaica observer. com/ business/ethiopia-to-issue-ids-for-rastafarian-community_106228.

Agunias, Dovelyn Rannveig, and Kathleen Newland. 2012. *Developing a Road Map for Engaging Diasporas in Development: A Handbook for Policy Makers and Practitioners in Home and Host Countries*. Geneva, Switzerland, and Washington, D.C.: International Organization for Migration and Migration Policy Institute.

Ashworth, Joanna, and Shaheen Nanji. 2012. *Diaspora Voices*. Vancouver: Simon Fraser University.

Associated Press. 2017. "Ethiopia to Give ID Cards to Rastafarians Long Stateless". 27 July2017.https://ghionjournal.com/ethiopia-to-give-id-cards-to-rastafarians-long-stateless-ap/.

Barnett, Michael. 2005. "The Many Faces of Rasta: Doctrinal Diversity within the Rastafari Movement". *Caribbean Quarterly* 51 (2): 67–78.

Bedasse, Monique. 2017. *Jah Kingdom: Rastafarians, Tanzania, and Pan-Africanism in the Age of Decolonization*. Chapel Hill: UNC Press Books.

Beyecha, Mahlet Ayale. 2018. "Rastafari in Ethiopia: Challenges and Paradoxes of Belonging". Master's thesis, African Studies Centre, Leiden University, Netherlands.

Bonacci, Giulia. 2007. "Pionniers et Héritiers Histoire du Retour, des Caraïbes à l'Éthiopie (19ème et 20ème Siècles)". PhD thesis, Paris, L'École des hautes études en sciences sociales.

_____. 2008. *Exodus! L'Histoire du Retour des Rastafariens en Éthiopie*. Paris: Scali.

_____. 2015a. *Exodus! Heirs and Pioneers, Rastafari Return to Ethiopia*. Kingston, JA: University of the West Indies Press.

_____. 2015b. "Mapping the Boundaries of Otherness: Naming Caribbean Settlers in Ethiopia". *African Diaspora* 8: 34–50.

Brinkerhoff, Jennifer M. ed. 2008. *Diasporas and Development: Exploring the Potential.* Boulder, Colo.: Rienner.

Christian, Ijahnya. 2012. "Return of the 6th Region: Rastafari Settlement in the Motherland Contributing to the African Renaissance". *CODESRIA Bulletin* no. 1–2, 30–42.

Ethiopian Government. 1995. *The Constitution of the Federal Democratic Republic of Ethiopia.* Addis Ababa.

Feyissa, Dereje. 2010. "More State than the State? The Anywaa's Call for the Rigidification of the Ethio-Sudanese Border". In *Borders and Borderlands as Resources in the Horn of Africa*, edited by Dereje Feyissa and Markus Virgil Hoehne, 27–44. London: James Currey.

_____. 2011. *Playing Different Games: The Paradox of Anywaa and Nuer Identification Strategies in the Gambella Region, Ethiopia.* Oxford: Berghahn.

Gebreluel, Goitom, and Biniam Bedasso. 2018. "Managing Ethiopia's Political Crisis". *Al Jazeera* (7 Feb). https://www.aljazeera.com/indepth/opinion/managing-ethiopia-political-crisis-180205113035729.html.

Gomes, Shelene. 2018. "Counter-Narratives of Belonging: Rastafari in the Promised Land". *The Global South* 12 (1): 112–128.

Hosein, Roger, Martin Franklin, and Samantha C. Joseph. 2009. "The Caribbean Diaspora—An Untapped Resource for Impacting Economic Development through Investments in the Caribbean". Dept. of Economics, UWI, Mona.http://sta.uwi.edu/conferences/09/salises/documents/M%20Franklin.pdf.

Ionescu, Dina. 2006. *Engaging Diasporas as Development Partners for Home and Destination Countries: Challenges for Policymakers.* Geneva: International Organization for Migration.

Leikola, Kirsi. 2014. "Talking Manjo: Linguistic Repertoires as Means of Negotiating Marginalization". PhD diss., University of Helsinki.

MacLeod, Erin C. 2012. "Water Development Projects and Cultural Citizenship: Rastafari Engagement with the Oromo in Shashemene, Ethiopia". In *Rastafari in the New Millennium*, edited by Michael Barnett, 89–103. Syracuse: Syracuse University Press.

_____. 2014. *Visions of Zion: Ethiopians and Rastafari in the Search for the Promised Land.* New York: NYU Press.

Otas, Belinda. 2012. "Why the AU Is Courting the Diaspora". *New African Magazine*, 26 July 2012. http://www.newafricanmagazine.com/special-reports/other-reports/10-years-of-the-au/why-the-au-is-courting-the-Diaspora.

Price, Charles. 2009. *Becoming Rasta: Origins of Rastafari Identity in Jamaica.* New York: NYU Press.

Robertson, Susan. 2008. "Bringing Diasporas to Market: Leveraging Talent (and Patriotism) for Nations' Economies". In *Symbolic Power in Cultural Context: Uncovering Social Reality*, edited by J. Houtsonen and A. Antikainen, 229–242. Rotterdam, Netherlands: Sense Publishers.

Yoshida, Sayuri. 2008. "Searching for a Way Out of Social Discrimination: A Case Study of the Manjo through the 2002 Incident in Kafa". *Nilo-Ethiopian Studies* 12:47–60.

_____. 2013. "The Struggle against Social Discrimination: Petitions by the Manjo in the Kafa and Sheka Zones of Southwest Ethiopia". *Nilo-Ethiopian Studies* 18:1–19.

Testimony

IVAN COORE, A RASTAFARI IN THE PROMISED LAND

DEREK BISHTON

Ivan Coore, Kingston Harbour, 13 September 2014

Photo © 2020 by Derek Bishton

IDEAZ—an interdisciplinary social science & humanities journal, vol. 15, 2020, pp.180-187

I van Coore—Brother Levi—who passed away on 7 September 2019, played a significant role in the early 1970s helping the fledgling Rastafari community in Shashemene, Ethiopia, to establish itself after the overthrow of Emperor Haile Selassie. He came from one of Jamaica's elite families. His father, David Coore, was a lawyer who helped draft the Jamaican Constitution in 1961 and later served as Michael Manley's deputy in the People's National Party Government of the 1970s. His mother, Rita, was a gifted musician and teacher, and his younger brother Steven "Cat" Coore was a founding member of the legendary Third World reggae band. Ivan became a Rasta in the early 1970s while still at school, and in 1973, at the age of 19, accompanied Vernon Carrington—Brother Gad, founder of the Twelve Tribes of Israel—on a fact-finding visit to Ethiopia. He subsequently decided to stay and study at the University in Addis Ababa. He returned to Jamaica in 1977.

I spent several weeks in September and October 2014 working with Ivan on Giulia Amati's film *Shashamane* (Blink Blink Prod., 2016). The main part of the interview reproduced here was recorded while filming in Jamaica. I have supplemented this with additional details that were either sent to me by Ivan, gathered in the many conversations we had, or posted directly by Ivan to his Facebook account.

As we drove around Trench Town, with Ivan at the wheel and Giulia filming from the passenger seat, he reflected on the social conditions in Jamaica in the late 1960s.

> This was a time of increasing wealth for the rich while the poor were getting poorer. Politics in independent Jamaica was centred around two parties and this tended to create divisions amongst people who would naturally have been united, but now, because of politics, became divided. So areas became marked as PNP or JLP areas, and there was inter-community violence based on which party you belonged to. And on top of that there was the ever-present threat of police intimidation and police brutality.

Most of this brutality, he said, was directed against Black consciousness movements.

> In the late '60s it was illegal to have any book that advocated Black power. If you were found with a book by Malcolm X, Stokely Carmichael or Walter Rodney, you could be arrested and imprisoned. And this is a *Black nation* and these are books by *Black people* written on behalf of *Black people*. But our government saw it fitting to ban these books. So all of this generated a sort of social antagonism that resulted in violence and people feeling dispossessed and that there was no future for them here.
>
> The people who live in a poor area, normally one would expect that they would be united in a common purpose, to escape from poverty; that they would be driven towards unity, but the reality was that they were encouraged to be divided by joining a political party. If you didn't join a party you would find yourself as a total outcast—which most Rastafari did. And politicians coerced whole areas to swear allegiance to them, and this could only be done if there was a violent enforcer, somebody who was armed who could turn threats into reality. So it was a political act that created antagonism in the ghetto. And on top of this you had the security forces who were programmed to oppress poor people and the principal way they did this was through ganja, the anti-ganja laws.

All these factors had the result of making the Back-to-Africa movement very appealing, reflected Ivan.

> The visit of his Imperial Majesty to Jamaica in 1966 caused a huge awakening of African consciousness and increased dramatically the desire and the number of people who wished to eventually get to Ethiopia.

In 1973, Ivan—aged just 19 and only recently married to Joan Hosang—was chosen to be part of an Ethiopian World Federation Chapter 15 mission to Ethiopia. The other members were Brother Gad (aka Vernon Carrington) and Brother Benji (aka Lascelles Laird). They left Jamaica on 23 May, spent a day in London and then boarded an Ethiopian Airlines flight for Addis Ababa, landing there on 25 May—Africa Liberation Day, which marks the founding of the Organisation for African Unity in 1963. Ivan recalled that the roads were decorated with the flags of all the member states along the roadway leading from the airport to the city centre.

> It was a magnificent spectacle. I remember feeling so good to know that we were so close to the Emperor and Addis was even more beautiful than I had imagined.

The delegation's mission was to discover what they could about Shashemene and other land settlements, but there were disagreements between Brother Gad and Ivan over the way the former related to some of the people they met—so in the end "it wasn't particularly successful in regard to its stated aims", Ivan recalled. However, when the time came to depart, Ivan made a decision to stay and applied to and was accepted into the Haile Selassie I University in Addis Ababa to study economics.

> I was supported in this decision by my family and so I went back to Jamaica for my wife and young son Daniel and started at the university on September 16, 1973—which happened to be the period just prior to the Ethiopian revolution. So right away there was tension and everything was not as we had been led to believe in the West, where we thought everything was going well with His Majesty's regime.
>
> However, by the end of my first semester, I had obtained good grades and I was very happy. In addition, I was able to get things done for the Shashemene settlement. Early in 1974 my father visited—he was the Minister of Finance in the Jamaican government at the time—and he agreed to provide support for the Shashemene settlement. Then Dudley Thompson, the Minister of Foreign Affairs, visited and he confirmed that they were going to provide financial support for Shashemene, and this was excellent because early in February, when the troubles really started, the university closed and I was now left with an uncertain future. Fortunately, I was offered a job with the embassy in connection with the expected aid that was coming. They would need a field officer and that was to be my job. The money came in June, so my wife and I agreed that we should move to Shashemene as life in Addis was becoming increasingly tense and uncomfortable.

Before they moved, however, Ivan and Joan experienced a very moving encounter with His Imperial Majesty and members of the Royal Family. Although the revolutionary movement was gaining pace with the arrest of many officials and former ministers, the Emperor and his family still attended church on 5 May 1974 for a thanksgiving service to celebrate the anniversary of the defeat of Mussolini's fascist invaders in 1941. Ivan and Joan and their son Daniel were also part of the congregation that day. Ivan recalls:

> Daniel, who I had in my arms, and was aged two years and four months, lifted his hand and pointed at the Emperor as he walked down the aisle to leave. He said, 'Ababa Janhoy', the name used by most Ethiopians when referring to the Emperor affectionately. I saw a short man but with excellent build and physique, not a mark of fat or excess anywhere, ramrod straight and upright. He had a youthful looking countenance and penetrating eyes that seemed to be filled with wonderful clarity. Our eyes met and I believe he smiled.

For Joan, the moment was even more special as Princess Tenagne Werk, the Emperor's oldest daughter, stopped and shook her hand.

The political situation became even more volatile and the Emperor was deposed on 12 September 1974, and on the following day the military council formed a new government, which became known as the *Derg*. Ivan recalled:

> We had been using the assistance in Shashemene to do our farming. This was a shocking time, a time of great self-introspection. As a group we were questioning everything. But we had faith that the scriptures were right and that this was part of the plan and we should just work with it. We had a lot of difficulty about how the revolution was carried out. They tried to spread lies and negate all the good things that the Emperor had done. The military government nationalized all the land, but we went ahead and continued planting our crops.

Some of the innovations made by Brother Clifton Baugh and his wife, Inez, who had arrived in Shashemene in 1969 from Jamaica, transformed farming techniques in the area. Brother Baugh showed how it was possible to plant and reap two harvests a year rather than one, which was the practice of the local Oromo farmers. Crops included *t'ef*—the high protein grain that thrives at high altitudes—and soya beans.

However, all the time the Ethiopian Revolution was fermenting, and on 1 March 1975 the land occupied by Rastafari settlers was invaded by Ethiopian peasant farmers. They had interpreted the nationalization of land decree to mean that this land should be confiscated. So they came and took it. Ivan recalled the day quite clearly.

> On that morning, I was awake because Joan was seven months pregnant with our second child and I had the habit of getting up early as water had to be fetched from the other room we occupied, which was separated by a courtyard from the room that provided our sleeping and bathroom space.
>
> I heard the commotion and went to the gate of the compound and saw literally hundreds of peasants, some on horseback, some on foot and others ploughing through our fields. In a few instances they had started at the doorway of some settlers, leaving only a small track to enable visits to the outhouse. I approached a couple of the Oromo horsemen because I recognized one who had worked with us

only a few months before, when we were cultivating our soya bean crop. Several of the invaders had worked with different settlers over the years, and the treatment meted out to individuals spoke volumes. Brother Baugh and Brother Dyer,[1] who had extensive gardens surrounding their houses, were allowed to keep these, although their fields were ploughed. Others were not so lucky as the ploughmen came as close as possible to their doorsteps. My Oromo friend explained that this was now their time, and Haile Selassie, our King, Patron and Emperor, had been dethroned and now it was a people's government and we should vacate the lands and return to Jamaica. In fact they could have driven us away there and then, but out of respect for our community and past associations they would allow us time to leave peacefully. We pointed out to him that we, Jamaican settlers, had lived here for years under the heel of James Piper[2] and had to fight to gain the right to use the land that had been granted to the Black Peoples of the West for assisting Ethiopia during the Italian occupation, and we considered ourselves to be Ethiopians. This statement again drew some sympathy as Piper was not generally well loved by the Oromos. In fact they had invaded his compound, and we heard that during the course of that day, he and his wife, Helen, fled to Addis Ababa and the safety of the US Embassy.

The following days were a great test of our faith, but in retrospect, collectively, as represented by the majority, defiance and determination to 'live over this temporary setback' became our resolve.

On Friday 6 March, Ivan went to Addis Ababa to give a report to Ambassador Foreman on the situation in Shashemene as it related to the Jamaican settlers and also to collect his wages. He was greeted with the news that there was a telex for him that had just arrived. The news was devastating. His mother had died that same morning. The telex had been sent within an hour of her passing in an attempt to catch the Ethiopian office before it closed for the weekend. Later that evening he spoke to his father by phone, who asked if he and Joan would consider naming the child she was carrying Rita, if it was a girl. Rita was born in Shashemene seven weeks later.

When Ivan reported the situation in Shashemene, the official response was to offer all the settlers a ticket back to Jamaica. Ivan knew this would not be a choice many settlers would want to make. An Ethiopian woman who worked in the embassy suggested that they do what other Ethiopian groups who had been similarly disenfranchised since the military takeover had done, which was to write a petition to the military government seeking to restore their land rights. When Ivan returned to Shashemene, he talked to all the settlers about the options available, and twenty decided to vote for preparing a petition. Eleven people decided to accept the embassy's offer of a flight back to Jamaica.

What followed was one of the most remarkable moments in the history of the Rasta community in Ethiopia. Ivan and Brother Noel Dyer travelled to Addis Ababa from Shashemene on 26 August 1975 to present a petition to the Ministry of Land Reform. The petition asked for the land seized by the Farmers' Association earlier in the year to be returned. Ivan and Brother Dyer presented the petition on 26 August, the day the *Derg* announced His Imperial Majesty's death. Ivan admitted:

> We heard the news as we were on the way to present the petition. It was a shock, but if anything it made us more determined to go ahead. We saw the surprise on the soldiers' faces that we had even turned up. Anyway, they accepted our petition and two weeks later the embassy was informed that it was not the military government's intention to take away the land, but the quantum had to be re-examined because we were living in an area where the average landholding was five acres, and there was no way they could allow us to have twenty-five acres each. They agreed to give five acres to each of the signatories to the petition, but we would have to work it communally and without hiring any local labour. So a month or so later government officials came down and surveyed the land, and we had one hundred acres instead of the original five hundred acres.

In initiating this action, Ivan Coore, with the support of the other pioneer settlers in Shashemene, ensured that the Rastafari community in Ethiopia survived its most perilous moment. Ivan recalled this period as one of intense tension:

> During this period, the resistance to the *Derg* was increasing and their response was to become more hard line. In some areas it was close to civil war. In Addis you had bands of urban militias roaming around looking for people who were breaking the curfew. It wasn't a good time to be an Ethiopian who had some money.
>
> My wife had our second child—Rita—in Shashemene in April 1975 and most of that year was a time of uncertainty, and by the end of the year my wife was pregnant again with our third child. We agonized over it and we decided, in early 1976, that it would be best for her to return to Jamaica with the children. To make even one journey to Addis at that time—for prenatal check-ups, for example—meant being stopped up to twenty times and there was sporadic violence all over the countryside. So Joan, Daniel and Rita left at the end of March 1976.

Although Ivan's degree course had been interrupted by the revolution, he applied to the Ministry of Education for a teaching job. There was a severe shortage of teachers and he was offered a post at Wolaita Sodo Comprehensive High School, which was located some one hundred thirty kilometres south-west of Shashemene. He took up his new post in September 1976 and arranged to rent a room in a small hotel—returning to Shashemene some weekends and during the holidays.

In spite of the fact that a civil war was raging between supporters of the *Derg* and the Ethiopian Revolutionary Party, Shashemene remained relatively peaceful.

We were happy that we had our little corner where we could stay quietly out of the way. Great things happened because Alan Cole, one of Jamaica's best footballers, came to Ethiopia. He made a great impression and he was offered a job to coach the Ethiopian Airlines football team.

Events took a dramatic, new turn for Ivan in May 1977, however. On 1 May, a May Day celebration in Wolaita Sodo turned into a violent confrontation between pro and anti *Derg* forces. Ivan was arrested by local militia along with many other teachers and students on suspicion of distributing anti-government propaganda. They were badly beaten and then loaded into trucks to be taken to a detention centre. Several times on the journey the militia stopped to discuss whether their prisoners should just be summarily executed.

We finally arrived at a gated compound where there was what looked like an administrative building with barrack-like structures in close proximity. We were ordered to assemble ourselves in three lines: one for students and teachers from the high school, another for other workers from the town and the third line for persons who had no specific ties to the town. The longest line by far was that of students and teachers. This compound was manned by the Ethiopian Official Military, the Army, and was not controlled by the peasants. A soldier walked along the line, confiscating all our possessions including IDs, wallets, watches and any jewellery we were wearing. While this was going on, one of my students who had also been arrested started telling the soldier about me as I was having difficulty communicating fluently in Amharic in response to the questions that were being asked of all of us. This soldier, may God bless him and his generations, looked at me intently and then started to question me in English, and when I confirmed all that my student had told him—that I was from Jamaica and had played no part in the demonstrations—he placed his right hand on his brow, made a deep sigh, and immediately asked all the teachers in the line to confirm or deny what I had said. When he saw that the confirmation was unanimous, he came over to me and immediately apologized for any hurt I may have suffered, returned my watch and ring and ordered me back to the truck, this time to sit in the cab, and await my transportation back to town. The relief I felt then was indescribable and I remember tears of joy and relief as I walked away from the captive area. I also felt incredibly saddened as I contemplated the fate that awaited my students and colleagues.

Although Ivan returned to teach at the school until his contract ended in July, it was obvious that he was not going to be able to bring his wife and family back to Ethiopia in the near future.

It was quite common going to Addis to see dead bodies stacked up with a sign saying this was the fate of the enemies of the revolution. Basically it was not a good time to be in Ethiopia because if you were with the *Derg* you could be killed, and if you were against the *Derg* you could be killed.

So, reluctantly, Ivan returned to Jamaica in the autumn of 1977. Although he never returned to Ethiopia, he retained a deep love for the country and an unshakeable faith that "the Lion of Judah shall break every chain".

Notes

1   Brother Noel Dyer's epic journey to Shashemene is told in my book *Black Heart Man* (Chatto & Windus, 1986). A version is available on my blog, https://www. derekbishton.com/noel-dyer-sets-out-to-walk-to-ethiopia/

2   Helen and James Piper were born in the early years of the twentieth century in Montserrat. They migrated to the United States where they became followers of Marcus Garvey and then converted to become Black Jews in Harlem—a faith they maintained in Ethiopia. They were also members of the Ethiopian World Federation, founded in 1937 in New York. In 1948 they settled in Addis Ababa, Ethiopia, part of a generation of pan-Africanists who were engaged in the reconstruction of the country after the war with Italy. A couple years later, they were the first settlers on the Shashemene land grant. (See Giulia Bonacci, "'It Would Have Pleased the Great Spirit of Mr. Garvey': Helen and James Piper and the Return to Ethiopia", *International Journal of African Historical Studies*, 51 (2): 293–316 (2018).

COMMENTARY:

Reflections on 2020 through a Rastafari Lens

MICHAEL BARNETT

IDEAZ—an interdisciplinary social science & humanities journal, vol. 15, 2020, pp.188-191

The year 2020 has been particularly mystical and bizarre. It ends, as it began, as a year of uncertainty, unpredictability and one which has been a test of character, fortitude and faith for most people.

Many Rastafari who make much of having a "far eye" (as may be inferred from the syllabic ending of the nomenclature itself, *Rasta-far-i*) proclaim their ability to have a far vision—in other words, the gift of second sight, or even better, such a very deep and clear vision that they could always see beyond the surface of things. For some Rastafari, the novel coronavirus did not just spring up organically, or via some freak biological accident (e.g. jumping across the species barrier to infect humans). The proponents of this theory argue that it originated in a laboratory. In other words, they hold to the view that the novel coronavirus is actually man-made, deliberately created for the purpose of biological warfare aimed at wiping out designated populations of the human family. The fact that it has effectively affected much of the world's human population is seen to be a miscalculation by some and a shrewd intended outcome by others.

Whether one subscribes to the conspiracy theory or not, one thing is clear. People's basic freedoms have now been compromised, economies globally have shrunk, and the gap between the have-nots and the haves has widened. On a macro scale, the economic gap between the Global South and the Global North has widened, and countries that were in a dependent state are now even more dependent. Those nations without adaptable economies and a strong technological infrastructure are going to find it increasingly more difficult to survive, as we plunge further into the future.

BLACK LIVES MATTER REIGNITED

The other major event that occurred in 2020 was the reigniting of the Black Lives Matter movement, with the tragic death of George Floyd at the hands of the Minneapolis police on a day that was celebrated as Memorial Day in the United States, May 25, 2020. Paradoxically, George Floyd became a martyr to a movement that was initially resisted and denigrated to a large extent by the powers that be (the establishment) when it first emerged in July 2013 in protest against the acquittal of George Zimmerman of the murder of a young Black teenager, Trayvon Martin. Now the movement has gained worldwide popularity, with different racial and ethnic groups coming together to express their disgust at not only the brutal killing of George Floyd, but the systemic racism that people of colour are exposed to in many countries in the world, but most blatantly in the United States. At the time of writing (August 10, 2020), the Black Lives Matter protests are still ongoing in the United States, with the critical region of the demonstrations being Portland, Oregon.

The killing of George Floyd seems to have reignited the consciousness of many around the world in the search for justice, the fight against oppression in all its forms, especially racial discrimination, and in advocating for the decolonization of public places and people's attitudes. Some argue that there has been a shift, a new awakening, the yearning to pursue what is right and just and to repudiate and expose the crimes, sins and oppression of the former colonial powers.

As an ostensibly anti-colonial movement, forged in the tradition of Black resistance against colonial oppression in Jamaica, the Rastafari movement notably has ideological aims and goals that are in alignment with those of the Black Lives Matter movement.

Let us briefly recap a few notable occurrences resulting from the Black Lives Matter protests of 2020.

• Push Back Against the Police

Within ten days of the protests, the State of Minneapolis bans choke holds, and their City Council votes to defund the police and fund investment and safety measures instead. The charges against officer Chauvin and his three accomplices are notably upgraded to second-degree murder, and all four officers are arrested and charged.

Dallas adopts a "duty to intervene" rule that requires police officers to stop other officers who are engaging in inappropriate force; while New Jersey's Attorney-General announces that the state of New Jersey is to update its "use of force" guidelines for the first time in two decades. In Maryland a bipartisan group of state lawmakers announces a police reform group. In Los Angeles, the City Council introduces a motion to reduce the LAPD's US$1.8 million operating budget. The Massachusetts Bay Transportation Authority agrees to stop making its public buses available to police officers to transport them to protests; while in the city of Ft Lauderdale in South Florida police brutality captured on cameras leads to immediate suspensions and firing of the officers involved.

• Monuments are Taken Down

Monuments celebrating confederate luminaries are removed in cities located in southern states such as Virginia and Alabama—something which previous agitation and activism have been unable to achieve.

After a Black Lives Matter protest in Antwerp, Belgium over the weekend of June 6 – 7, 2020, the authorities decide to remove the statue of colonial king, Leopold II. Notably one of the most brutal European leaders who exercised colonial authority in Africa, Leopold inflicted immense human atrocities on the Congolese population—such as, for example, the mass amputation of the hands of those natives considered not to be working hard enough on the rubber plantations as they extracted latex from the trees.

In Bristol, England the statue of notorious slave trader Edward Colston was dismounted with pieces of rope by Black Lives Matter protesters. It was then rolled along the ground and thrown into the harbour. Protesters jeered and cheered as this symbol of oppression was removed. As a result of this action, all over England various city councillors debated removing statues of slave traders and imperialists that progressive minded folk would in all likelihood deem offensive.

• British Companies Own Up to Being Complicit in the Slave Trade

Pub retailer and brewer Greene King, and corporate body Lloyd's of London reveal their involvement in the transatlantic trade in enslaved Africans and pledge reparations by making payments to members of the BAME (Black, Asian and Minority Ethnic) community in England. They do this as a result of Black Lives Matter protesters expressing their outrage against continuing racism in England and the lingering legacy of the extensive involvement of England in the slave trade and its imperial project, (notably having colonized more of the world's peoples, their territory and wealth than any other nation on earth).

• Black Lives Matter Plaza Comes into Being in Washington D.C.

In Downtown Washington D.C. near to Pennsylvania Avenue by the White House, a two-block long section of 16th Street NW is renamed "Black Lives Matter Plaza", and the Department of Public Works paints the mural "Black Lives Matter" in large 35-foot-tall yellow capital letters across that section of the street. This is commissioned by the mayor, Muriel Bowser.

• The National Football League (NFL) of America Changes their Stance on Protests During the Playing of the National Anthem

The NFL in a major turnaround in policy announces in early June that football players should be allowed to protest during the playing of the national anthem, in the wake of national and worldwide protests against the killing of George Floyd. Thus, importantly, they have indirectly absolved Colin Kaepernick of any wrongdoing. Kaepernick was brave enough to sacrifice his football career by taking the knee during the playing of the National Anthem at the start of the football season in the fall of 2016, as a show of protest against police brutality and racist oppression of Black people in the U.S.—following in the tradition of Black activist athletes like Muhammad Ali who in 1967 refused to be drafted into the Vietnam War, as well as Tommie Smith and John Carlos who gave the Black Power Salute at the 1968 Olympics held in Mexico City, in a similar show of protest against racism in the U.S.

As the Black Lives Matter movement continues to rage (at the time of writing), unprecedented change is sweeping through the world. Hopefully, the end result will be that we all find ourselves living in a world of greater material equality, free of racial and other forms of oppression and discrimination, and significantly more connected as a global family through our common humanity.

SUPREME COURT RULING IN JAMAICA
SUPPORTS THE BANNING OF DREADLOCKS
BY KENSINGTON PRIMARY SCHOOL

On July 31, 2020, on the eve of Emancipation Day in Jamaica, the *Washington Post* was the first newspaper to drop the bombshell that the stance taken by Kensington Primary School to bar the daughter of Dale and Sherine Virgo from attending their school on the basis that her hairstyle, dreadlocks, was not allowed at the school, was upheld by the ruling of the Supreme Court of Jamaica. Kensington Primary School had maintained that they had an unwritten policy against the wearing of braids, beads and locks (notably all modes of African oriented expression). The justification for banning locks (dreadlocks) at the school was that they had a propensity to attract head lice and junjo (a form of mould), and were a distinct source of bad hygiene.

The upholding of this unwritten school rule by the Supreme Court revealed the extensive prejudice against dreadlocks in Jamaica, which paradoxically is the nation that gave birth to the Rastafari movement which, in turn, popularized dreadlocks globally. The wanton discrimination and prejudice against dreadlocks in Jamaica (where it has been publicly proposed that dreadlocks are synonymous with lice and poor hygiene, even now, well into the 21st century) has created a significant degree of moral outrage in the country and has even led to the emergence of a "Black Hair Matters" movement. The irony I'm sure is not lost on the reader—that in Jamaica, the land of Marcus Garvey and Rastafari, a Black Hair Matters movement has had to emerge (at the time of writing) to combat the severe discrimination and stigma that the wearing of dreadlocks (natural African locks) still provokes, demonstrating in open view the schizophrenic nature of Jamaica in 2020.

For some Rastafari this is indicative of the fulfillment of biblical prophecy and the Last Days—where all that was hidden will be revealed to all, even to the babe and suckling.

NOTES ON CONTRIBUTORS

SHAMARA WYLLIE ALHASSAN specializes in Rastafari Studies, Black women's intellectual history and Black radical politics. She is currently Assistant Professor of the Black Experience in the Americas in the School for Historical, Philosophical, and Religious Studies at Arizona State University. She earned her PhD in Africana Studies at Brown University.

MICHAEL BARNETT, CSE is Senior Lecturer in Race and Ethnicity, African Diaspora Studies and Social Theory in the Department of Sociology, Psychology and Social Work, The University of the West Indies, Mona. He was vested with the Commander of the Order of the Star of Honour of Ethiopia, by the Ethiopian Crown Council for service to Ethiopia and the Crown Council. In terms of notable publications on Rastafari, he has authored *The Rastafari Movement: A North American and Caribbean Perspective* (2018), co-edited the Rastafari Anthology, *Leonard Percival Howell and the Genesis of Rastafari* (2015), and edited the Rastafari Anthology, *Rastafari in the New Millennium: A Rastafari Reader* (2012). He is co-Guest Editor of this issue (*IDEAZ,* vol.15, 2020).

DEENA-MARIE BERESFORD holds a Doctor of Education (EdD) degree specializing in Educational Leadership and Higher Education Administration. She is currently Librarian Manager for public schools in Washington, DC and an adjunct professor at the Catholic University of America in the School of Library and Information Science. She is an active member of the global Rastafari community and a member of the Ethiopian World Federation, Local # 1-Haile Selassie I Local. She is the current President of the Iniversal Development of Ras Tafari, Inc. (IDOR) which is a nonprofit cultural and socio-spiritual community service and development organization located in Washington, DC and Baltimore, Maryland. She is the owner of Yeshimabet Books and Things which is a vending/mobile business devoted to supplying African/Rastafari centred literature, editing and proofreading services, research, cultural clothing, crochet, and incense from Ethiopia. Dr. Beresford is the author of *Gurage! Gurage! Gurage! The Story of a Wollo Princess: Yeshimabet Ali Abajifar*, a book about the mother of Haile Selassie I, Emperor of Ethiopia.

DEREK BISHTON is a writer, journalist and photographer. He was a founder and contributing editor of the radical photography journal *Ten.8* (published from 1979 to 1992). He worked for many years as a community activist in Handsworth, Birmingham—co-founding the Sidelines Agency which produced the award-winning Handsworth Self Portrait project. In 1981 he spent six weeks living with the Rastafari community in Shashemene and he recounted this experience, along with work undertaken with Rasta communities in the UK and Jamaica, in his book *Black Heart Man: A Journey into Rasta* (1986). In 1994 he became part of the launch team of the UK's first Internet newspaper, *Electronic Telegraph* (now *Telegraph. co.uk*) and went on to edit and develop digital services for the Telegraph Group until 2012.

GIULIA BONACCI is a historian, researcher at Institut de Recherche pour le Développement (IRD), and posted at URMIS, Université Côte d'Azur, France. She studies the intellectual history and popular cultures that circulate between Africa and the African Diaspora since the 19th century. Her book *Exodus! Heirs and Pioneers, Rastafari Return to Ethiopia* (2015) received two awards in the USA. She has co-edited various books and special issues (*Annales d'Ethiopie, African Diaspora, Northeast African Studies*) and her latest papers, in English and in French, were published in *Esclavages & Post-esclavages, Tumultes, The International Journal of African Historical Studies, Volume!* and *New West Indian Guide*. She is co-Guest Editor of this issue (*IDEAZ*, vol.15, 2020).

ENNIS B. EDMONDS teaches courses on African spirituality in the Americas, religion and society in the United States, and religion and popular culture. His research and publications have focused primarily on Rastafari, but also on other religious traditions in the Caribbean. Current research interests include the conversion of Rastas to Evangelical Christianity, religion in Afro-Caribbean and African American popular culture and literature, and issues of identity among Rastas who have repatriated to Africa. His publications include *Rastafari: A Very Short Introduction* (2012), *Rastafari: From Outcasts to Culture Bearers* (2003), and *Caribbean Religious History: An Introduction* (with Michelle Gonzalez, 2010).

CLINTON HUTTON is a retired Professor of Caribbean Political Philosophy, Culture and Aesthetics at The University of the West Indies, Mona. He is presently Director of the Institute of Technological and Educational Research at Mico University College, Kingston, Jamaica. His most recent book publications are: first editor, *Rupert Lewis and the Black Intellectual Tradition* (2018); author, *Colour for Colour, Skin for Skin: Marching with the Ancestral Spirits into War Oh at Morant Bay* (2015); and first editor, *Leonard Percival Howell and the Genesis of Rastafari* (2015).

ERIN C. MACLEOD teaches in the English department of Vanier College, Montreal, Canada. She is co-editor with Moji Anderson of *Beyond Homophobia: Centring LGBTQ Experiences in the Anglophone Caribbean* (2020); author of *Visions of Zion: Ethiopians and Rastafari in the Search for the Promised Land* (2014); and co-editor with Jahlani Niaah of *Let Us Start With Africa: Foundations of Rastafari Scholarship* (2013). She is also an award-winning journalist who has written for many publications, including *The Guardian, Rolling Stone*, and *The New York Times*. She is co-Guest Editor of this issue (*IDEAZ*, vol.15, 2020).

DEAN MACNEIL is the author of the groundbreaking work, *The Bible and Bob Marley: Half the Story Has Never Been Told* (2013). He holds an MA in Theology from Loyola Marymount University and a BA in English Literature from the University of Michigan Honors Program. His interests lie in the intersection of music and theology. MacNeil is a music industry veteran, lifelong musician, and former technology executive for the world's leading music company. He currently advises some of the world's largest and fastest growing companies on product development and execution strategy. He lives in Los Angeles, where he drums in jazz and reggae bands, and enjoys hiking, biking, and sailing with his son.

JAHLANI NIAAH is lecturer in the Institute of Caribbean Studies, and former coordinator of the Rastafari Studies Unit at The University of the West Indies, Mona. He is an embedded Rastafari scholar with research interests in African religious retentions, Rastafari, reparation for Africans and repatriation to Ethiopia, among other areas. Niaah has recently completed his first publication as solo author, *Lamb's Bread: Rastafari and Ganja in Jamaica* (forthcoming).

CHARLES PRICE is an Associate Professor in the Department of Policy, Organization, and Leadership Studies in the College of Education of Temple University. His research, writing and activity focus on identity formation (racial identity; personal-individual identity; collective identity; Rastafari identity), life narrative genres, action research, community organization and community organizing, people-centred community development, and social movements, with a geographic concentration on the United States and Jamaica. Price is author of *Becoming Rasta: Origins of Rastafari Identity in Jamaica* (2009), and co-author of *Community Collaborations: Promoting Community Organizing* (2009), and he has published many journal articles and book chapters. Price recently completed a joint NSF-funded pilot study of Black men and resilience in Greensboro, North Carolina, and Hartford, Connecticut. He is currently completing his book *Rasta: The Evolution of a People and their Identity* (forthcoming).

RICHARD SALTER is Professor of Religious Studies at Hobart and William Smith Colleges, where his teaching responsibilities include global Christianity and American religion. He also has a strong interest in issues of human rights and genocide. It was this interest that led him to teach at Five Points Correctional Facility, a maximum security prison located in Romulus, NY, and led him to think about Livity and the Law. His work on Rastafari began in the 1990s with fieldwork in Dominica, where he explored how Rastafari and Pentecostal groups formed as the traditional Roman Catholic structure of the island changed. He has subsequently written several articles and book chapters on Rastafari, including "Rastafari in a Global Context"—his Introduction to *The Globalization of Rastafari*, the 2008 special issue of *IDEAZ* (vol. 7), as well as his essay "Rastafari in a Global Context: Affinities of 'Orthognosy' and 'Oneness' in the Expanding World", published in the same issue.

SECONDE CHANCE (aka Dominique Mark) is a self-taught artist and portraitist from the Republic of Mauritius. The beauty of her island inspires her production. She started painting as a child and has been a professional artist since 2018. Her work can be seen on Instagram at secondechance7732. Her portraiture of Emperor Haile Selassie I and Empress Menen appears on the cover of this issue (*IDEAZ*, vol.15, 2020).

www.ingramcontent.com/pod-product-compliance
Lightning Source LLC
Chambersburg PA
CBHW061735270326
41928CB00011B/2247